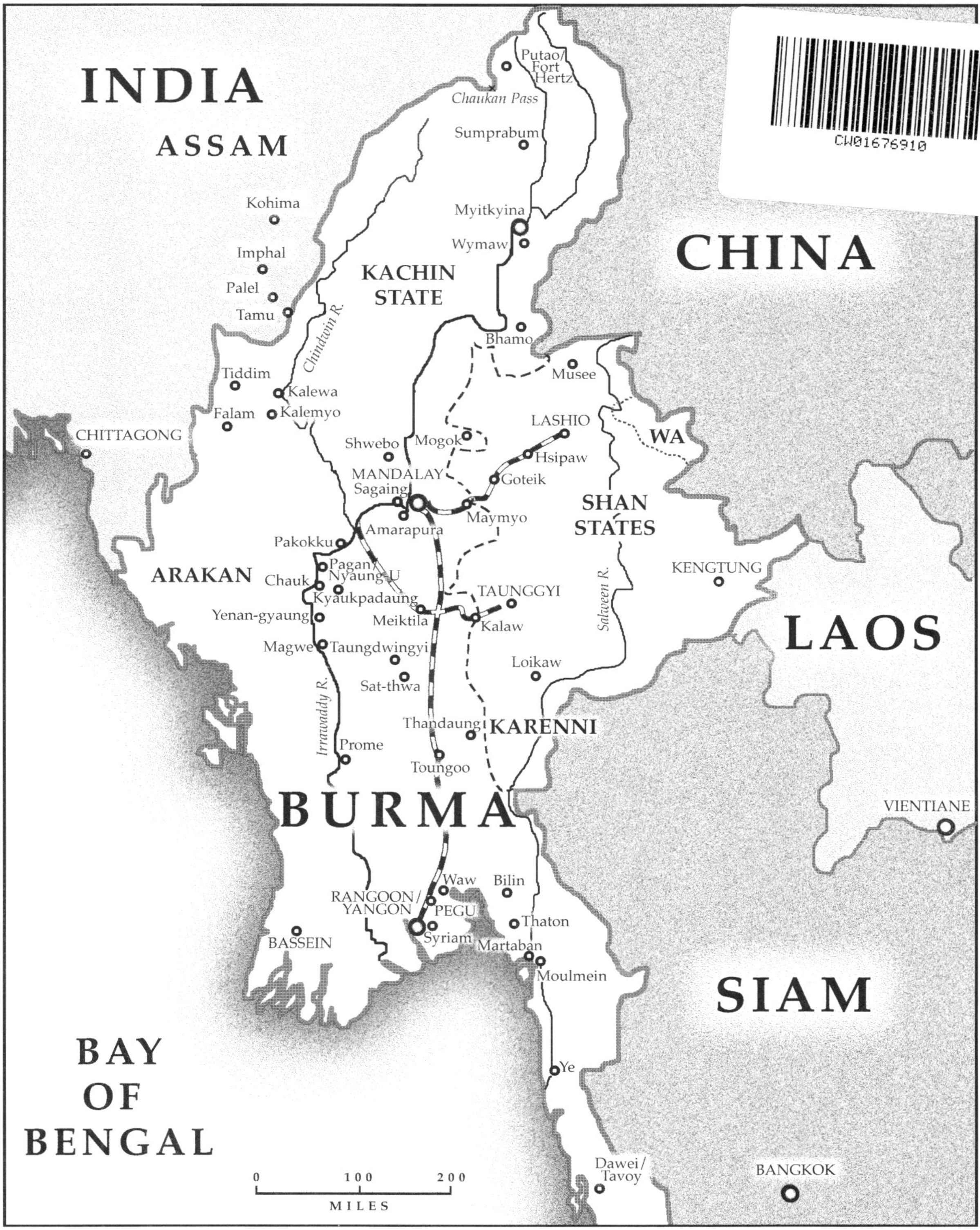

Map of Pre-War Burma (can be folded out to accompany text).

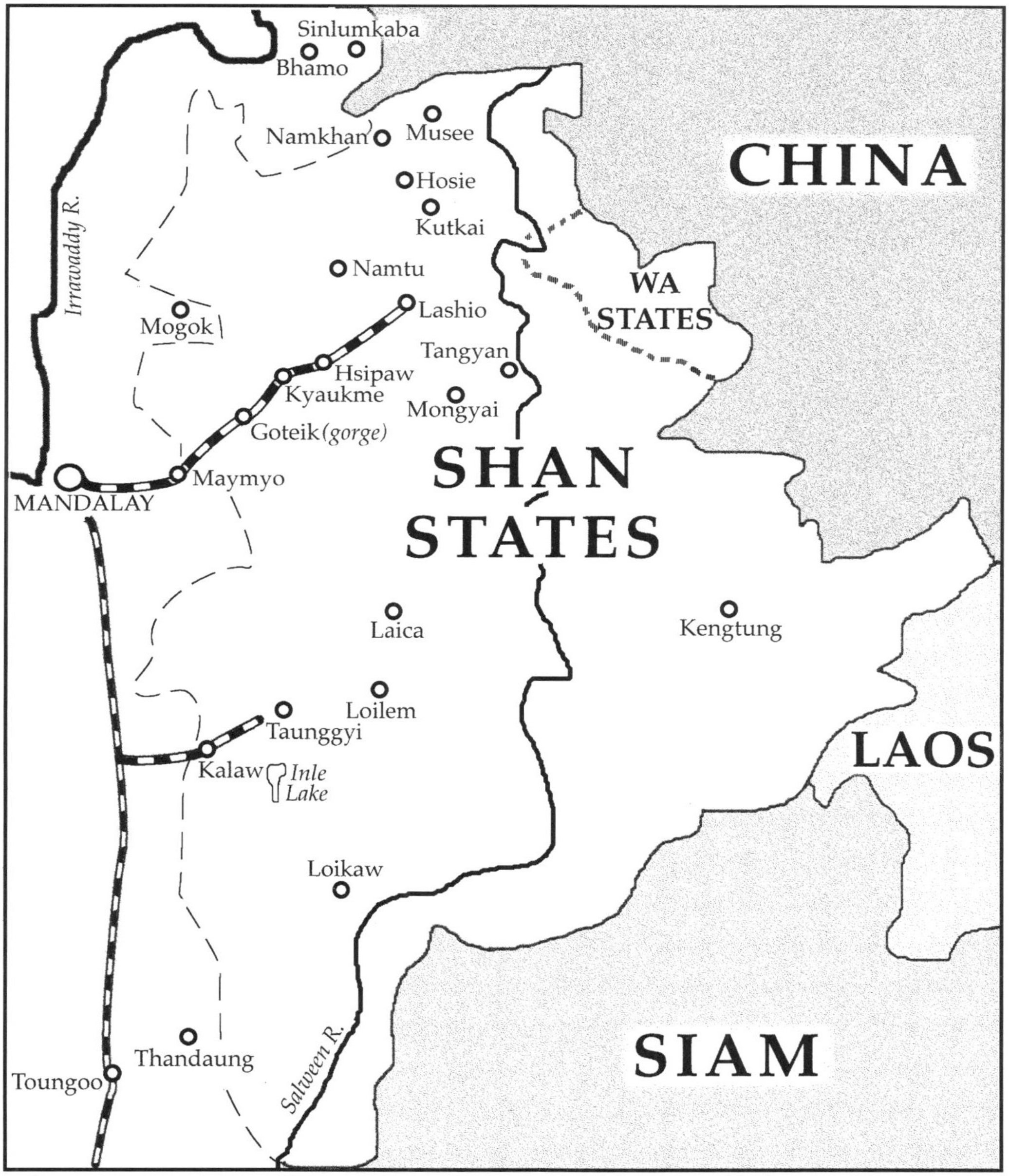

Close-up of the Shan States.

LINES FROM A SHINING LAND

Lines from a Shining Land

Friends at Inya Hall, Rangoon, in 1953.

Lines from a Shining Land

Compiled by Derek Brooke-Wavell

THE BRITAIN-BURMA SOCIETY

Published in Great Britain 1998 by the Britain-Burma Society
40, Kidmore Road, Caversham, RG4 7LU, Berks

ISBN 0 9534054 0 0

Printed and bound in the UK
by Antony Rowe Ltd, Portman Road, Reading.

List of Illustrations

POW "The Prince of Wales Eastern Book, Hodder & Stoughton, 1922"
In addition, there are many portraits of contributors, from them or their children.

Acknowledgements

We have quoted liberally from two excellent books of personal experiences of Burma published in the last two years, and which we would thoroughly recommend for your bookshelf.

All quotations attributed to "Maureen" are taken directly from *A World Overturned - a Burmese Childhood* by Maureen Baird-Murray, published by Constable in 1997 at £15.95. Copies can be obtained from: Constable Publishers, 3 The Lanchesters, 162 Fulham Palace Road, London, W6 9ER, United Kingdom.

All quotations attributed to "Sylvia" are taken from *Burma Bride* by Sylvia Molloy, published by Molloy Publications in 1996 at £9.99. Copies can be obtained from her on (+44) 1462 627986 - P&P (UK): £1.75.

Our thanks to BMJ Publications for permission to quote extracts from Professor Alan Woodruff's article *Medicine in Burma Today*.

All quotations attributed to "Stella" come from the recollections of Stella McGregor, for which I have to thank her daughter Pauline Currien. They may later appear in print under the title *Radiant Star*. Look out for it!

We would like to thank all contributors, in and surrounding the Britain-Burma Society. Their details are in Appendix I; they are Gerry Abbott; Anna Allott, OBE, Euan Bagshawe, Maureen Baird-Murray, Bruce Beale, Evelyn Broughton-Smart, Derek Brooke-Wavell, Dr Glyn Court, Pauline Currien, Mavis Edwards, Sir Nicholas Fenn, GCMG and Sue Fenn, Amy Fitzgerald, Tony Foucar, Patricia Herbert, Noel Holmes, Bill Howe, Dr Desmond Kelly, U Khin, Sir Nick Larmour, KCMG and Nancy Larmour, Daw Kyi Kyi May, Sylvia Molloy, John Okell, Philip Plumb, Maeve Reid, Lewis Shaw, Elizabeth Shepherd, Peter Smart, Kenneth Watts, H. E. U Win Aung, Helen Woodruff and Ken Wootton.

In particular, thanks to the Officers of the Britain-Burma Society for their contributions - our Patron, H.E. U Win Aung; our President, Sir Nicholas Fenn and our Chairman, John Okell for their contributions; also thanks to Patricia Herbert, whose original idea this was, for some marvellous help and inspirations, often at the most awkward times for her.

We must also draw the reader's special attention to the following contributors, whose very substantial writings may well find publication elsewhere at a later date:

Sir Nicholas Fenn, GCMG; Dr Desmond Kelly and his sister Pat (*nom de plume*: Maeve Reid); Sir Nick Larmour, KCMG; Philip Plumb; Lewis Shaw.

Last but not least, a tribute to those who contributed some excellent photographs, particularly Mrs Caroline Donachie, but not forgetting any of those mentioned on the list of illustrations.

CONTENTS

PREFACE

by Derek Brooke-Wavell

In 1998, Burma (officially known as Myanmar) celebrates 50 years of Independence.

Burmese culture is one of the world's most attractive, yet difficult to grasp. To many who have lived there this has been a shining land, whose light has touched them in ways they find hard to communicate to friends and countrymen. So they meet periodically, in groups like the Britain-Burma Society, or over the Internet. But the generation that still remembers colonial times in Burma will soon be gone; and foreigners who have lived in the country since Independence in 1948 are also few because the country's leaders consciously sought seclusion.

Lines from a Shining Land allows the privileged few to pass on their experience to the many, before it is too late. You could regard it as the collected highlights of two dozen autobiographies; or as a patchwork history of the most direct kind; or, if you like, a rare viewing of the "hive truth" of the Britain-Burma Society. Nearly all the authors were ordinary young people at the time of which they speak, though many subsequently achieved eminence. Accounts range from 1910 to 1980, and a bit further. All are telling their own stories, and all are members of the Britain-Burma Society or their families. The writers' original words are reproduced, down to variations in style and spelling. Here you will find no well-known gems of the literature, nor - outside this introduction - sentimental generalisations. Nor yet do we touch the open wound that is Burma's last decade. Within our chosen area, we offer real history in snapshots - the eye-witness accounts of a very broad sample of people over a long period of time.

Some of these scenes come from letters or diaries of parents or grandparents. One old lady's account was found after her death, painstakingly scribed onto sheets of lavatory paper - the only writing paper she could find by her hospital bedside. Her son was so moved that he pieced it together and sent it to me.

Fairy-tale Lives. In English literature, and particularly children's literature, there is a long tradition of stories about a secret, magic land - Oz, Middle Earth, Narnia, the Never-Never Land. Through some miracle, an ordinary grey person gets swept off to this marvellous place - and suddenly everything is in colour; the sun shines bright and warm; they talk with princes, ride elephants; there is evil to fight, virtuous maidens to rescue - and when eventually they return to the greyness of home, they feel somehow nobler for the experience.

For a great many British people, Burma was a real-life fairy tale of that kind. Such was the story that Jessie Beale - for it was she - left on lavatory paper for her son to inherit. Burma, walled by mountains, fits the minimum criteria for a "lost kingdom" very well. And where there are warm and gentle people - like the villagers - there will also be cold-hearted rogues, such as the Japanese invaders, to exploit them.

An Alien Land. It has often been observed that Burmese culture was not changed nearly as much as it might have been by a century or more of British rule (from 1826 to 1945/48). The Burmese had an old culture based on Buddhism, in which prestige was gained by giving to monks, not keeping things for oneself. They had a kind climate, and plenty to eat. Few were interested in Christianity or inducements to rise in the colonial establishment, through wealth or English education. And so their ancient culture was preserved, more than almost anywhere else. Even so, the inhabitants of Burma were beneficiaries of the period of peace and prosperity that was maintained under British rule.

Independence, on January 4th 1948, meant a brief period of happiness for all Burmese. Here was freedom from the foreigner, freedom from subservience. As it happened, though, it also meant freedom from wealth - since the economy had been pretty well destroyed during the four years in which the country was a battleground between Japanese and Allies. And it also meant freedom from peace, as the Communists and a number of different ethnic armies waged war in pursuit of various aims.

To Burmese Buddhists, lack of wealth was a situation in which they felt at home; nor would they ask for outside help with the insurgencies. So there followed a long period of isolation from the world - in which to go back to cultural roots, under the banner of non-alignment.

For many of the British in Burma, the Second World War followed by Independence also meant a grim kind of freedom - freedom from everything they had known and loved. As one of our writers puts it, "arriving in a cold distant land; alien culture; freezing winters; rationing; English boarding schools; loneliness, isolation. One locked up experience and silently mourned the loss."

Since Independence, far fewer outsiders have ever had the chance to know Burma in depth - and there is a real difference in their accounts. For the Burmese no longer have to fit in with a British system; they appear in their true colours. Understanding requires a greater effort - but is all the more rewarding for that.

The Background - History and Geography. Burma is a diamond-shaped country of 261,000 square miles, a little larger than its next-door neighbour, Thailand. At its high borders, three of the world's great regions meet - China, India and South-East Asia. Before the arrival of British rule from 1826 onwards, Burmese history was a story of warlike kings, pagoda-building and

A Burmese Festival of the 1930s.

Buddhism. The British swallowed Burma in chunks, completing the process in 1885; and then Burma was under British rule for another 56 years before the Japanese drove them out in 1942. Burmese forces welcomed in the Japanese - but later joined with the British to complete their defeat. The British briefly resumed government in 1945, but in the face of a strongly-supported independence movement, handed over power in 1948. There was one trauma during the handover period that no Burmese can forget - the assassination in 1947 of General Aung San, the man who had almost single-handedly pushed the British into leaving, and laid out the future blueprint for his country.

Politically, the 1950s were a time of democracy under U Nu, based on the British system but looking very frail in the face of massive insurgencies. After that time, Burma has been continuously under army control. General Ne Win ruled, under one guise or another, from 1962 to 1988, when he resigned.

1988 also saw the rise of a pro-democracy movement, in which Aung San's daughter Aung San Suu Kyi Suu Kyi became central, followed by a hard-edged re-imposition of military control by the SLORC. The years since then have seen repeated attempts by the military government to put down opposition and gain acceptance for a new constitution based on army-guided democracy. From outside Burma there has been condemnation of alleged human rights abuses.

Times and Places. Many times and places are woven into this Burmese tapestry. Some jump out with particular clarity because of the number of our contributors who had experience of that area. The short period between the end of the war in 1945 and Independence in 1948 probably gets more attention than it deserves; on the other hand, we are fortunate to be able to depict the pre-war Shan States in such detail, since this large area is the most diverse in Burma, both ethnically and geographically. It was also the area where Europeans came into the most daily contact with villagers in their own environment.

Our first contribution of all is right off the normal map - in terms both of date and place. This is an entry from the diary of Elizabeth Bagshawe, a 27-year-old English bride who, with her husband, ran a remote tea estate in Cachar in 1866. Cachar is actually just across the border from Burma, in Assam; but the area had been tributary to Burmese kings until not long before and, like Rangoon, it was then administered as part of British India.

For Dippers and Skimmers. This book is good for those who only have time to dip, because it is made up of separate scenes only a page or so long. Even a run of scenes does not go over five or ten pages. But please read in sequence if you want the full experience!

Scenes follow each other in an order that is not always what is expected - so that we move in turn forwards, backwards and sideways. In the process, we gradually construct the intersecting lattices of place, time and experience that make up Burma over the last hundred years.

DIFFERENT PEOPLE, DIFFERENT TIMES

1866* Elizabeth Bagshawe (aged 27)

Here is Elizabeth's diary entry for 27th February 1866. She is running a tea estate in a remote part of Cachar, just across the Indian border from Burma, and describes her daily routine. 76 years on, in 1942, this area will be traversed by hundreds of starving Europeans on the run from the Japanese invasion of Burma.

We get up about half past six, when the gong sounds for the coolies to go to work, and the moment we dress we have *'chota hazree'*, little breakfast, tea, biscuit and an egg; we have no bread here; then I look after my chickens, ducks and geese, pigeons, rabbits, goats etc, talk to Ramu Sammy (the cook) and give out whatever is needed from my store room; Clem generally has a good many people to see him and then he goes round his *teelahs* (the hills where the tea grows) and I go for a canter in the jungle with a syce; we are at home, bathed and dressed and ready for breakfast at eleven...

We go out again in the evening, walking, riding, or visiting the coolie lines, dine at seven, after which Mr McNaughton (the assistant) and the baboo, who is the head native, come in and the latter reads the report of the day's work and orders are given for the following day and all the affairs are talked over and any disputes among the coolies settled. Then the work is done and we can play the harmonium and do as we like till bed-time.

One day is very much like another, but I think we have both of us too much to do to get tired of our life, and we are happy and as well as possible. We have more than 300 coolies here, but a large proportion of them are women and children, and of course many of them are utterly useless. We are establishing a nursery and have got two women to take care of the little children while their parents are at work, for they are utterly neglected and two or three of them have been terribly burnt. They are all to be brought up to the bungalow every day for me to inspect them and see that they are kept clean and tidy! It is not easy to do much for these people; one cannot look after them the way you can after poor people at home, except when they are in hospital.

***Important - please note the date at the top of each extract.*

1922 **Stella**

(aged 9 in text) - she will be introduced later.

On the train journey back to Rangoon the monsoons had broken and the scene was quite different. The paddy fields were covered with water, water buffaloes plodded along and large white birds almost like gulls or herons sat about - they were called paddy birds.

There is one thing that makes me smile even now - small Indian children ran around almost naked except for a medallion of a silvery metal covering their private parts. A friend of our family was returning to England and sent her servant to buy one of these medallions so she could have it as a souvenir. When he returned without it she wanted to know why - "Sorry, ma'am, I looked everywhere but could not find one large enough for you."

1941 **Sylvia** *(aged 26)*

At this year's *"Thingyan"* Water Festival all the villagers filled buckets and bamboo sections with water and sprayed water over anyone passing by. Many of them poured whole buckets of water over each other amid great fun and shrieks of merriment.

So seriously is *Thingyan* taken in Rangoon that during the festival the Corporation installs pipes all over the city so that people can easily obtain water. In April 1940, the city used 83 million gallons more water than the usual monthly supply.

The festival lasts from the 13th to the 17th April. On the third day we were walking past the spring from which people got their water from a bamboo pipe. They were filling up their containers and were doubtful as to whether they should throw some water on us. One woman took courage and sprinkled some on me, whereupon I put my hand in her pail and threw some back; my husband Pat also gave the woman a thorough drenching and then we ran away. Screaming with delight and laughter she pursued us home. It was great fun, especially for the onlookers.

On the 17th we were told that a number of people had come to show their respects to us. We were surprised to see at least fifty people all supplied with water. They had three bowls of gifts for us with bananas and jelly sweets made from rice. The Revenue Minister blessed the gifts with prayer.

Then we were told that they wanted to wash our hands and legs, as it was the custom for them to visit officials and do this during the festival. We took off our shoes and stockings expecting a light sprinkling of water, but they came up and poured it over us. I retreated after a while, but Pat stood and let them pour water over him till he was like a drowned rat, just dripping with water. The people were highly delighted. They say they do it to make you cool and contented all year round.

1961 John Okell

When I was in my twenties I stayed for a few weeks with a friendly family in the village of Ywama on Inle Lake. I was enchanted by the beauty of the lake and the village, and the openness and warmth of the people. And the need to paddle your boat along the creeks wherever you went - to the village shop, to visit friends. One evening, three of the young men of the neighbourhood took me outside without saying why. One of them was a thin and scruffy but lively and comical youth called Pwe-sa Pu. He was called that because he made a meagre living (*sa*) by working as an attendant at the gambling fairs *(pwe)* that were held from time to time. But a "*pwe-sa*" is also a broker, usually wealthy, so Hla Pu was called Pwe-sa Pu by his friends to tease him.

We were to go fishing, but we had to be extremely circumspect: if we were found breaking the Buddhist precept against taking life the elders would be severely disapproving. One of Pwe-sa Pu's many skills was spearing fish, so he was installed in the bows on his haunches with a torch and his illicit spear (only brought out of hiding in the dark), and we paddled noiselessly along the reedy banks of the creeks looking for fish. Pwe-sa Pu had several near misses, but no catch, so we decided to go to the monastery.

Like all Inlay houses, the monastery was built on teak posts embedded in the lake bed, with its floor about six feet above the water level. The best and biggest fish were to be found in the water under its floor. But fishing there was extremely dangerous, because the head of the monastery was an irascible monk who had been known to belabour people with a cudgel if he caught them under his monastery breaking the precept.

We held our breath as we glided silently in the dark water between the posts. Sure enough Pwe-sa Pu soon spotted and speared a good fat fish. It took two of us to hold it down on the floor of the boat, terrified that the noise of its thumping would alert the Sayadaw. Fortunately we escaped without being detected. We paddled swiftly away from the monastery until we were well out of sight and hearing. Then we found a clear patch on the river bank, where we made a fire and roasted and ate our catch. Possibly the tastiest piece of fish I have ever had.

A LIFE IN BRIEF - 1906-1939: UK - BURMA - UK

by Jessie Beale née Bruce

This was the account that was written by a dying woman on exercise books and lavatory paper, and left for her son to find. Bruce Beale sent it to me with the comment that he was himself now incapacitated by strokes, but it was his dearest wish to see it in print. This narrative (5 pages long) is the longest unbroken story in this book, and the only one which describes the UK as well as Burma - but it is worth reading from beginning to end, as a remarkable introduction to all that follows.

I was born in a tall thin house in Vauxhall Walk, Lambeth in 1906. My mother was twenty-two and my father thirty-two. I faintly remember my father who taught me to read when I was three years old. He was a very sick man with Tuberculosis and sat all day in a chair coughing. The two babies, William and Lillian were also very ill with TB. In 1910 my father died and so did the two babies and mother was left a widow. She was given a lump sum of £200 on my father's death. My father had been a foundation member of the Post Office Workers' Union and a strong Socialist.

After visiting relatives in Scotland we went back to London where my mother had to find work. This was very difficult as she was quite untrained. She applied to the Post Office and was given a char's job scrubbing corridors for twelve shillings and six pence a week and having to work very long hours.

My grandfather had a habit of starting at Brixton and stopping off at various places picking up grandchildren until he reached us at Blackfriars. There was a tram which ran all the way for 1d from 9 a.m. until 4 p.m. Gathering up all the Grandchildren we would be marched off to a museum or art gallery or some place of interest, walking miles and not allowed to bleat at all or a sharp tap with his walking stick would soon shut us up.

He not only went to museums but anywhere in the history of London. For instance we were taken to Clapham Common where we had a paddle and then were shown where Stevie Morris killed someone. I love thrillers and I think this is where I got the bug. I also love museums. Grandfather was a Fabian and an outdoor man and died at the age of eighty eight. He was knocked down by a bus whilst going to a museum, the one near Camberwell.

I like to remember the Southwark streets I knew as a little girl also Lambeth where my grandfather had a lovely house on Brixton Hill with a curving gravel drive and a small pony and trap kept at the side. My Grandfather was married twice and had a lot of children. His first wife had nine children. One every year and then died. I am not surprised. Then after being a widower for a few years he married again and had four more children. The children of the first marriage hated their step mother and would not have anything to do with her. Most of the family were hard working and strong, the delicate flower of the family being my Aunt Maude the eldest daughter. I was told that she was always ailing and delicate even though she has only recently died at the age of ninety five.

Mother was always told "Poor Maude, not at all well, she'll never get married it would kill her."

Maude became a rather dried up little spinster, a strict teetotaller and Rechabite. Then just before the outbreak of the 1914-18 war she met a young House Painter, twelve years her junior and they married. I was a bridesmaid. I remember all the Aunts shaking their heads over their tea, "What a disaster, she'll never last, at least there would be no children." There were six, and several miscarriages. Each time the family was alerted to each hospitalisation the whole family would troop off to Lambeth to wait near St Thomas's Hospital for Maude to die, but she always got over each little medical problem.

The Great War came and all my uncles went off to the war except my mother's youngest brother George who was only sixteen. Poor old Lou was very badly gassed. Most of my mother's brothers were killed storming Hill 60 on the Somme. Then Uncle George was taken. He had been driving a van horse dray and so was put into the Gunners. This meant drawing the horse drawn guns through a hail of shot to the front. He came home a complete wreck having been wounded time and time again, deaf and dreadfully shell shocked.

For my honeymoon I went with my husband to Burma. He was a forest manager for a teak firm and had been on leave in England. We were married in August at the Caxton Hall in Westminster. In September, 1932 we sailed for Burma from Liverpool in the SS Pegu. This ship carried about one hundred passengers and a certain amount of cargo. After a few days we reached Marseilles. The Bay of Biscay was very rough and all the passengers were sea sick.

We then sailed through the Mediterranean Sea passing the live Volcano, Stromboli which was clearly visible and a wonderful sight at night, before arriving at Port Said where we stayed for one day whilst the ship was coaled. At Port Sudan many of the passengers disembarked as they made their way to the Sudan Cotton Plantations. It was so hot at twelve noon that you burnt your hand if it touched bare metal and the heat came through the soles of your shoes.

As we neared the Gulf of Martaban in the Indian Ocean the colour of the sea changed to muddy grey with lots of debris in it, more and more as we neared the mouth of the great

Irrawaddy River which runs through Burma and is enormous. The nearer we got to Rangoon the more tree trunks, coconuts and rubbish we saw. We steamed through this and at four a.m. my husband woke me up to go on deck to see the Great Golden Pagoda with the dawn just breaking over a pink, pearly sky. As we sailed up the river the sides were covered in dense forest with little villages here and there complete with smaller golden topped pagodas. The stubby trees covered with vines. Gradually a house or two raised on stilts made of bamboo and wood thatched with palm leaves. A tiny village with mango trees and a tiny pagoda at one end built on a little knoll. The Great Pagoda is very awe inspiring as it is so huge and as the sun rises its glittering golden cover shines brilliantly soaring into the heavens.

On disembarkation we motored to a friend's house going past this great Pagoda surrounded by smaller ones all covered in Gold. Many people were going to the Pagoda and they all took off their shoes before climbing the steps. Most of the women carried bowls of fruit or various gifts to place in front of the Buddha. The people looked very attractive to me. The women very dainty and prettily dressed wearing a thin white muslin jacket type of blouse fastened with tiny jewelled buttons and a long brilliantly coloured silk skirt wrapped tightly around them. They had oiled their hair with coconut oil and taken it up with two wooden combs into a small tower on top of their heads. The men wore plain white jackets and brilliant coloured silk skirts and a silk type of head gear with a small tail at one side.

After passing The Great Pagoda we went to the large market. Most of the stalls were kept by Burmese women, who had a very free life compared with other women in the East. Nearly all business was carried on by women and they were protected by law and by various inheritance laws. Most Burmese were Buddhists when I lived in the country but there were a large number of Roman Catholics and Baptists.

When I first arrived I went to live with my mother in law who lived in a very nice house with a beautiful garden in a hill station called Maymyo. May was the name of the District Commissioner who first settled on the hill and Myo means township. It was a very Edwardian Society with very set rules. I had to go and drop cards on certain people who then called on me and there was a great deal of protocol as to who went in first to dinner and who took which wife in. As a bride I was given precedence for one month and then abruptly found myself assuming a very lowly position as my husband was in business. It didn't matter how important your job was you simply could not take precedence over the Army or Government officials no matter how incompetent.

I found this all very difficult and ran away by train to Toungoo four hundred miles down the line where my husband met me and we went by car for about one hundred miles in his T model Ford and met up with his elephants. About five or six old ladies with one *Butcha* (baby) with them. We marched into the jungle for about six miles before making camp. There was some sort of rebellion going on in the jungles so we had to be careful and my husband trained two Scouts to go ahead and see that our way was clear.

We would get up at four-thirty having slept on camp beds under a canvas slung between the trees. Our bath water was heated on fires in paraffin tins. Our servants were experts at chopping down bamboo and making shelters of this as well as tables and chairs. Next day and for a further four more days we marched about fifteen miles each day and then made camp. We had a bath and a meal and went to sleep. Then a cup of tea at four thirty and my husband and I would go shooting. Usually a Peafowl or Jungle Fowl to give us food. We carried a few vegetables, rice, flour, sugar, tinned milk and fat. The cook would bake the bread over a fire in a tin can.

We then came in sight of a large wooden building on high stilts. All the houses up country or in native towns and villages are built on piles to keep them out of the flood water. When the monsoon breaks the rain comes for nearly four months and makes things very uncomfortable, steamy and gives one a very irritable prickly heat rash all over the body.

As you walk through the jungle leeches fall on you and swell up from a little black thread to a large round knob, my husband used to light a cigarette and touch each one with the lighted tip and they would fall off. We saw very few people and only very occasionally a small cluster of shacks, not really a village until we began to get up into the foothills where some Karen and Kachin tribes lived. The people were living in small bamboo houses and in some cases the whole village lived in one long house made of bamboo and raised on stilts. They would clear a small area of jungle and then plant it and did this until the ground was worked out when they would move on to another patch of jungle. We would distribute Epsom Salts, Boracic washes and

aspirin. There was no chance of these people getting proper medical attention as we knew it, and some of the things that happened were pretty grim. I once saw a poor girl who was being looked after by some old women in childbirth. They put a plank on her stomach and jumped on it to force her baby out.

I did not feel too frightened in the day time but lying in my tent at night I was terrified that a herd would just come through the jungle trampling everything including our poor little tents. In the morning we would move off into deep jungle with no fears. The mist rising thickly, the gibbons leaping overhead from tree to tree and our placid old lady elephants walking sedately along with us and all our belongings packed on them. We would have to start early as we could not march after ten a.m. Elephants need a lot of time to feed. The elephants would be unloaded and led down to the river to bathe. We always camped near a river and a small chain would be linked from leg to leg so that the elephants could walk but not run away. Before this was done the elephants would be allowed to bathe and splash in the water. Then for the rest of the day they grazed. All of them had large wooden bells around their necks. In the evening the men would go out into the jungle to bring them back to near the camp. They were tempted with pieces of sugar cane which they loved.

All our elephant men came from Laos since my husband recruited from there. We lived up by the Mekong and Chindwin Rivers. Later we were posted to the Pegu Yoma forests which bordered the Sittang River and was in the Karenni District. All the tribes ruled themselves, seldom seeing an Englishman or Government official. In the Triangle where we lived the Wa Tribe lived. They had been noted as head-hunters and supposedly still were if the harvest was desperate. A head man in each village administered what law there was. Opium was grown but the British Customs tried to prevent smuggling. We were forced to issue a ration of opium to our elephant men. We also gave them Marmite to prevent them getting Beri Beri.

Bruce Beale notes: Just before the outbreak of the 1939 War my mother Jessie and her husband retired to England and built a house in Angmering village for £950. Almost as soon as War broke out her husband was called up and because of his knowledge of Burma, elephants and native languages was shipped out to Burma with the East African Division. After the war Burma became independent and they lost the pension they hoped to live on. It was a very difficult period for them. The family had lived in India and Burma for generations and simply could not cope with the UK.

Jessie, with the help of her sister Nell and brother Harry, managed to sort things out and at length the family settled in a bungalow in Rayleigh, Essex.

She eventually retired to live in the village of Debenham in Suffolk with her husband. After burying him in the graveyard in Debenham, Jessie went to live in Ipswich where she was given a great deal of help and support by her neighbours. She continued to lead a very active life and even though sick, and in great pain from bone cancer worked as a housekeeper from time to time for the local Abbeyfield Society.

INTRODUCTIONS

to some of our guides: Maureen, Sylvia, Stella, Nick and Sue Fenn, and Evelyn.

Introducing Maureen (Rossiter)

I was born in 1933. My mother was Burmese. Her family were poor peasant folk from Taungdwingyi in the dry zone of Central Burma. She was seventh in a family of eleven. Surprisingly only two of this large family did not survive early childhood.

My father was Edward Rossiter, Irish by origin, an Assistant Superintendent in Shan States. It was while he was on tour and passing through Taungdwingyi that he stopped at a cheroot factory and caught sight of my mother. Struck by her beauty, he made several attempts to engage her in conversation, but it was to no avail as she kept running away to her mother, for she spoke no English and stood in some awe of the foreigner. My father, however, was not easily deflected, spoke fluent Burmese, as well as Shan and several dialects of the hill tribes. All his direct efforts being in vain, he was to have recourse to the headman of my mother's village to make the necessary arrangements for the meeting. This must have been something of a success because eventually permission was given for a marriage to take place.

Making cheroots and cigars was a traditional occupation of young Burmese women.

The above account, and others that appear here in the name of Maureen, are all taken from "A World Overturned", published in 1997 by Constable, in her married name of Maureen Baird-Murray.

Introducing Sylvia (Molloy)

The blackout in Europe in 1939 put an end to my play production and my painting classes in Paris. It also seemed to put an end to my marriage plans. After two years in England, Patrick Molloy returned to Burma to take up his appointment as Assistant Superintendent and it was his intention to return in three years time when his leave was due, to marry me.

The war put an end to that plan, as he was no longer allowed to leave Burma, but I was free to travel to Burma if I chose. Being of an obstinate disposition and against all family advice, I booked my passage in August 1940 on the Henderson boat, *S.S. Burma*. Strangely enough it was this ship that had brought Pat to me from Burma, when he came as a fairly tall young man to Cambridge. We had fallen in love at first sight and, being given to versifying, I well remember his first love message to me, found written on the typewriter, "I wonder how I could be so fond, as to fall in love with a blue-eyed blonde", to which I replied in typing, "I wonder how I could be so mad, as to fall in love with a Cambridge lad"...

After a month at sea in U-boat-infested waters it was sheer delight to me to land in Rangoon and discover to what a colourful and charming land destiny had brought me. My first impression was of a mass of colour on the quayside. This was a group of Burmese girls in their multi-coloured *loongyis* (pronounced loonjies) and white transparent *aingyis* (ainjies). The *aingyi* or blouse was worn over a lace bodice and contrasted beautifully with the bright colour of the *loongyi* or skirt. The Burmese girls wore fresh flowers in their jet black hair and their blouses were fastened with beautiful buttons, often real jewels. They also wore gold bracelets and necklaces of real stones such as ruby or jade. Burma of course has a wealth of ruby and jade mines.

I arrived in Rangoon in October, which is the cool season as in England. The days were a little hot, but the evenings were enchanting. We drove along roads with huge palms like sentinels to the beautiful lakes of that city, the Victoria and Kokine lakes. Above the city stands the Shwe Dagon Pagoda all faced with gold leaf, donated by Burmese who wish to achieve merit in the next life.

My first impression of the East was the continual chirruping of the crickets in the evenings, and this sound will always suggest the Orient to me. I was thrilled with the huge bazaar called the Scott Market. There I saw the opulence of the East in wonderful lengths of Mandalay silk, beautiful silverwork and carving and painting on plates of mother-of-pearl. Everywhere were silk and even paper sunshades, hand-painted. The low prices were astounding to an English girl, but even then they were not cheap enough for my future mother-in-law, who astonished me with her long-drawn-out haggling to reduce the price. I quickly learned the art of bargaining in the East. I really believe that both seller and customer enjoyed the haggling; it made the sale so much more interesting and more of an achievement for both parties.

From Rangoon, Pat, his mother and I travelled north in a very old Essex car acquired by Pat at the price of 400 rupees (£30). It was a tourer of the old fashioned type, and was destined to do the most astonishing feats at a later date. We planned to marry in Maymyo in the Northern Shan States, as we were to be stationed in Kyaukme (pronounced chowmay).

Sylvia's accounts are all taken from "Burma Bride", by Sylvia Molloy, published in 1996 - see details at end of book.

1913 Introducing Stella (McGregor)

My earliest recollection is of a two-storey wooden house, set in a large garden on a quiet, tree lined road. "No. 2 Kandawglay Road" Rangoon, Burma, now called Myanmar. This house was too large for us and to supplement the family income my parents took in Paying Guests or PG's as they were called. They were usually young Scots working abroad who found hotels too expensive. They soon became part of the family and good friends. It was because of these PG's that my Mother only ever employed two Burmese Nannies to look after us children. The Burmese National costume is a tight long *longyi* or skirt in bright colours worn with a loose white blouse. The women wore their black shiny hair up in a high smooth pile on the top of their head with sweet smelling flowers over one ear. To keep slippers on their feet and because of the tight skirt they have a very provocative walk. Mother soon noticed that Nanny found excuses to walk through the rooms where the young men were and so as she felt responsible for their

Picture of a Burmese nanny? The postcard from which this photograph was taken was posted in 1912 - one year before Stella was born.

welfare, out went the Nannies!! In fact when these young men lived in bachelor establishments or "chummeries" as they were called, some of the young men were said to take "Burmese Dictionaries" to bed with them - to help acquire a knowledge of the language!! So we had older "Ayahs" to look after us until we were about three or four years old.

In this Kandawglay garden there were large clumps of bamboo trees, twenty or thirty feet tall, which groaned when the wind blew and rubbed the trunks together. One night after dinner my Mother saw what she thought was a length of cord by her chair. Then she realised that the cord she was sewing was spiral whereas this was banded. Quick as a flash she whipped off her high heeled shoe and brought it down on the snake's head instantly - it was a deadly "Krait". We jumped out of bed to see what the excitement was about. Mother was the heroine of the evening. Scorpions too used to be found lurking in cool places or crawling over the floor. It was second nature to watch out for creepy crawlies.

Stella McGregor was born and brought up in Burma. Her father was in Bulloch Bros, a shipping company In the oval picture she is about sixteen, and carrying her pet gibbon, Jacko. Stella died in 1995, but her daughter Pauline Currien has put together the letters she wrote on her early life, and they may one day appear in print under the title "Radiant Star".

1936 — Maureen

As time went on I was aware of a change coming over my parents. My father's looks grew more stern and set, while my mother frequently appeared to be crying, but I did not know the cause of this change. Then one day the three of us got into the car and drove away from the house and Loilem. The destination was Kalaw, another town in the Southern Shan States. As I see it on the map today the distance does not appear great, but at the time I was sure that it was a long journey, lasting three days, stopping at night with friends. Not much was spoken during the journey; my father serious and stern, my mother quietly dabbing her eyes. Not an inkling did I have of what was in store for me.

At last we approached enormous iron gates and drove through them. On one side was a high bank cut into terraces on which grew a profusion of beautiful tall flowers. We came to a stop in front of low dark timber building. As we stepped out of the car a door opened out of the low building and a figure, quite unlike anything I had ever seen before, came to greet us. She was dressed entirely in black from neck to foot and wore a starched white bonnet tied under her chin with long tabs, reaching to her waist. The impression was that of a crow, a very old black crow, though her face was white with a lot of wrinkles and a couple of large moles. She tried to smile encouragingly at me but, still terrified, I gripped my mother's hand even tighter. The black robed figure and my father carried on a conversation in English of which neither my mother nor I understood a word.

After a while, to my surprise we were joined by a Burmese lady who was dressed just like my mother and they carried on a conversation in Burmese. Then turning to me, she asked if I would like to go for a little walk with her. Not wanting to leave my mother, I shook my head. In the distance I could hear the voices of children at play.

"Wouldn't you like to go and see the other children?" she coaxed, to which I replied, "No." Then, producing some sweets, she held them out to me and repeated the invitation.

Won over by the sweets and curious to see what the children were doing, without a backward glance at my mother, I took the Burmese lady's hand as she led me up some wide smooth stone steps. Looking back it seems to me that the whole of that terrible day is forever linked to those wide smooth stone steps. The children's voices were getting nearer and nearer... But I suddenly realised my mother was not with me. Turning to the Burmese lady I said firmly that I wanted to go back to my mother. Smiling, she led me down the steps only just in time to see my parents driving away. In frantic desperation I broke away from her, running to catch up with the car, but it kept driving on with my parents looking straight ahead. Unbelieving, stunned and frightened, I watched till it disappeared from view, then, screaming and crying my disbelief, I turned and faced the black figures, for by now the place seemed to be full of them. In the end they were too much for me, and four of them carried me to the playground where I was soon surrounded by jeering children. This then was my introduction to St Agnes's Convent English High School for Girls, Kalaw. It was also the last time that I was ever to see my parents together, a day I remember as if it were yesterday.

Maureen was to stay in that convent for many years - throughout the Japanese invasion and occupation, in fact.

Introducing Nick and Sue Fenn

In the early 1960s - of which he writes in the present volume - Nick Fenn was a junior British diplomat in Mandalay and Rangoon.

At the University of Mandalay in 1960 my wife Sue and I taught spoken English to classes of 70. We wanted to learn Burmese from our students. So at the end of every lesson we invited them home: "No 29 University Estate - any time." Nobody came. The teacher is on a pedestal and you do not visit him at home. After six weeks, one bold spirit came timidly to the door. We welcomed him in and explained the ground rules: half an hour English in exchange for half an hour Burmese. After that they came for breakfast, lunch and dinner.

Three of them invited us to visit them at home in April. They came from Pakokku, notoriously the hottest place in Burma in the hottest month in the year. No matter. We went.

They welcomed us at the airport with long faces. The local English Methodist missionary had said their homes were not good enough for us: we must stay at the manse. We left our luggage at their house, went to pay our respects to our compatriot and declined his hospitality.

Back with the students, I belatedly recalled a session we had had with them the previous week when they had asked me to describe to them a day in the life of an Englishman in Burma. I had mentioned that I took a glass of whisky before dinner in the evening; and there on the dressing table in our bedroom was a bottle of whisky which must have cost them a month's income. I had mentioned that in the morning we took a bath - not a splash in the well but total immersion. And behind their house they had built a bathroom in our honour. All the children in the village knew of this phenomenon. As soon as we emerged from the house with our towels they came running to peer through the slats to see if we really took all our clothes off. Fortunately their parents soon shooed them off and we took our baths in privacy.

We had been given a lesson in hospitality. And shortly afterwards the Methodist missionary was posted to Cornwall.

Nick Fenn - or Sir Nicholas Fenn GCMG, as he is now properly titled - went on to a most distinguished diplomatic career - including Ambassador in Rangoon in the early 1980s, and more recently British High Commissioner in India. His Burma experiences will no doubt find a place in his memoirs at some future date.

1930s Introducing Evelyn (Gaudoin)

In the late 1930s, Evelyn was in her teens - the daughter of an Anglo-Indian Deputy Commissioner and a Shan princess.

We took the fantastic mountain scenery of the Shan States for granted - looking out of the dormitory window the moon rose above Myin-Ma-Ti, 5000 ft above sea level. The school's forty acres had no fences as we were surrounded by virgin pine forests. We seldom went into the single High Street of the small holiday resort, except for walking in the 'crocodile' on Sundays. There were about a hundred pupils then, mostly girls - the few boys there were either those with sisters there or American citizens. One thing we learned that was not taught in other schools (English-speaking) was about the country we were living in - the flora and fauna, tribal customs, local religions etc. Other schools lifted the curriculum straight from the English system with no reference to Burma.

We had samples of the local timber and could differentiate between teak, *pyinkado, padauk* etc. From our bird watching expeditions I recollect the names of some of the birds: hoopoe, golden oriole and scarlet minivet. We all had the same amount of pocket money regardless of what the parents' income was but we seldom had occasion to spend it, except at the school fairs. I recollect a highlight of the school year when Captain Rushall, Mayor of Rangoon, paid Kalaw a visit. He took us all to the one main store and said we could each choose any sweets we wanted to the value of 8 annas (about 6d.) The store was Shirazee's (run by Iranians). I chose chewing-gum and sugared almonds as long-lasting. We went home only once a year at Christmas for 8 or 10 weeks. In my case we lived about 600 miles from school as father was in the Burma Frontier Service. Our Easter break was in the dry season and we had wonderful picnics - the Americans were quite inventive and imaginative - there was the 'One legged Pirate picnic' and the 'Kidnapping picnic' which due to a misunderstanding turned into the 'Police picnic' when the Assistant Superintendent of Police and his posse of armed constables turned up. Many years later I married the man.

This is Evelyn Broughton-Smart née Gaudoin. These recollections were written specially for the present work.

1940 **Sylvia**

The Northern Shan States is a high plateau on the eastern border of Burma and China. I believe Pat was given this job out of consideration for me, being a new bride from England, because the climate was so pleasant.

Waking up in the morning at Meiktila, I was amazed at the glorious sunrise reflecting in the lake. I think I have never seen more wonderful skies than in Burma at the rainy season. When the clouds bank up at sunrise or sunset, the heavens seem aflame...

We were delighted to arrive at our new home situated on a hillside and standing alone in a spacious garden, a two-storey house, unusual in that land of bungalows. I was greeted on arrival by the cook and his wife (Anthony and Mary, very dark Madrassi Indians, who later shared our many vicissitudes) and Thaw Ma, the Burmese *lugale* (loogalay) or butler. Next we met the *mali* (gardener), an Indian. Apart from these servants we also had as part time workers the dhobi, who took away the clothes for washing (banging them on the stones), and the Indian sweeper who came every day to clean the floors and the bathrooms, there being no sanitation or running water in those parts. In our bungalow, as was usual in Burma, every bedroom had its own bathroom, provided with a tin bath and a huge earthenware jar of water big enough to conceal one of the Forty Thieves. We used to sing together as we bathed in the adjacent bathrooms, songs such as *Ain't Misbehavin*, and *Dinner for one, please James*. The bath water was prepared by our *lugale,* Thaw Ma.

1946 — Philip Plumb

A 21-year-old British officer who will later describe the transition period between the surrender of the Japanese in 1945 and Burma's Independence in 1948.

At this time Rangoon Radio was housed in most inadequate premises at 228 Lowis Road. From time to time at the studios we caught glimpses of a Westerner attired in Burmese *longyi* and jacket who, according to our colleagues in Intelligence "had gone native" and was regarded with some suspicion. This was Ft. Lt. Hugh Jenkins, who had been seconded to the Government of Burma in 1945 as Director of English programmes, Rangoon Radio. He later became Minister for the Arts in the Labour Government, 1974-6 and is now Lord Jenkins of Putney. He has written various radio plays including *Lost Tune from Rangoon*. He was highly delighted to hear of Intelligence's view of him when I told him a few years ago.

1950s - A Bo-Gyi in Dawei — U Win Aung

Dawei, formerly known as Tavoy, is a coastal town on the Tenasserim Coast. It is my birthplace where I grew up. One would be surprised to know that an Englishman lived there even many years after Independence. I did not know his real name, because we all called him Bo-gyi ("Sir"), and that was enough to remember him. He was not married, but lived with his adopted son, U Shwe Lann and his family. U Shwe Lann had a very beautiful young daughter, who was the same age as me. Her name was Aye Aye. Bo-gyi was very proud of his grand-daughter and every morning they used to walk together hand in hand along the road where we lived. He was a very gentle hearted man and the reason we liked him most was because of his fondness of children. Whenever we saw him, with Aye Aye beside him, we chased after him and greeted - "Good Morning Bo-gyi". He would give us some sweets, which he always carried in one of his trouser pockets.

We always greeted him without fail for two reasons - beautiful Aye Aye and of course the sweets.

Bo-gyi passed away in our home town when I was still young. We were very sorry to learn of his death. Because Aye Aye would now always be accompanied by her rather strict mother and also there were no more free treats from our dear Bo-gyi.

After many years, one day in Yangon (Rangoon) I met Daw Aye Aye who is now happily married to a friend of mine, a Senior Naval Officer, at the school where our children studied. Though she was alone, waiting for her son, I thought I saw Bo-gyi beside her. Of course that was just an imagination.

H.E. U Win Aung is currently Myanmar Ambassador in London - as well as patron of the Britain Burma Society.

1961 - Mrs Childers

Nick Fenn

One of the most rewarding things about the diplomatic service is the way in which it brings us into contact with compatriots all over the world who have been left behind by history. I once paid a consular visit to a retired British merchant seaman who lived in a garage in the Sahara desert. In much the same spirit, my wife and I called on Mrs Childers in Kalaw in 1961.

Mrs Childers was the widow of a British Army Officer who had died in 1926. She still spoke not a word of Burmese and actually told us that "if they do not understand, you shout". She and her niece had been on the first plane which failed to get out of Myitkyina in 1942. Her niece had been killed beside her and she had been sent by the Japanese to sweep the streets. At the end of the war she had gone back to her cottage, replanted her garden and resumed her life.

The view was spectacular. The garden was "made in Hampshire". The door was opened by her Indian manservant who had first been engaged by her husband when he was a lion tamer for the Kaiser in the Berlin zoo in 1912. He said "Mummy will be with you directly" and showed us into a drawing room dominated by an immense ancient wireless permanently set to the World Service of the BBC. Last month's issue of the Tatler was open on the table. Mrs Childers served us tea out of a silver teapot and cucumber sandwiches. We talked about this and that. She disapproved almost equally of post-socialist Britain and of post-independent Burma. But her heart was in Kalaw and she would live and die there. By the time we rose to leave, I had enjoyed my contact with this dinosaur but had concluded that she did not have much to teach me.

In the hall she gave me a copy of Teilhard de Chardin's *Phenomenon of Man* which had then been published for about six weeks. She had read it and enjoyed it. Would I like to borrow it? It was one of the most seminal philosophical works of its generation. I had misjudged Mrs Childers.

1960 - A British *Nat?* — Nick Fenn

Nats are animist, pre-Buddhist spirits of the countryside who co-exist in many Burmese minds with the sophisticated teachings of Buddhism. There are the 37 great *Nats* with a secure place in Buddhist mythology. But there are also local *Nats* in many Burmese villages.

In 1960, the northern Shan states were closed to foreigners for security reasons. We could not go beyond Maymyo. But once we went with Burmese friends in their jeep to see the spectacular feat of railway engineering at the Goteik gorge. Just before Goteik on the right hand side my friend indicated the outskirts of a village. "Some time you must come back and visit that village," he said, "it contains a British Nat." He told me the following story.

The Goteik Gorge.

In 1942 the retreating British Army had passed through that village. One Sergeant had been wounded and had been left behind in the village by his mates. The villagers had tended his wounds and hid him from the Japanese. In turn, he had placed his university degree in engineering at the villagers' disposal and had designed a sophisticated irrigation system which had greatly enhanced the profitability of their fields. He also knew a thing or two about first aid. The villagers loved him.

But eventually he was betrayed to the Japanese. They took him out of the village and shot him under a banyan tree. His spirit lives in that tree. There is a shrine in his honour. His army webbing belt and his gleaming cap badge hang in the shrine together with a wooden rifle. And each morning they bring him not rice but a steaming mug of NAAFI tea. He is the British *Nat.*

Years later I went back to the northern Shan state but I could not find the village with the British *Nat.* I hope my Burmese friend was not pulling my leg. It is a good story.

1941 - Mrs Childers Before the War — Maureen

Sometimes I loitered near the boundary of the school compound, often seeing a very pretty English girl on horseback, rather older than me. Once I plucked up enough courage to say hello to her, and she told me that her name was Gemma, the niece of a Mrs Childers who lived near the convent and was a good friend of the nuns. I thought Gemma was the epitome of Englishness, with perfect poise, looking so elegant on her horse, and I was happy to worship her from a distance.

April 1942 - Flight from the Japanese — Sylvia

Travelling on the Burma road was slow torture - like the jam on an August Bank holiday in England, but there was no holiday spirit among us, only a grim determination to get away as far as possible from the Japs. Most of the vehicles were lorries packed with people and goods; all along the road were traffic jams, the tension of knowing what was behind was almost unbearable. Chinese soldiers were travelling to the front line in the opposite direction to us; when we met these convoys we all had to stop. We also met these convoys on the first day's journey as well as soldiers laying dynamite to blow up the road. The road was also blocked with trees at certain points. On our second day's journey we were held up for hours because we came to a bridge where only one vehicle was allowed to cross at a time. Considering the thousands of lorries that had to cross, the delay can be imagined.

June 1942 - Mrs Childers Reappears
Maureen (living under Japanese occupation)

It was almost dusk one evening and Lucy, Mary and I were playing a last game of General Post, chasing each other round the solid wooden pillars of the portico under the teachers' dormitory when we were startled by the ghostly appearance of a tall woman in European dress gliding out of the shadows. She was in a pathetic state, her clothing torn and filthy, her face too blood-stained and bruised to allow her to speak, but I recognized her almost at once as Mrs Childers, the aunt of Gemma with whom I had struck up an acquaintance in those lonely Christmas holidays. As I whispered her name, she put her hand cautiously to her lips and then fell senseless to the ground. We ran to get the nuns and they carried her gently up the stairs to what had been the teachers' quarters. With great kindness they nursed her back to health, for they possessed excellent nursing skills, taking all her meals to her room and keeping a watchful eye out for any sign of the Japs, as we now called them. She never came out until after dark, sometimes watching us play by the light of the hurricane lamps, now and again managing a faint smile, but not much more.

We learned from Teresina that Mrs Childers and Gemma had made their way to Myitkyina right up in the north and got on the last flight leaving Burma before the Japanese invasion. But the plane had been shot down, killing Gemma. Stricken with grief, her aunt had decided against attempting the perilous border crossing on foot and had somehow made her way all the way back to Kalaw. Often she travelled through dense jungle so as to avoid villages for fear of bumping into the Japs, sometimes she met helpful villagers, others drove her away for fear of retaliation. Miraculously she evaded the enemy, and, so full of admiration were the nuns for this brave lady, that they were prepared to risk a great deal to keep her safe.

Later 1942 - Mrs Childers

Maureen

We were left unmolested at the convent for most of the time, but every so often the Japanese soldiers would swoop down on us to make a random check, remembering that we had once harboured a Chinese. On one of these swoops, Mrs Childers was discovered. How, we never found out. Perhaps we had been watched as we played in the dusk when she was wont to come down and silently enjoy watching us. There was no warning. Four soldiers burst in among us one afternoon and without any hesitation marched their way to her room at the top of the stairs. Another soldier stood at the bottom barring the way up and thus we all stood helplessly below, hearing the guttural voices shouting and giving orders. They emerged some minutes later, surrounding her completely, but as she was taller than they, we saw that her head was bleeding profusely and her clothes were in disarray. We had not heard her utter so much as a cry, although she must have received quite a battering to be in such a state. Powerless to intervene, and greatly shaken ourselves, we looked on as she walked away, bayonets prodding her unnecessarily. As they passed, Mother Superior stretched out her hands in a gesture of sympathy towards Mrs Childers, hoping she would realise that we would not have betrayed her for anything in the world, but one of the soldiers butted her away with his rifle as a warning. We felt the brave lady understood, as with bloody head held high she was marched away. We never saw her again, although once or twice word got to the nuns that she was held prisoner in an unknown camp, impressing everyone with her dignity and courage, and still managing to be as fastidious in her dress and appearance as ever.

CHRISTMASES (& OTHER CHRISTIAN FESTIVALS)

Christmas 1931 - Rangoon — Stella

Christmas, occurring in the cool season, was always especially wonderful - with picnics, fancy dress parties and visits. On Christmas morning, the merchants and Brokers that my Father had dealt with during the year, came to pay their respects and (in a way) to say thank you for his kind attention. They arrived one or two at a time followed by their retainers carrying trays and baskets of goodies (these were known as Dollies). On the trays were large iced cakes, chocolates, Indian sweets, grapes, almonds, apples and dates. A couple of squawking chickens and very often a turkey were also presented. But first of all garlands of flowers (mostly marigolds) twined with silver tinsel would be hung around the necks of my parents. As you can imagine we children loved the performance. The turkeys would be kept and fattened for some other occasion. The rest of the day would be spent either receiving guests or visiting. Being a very Scottish community New Year's Eve (Hogmanay) took precedence over Christmas. First Footing was very important. The Scottish people stuck together.

Christmas 1937 - Near the Burma-India Border — Evelyn

On one Christmas break my father had to meet the Political Agent, Mr Gimson, on the border at Tamu via Kalewa and Kalemyo and we all went along too (six children). My father took the first car ever up that road to Tamu (this road was very useful during the British retreat from Burma in 1942). In our retinue there were two cars, horses, bullock carts and a mule train for staff and servants and incredibly two bicycles, ridden by my brother David and me - quite unsupervised - we were barely into our teens. It was hard going and I was quite nervous when we overtook the mules in case they panicked - especially on the roads with sheer drops on one side. Lifting the bikes over the *kazins* (ridges between the paddy fields) in the Kabaw Valley was tiring. But the final straw was when a bicycle-riding vaccinator, journeying from village to village, was chased by an elephant. I abandoned my bike and continued the journey on horseback - poor David (younger than I was) soldiered on alone. (Ironically, David later joined the Burma Rifles and did not survive the trek to India - he was still in his teens.) The horses would suddenly stop and refuse to move when we came across fresh elephant dung and our competent syces would come to our aid. I never talked about these experiences at school because no-one else seemed to do this sort of thing.

Christmas 1940 - Shan States

Sylvia

On Christmas morning we had a great surprise when the cook and his wife walked in as we were having breakfast and presented us with a dish of fruit and a bouquet of flowers, also a posy for each of us made of a rosebud with maidenhair fern. Such trifles as this touch the heart. Our house looked gay, decked up with the coloured chains I had always associated with Christmas as a child. We had our Christmas dinner in the evening, an innovation for me as coming from a middle class home in England I had always dined at midday. The goose was a great success, but the Christmas pudding was a failure. Probably my poor Anthony had never been called upon to cook such a thing before. To give the festive touch we had crackers and dined in evening dress, finishing up with a party on our own, dancing to the gramophone and singing Christmas carols - two English people quite alone in their festivities in that village of Buddhists.

The Superintendent of the Northern Shan States, Arthur Porter, spent New Year with us. He was a very lonely man; his wife chose to live in England with their son. Many men lived lonely lives because their wives would not stay in Burma. The children had to be sent to England or India for their education and it was a very difficult situation for any woman to face. However, the men can hardly be blamed if many of them took Burmese mistresses for their comfort.

Christmas 1941 - Shan States

Sylvia

The day I made the Christmas cake (that is, Christmas 1941) we were invited to the wedding of the Chief Minister's niece, but I could not go as I was in the middle of cake making. We had no warning of the wedding beforehand. Pat went along and saw the girl of twenty married to an Anglo-Indian called Kelly who was about 48 and divorced. They had met only three times. I believe the girl's father made this match because Kelly was a rich man.

We were giving a large party on 26th December, inviting about 25 people. There would be Buddhists, Mohammedans, Hindoos and our Christian selves. The problem of giving a dinner party among so many religions was no light one. The doctor, a Mohammedan, could not eat pork. The P.W.D. subdivisional officer, a Sikh, could not eat beef. The Buddhists ate anything and were particularly fond of pork. The doctor could not eat the meat of any animal or bird unless it had been killed by himself or another Mohammedan, and it was arranged that he should come to do the killing. We would have a number of different curries so that all could be suited.

Christmas Day was quite different from our English Christmas Day. We were invited to the christening of the daughter of the *Kyemong* (eldest son of the Sawbwa). The baby of three months was in a decorated cradle suspended from a beam in the ceiling and two children sat at the sides and rocked it by means of ropes tied to the sides of the cradle. Hanging on the ropes from the ceiling were various gifts including gold bracelets. The priest dressed in white said some prayers at an altar and then blessed the child, sprinkling it with water as in our own ceremony. It was a pleasantly short ceremony and afterwards we were given *khowkshwe,* a Chinese dish made from noodles and various spices and pieces of pork, a very tasty dish.

Christmas 1941 - Rangoon — Sylvia

The air attack by Japan in December 1941 came as a terrible shock, though our troops seemed to be recovering a little. We hoped that aeroplane reinforcements would be sent. Singapore had been bombed and the Japs were fighting in Malaya. We heard to our satisfaction that Jap planes approaching Rangoon always departed at the sight of our RAF planes. Looking back at this time, I fear we were suffering from wishful thinking.

Later we heard from Rangoon that Pat's mother had had a narrow escape from the bombing by Japanese planes, fire from incendiaries came into their trench and they were covered with dust from bombs falling around. Several buildings nearby were hit. In that first raid there were one thousand deaths due mostly to people standing out in the open to watch the planes. In the next raid on Christmas day there only fifty deaths, which showed that people had learnt a bitter lesson. Oscar (Pat's brother) was a 2nd Lieutenant on anti-aircraft guns and his battery brought down four Japanese planes. Altogether in the two raids we heard there were 41 Japanese planes accounted for and there might have been others shot down into the sea.

We did not think Mongyai was important enough to be bombed but nevertheless went ahead with blackout preparations. As we had only lace curtains, our brilliant kerosene lamps could be seen for miles. I therefore blacked out the lamps with half a kerosene tin. I blacked out the top small window with Shan paper which was quite thick.

Christmas 1945 - after Allied victory Lewis Shaw

In the Karen church, I was already reading the lesson, and it was not long before they persuaded me to give a sermon. This was a bit nerve wracking the first time, when I found that my Sergeants had all turned up to hear me! However, I did it six or seven times after that, and on one occasion actually took the whole service in English while one of the Karens repeated my words in Burmese.

On Boxing Day I witnessed my first display of Sumo Wrestling, by Japanese Surrendered Personnel. The wrestlers were serving soldiers of course, and therefore not the great fat men we see performing today, but nevertheless it was a fearsome show of strength. We had our main meal of the day in the evening, and our guests were six of our Karen friends. The sing song afterwards lasted till one o'clock, then having taken them home, we had another little party with the Sankey's. Once again it was after two when we eventually got to bed, the two days making the most memorable Christmas I had ever had.

Christmas 1945-46 - the Far North Mavis Edwards

"In return for roof repairs, due to the strong winds that swept the coast of Venezuela, washing and feeding the children and hungry of all ages, the local people shared the little they had and came bearing gifts of eggs and bananas for the sisters".)

On reading this paragraph in *Mother Teresa* by Kathryn Spink (p 83), I was immediately taken back to the long 'bamboo basha' which served as the Civil Hospital and our four wonderful rewarding years in Myitkyina. My dear husband, Robert was CMO, GS and 'General Factotum' in the capital of the growing Kachin State, with the Burmese Government after the Japanese left. In a similar fashion the very grateful poor came sharing their bananas, eggs and on one occasion a chicken, with us.

Myitkyina was unexpectedly cold, being on the very borders of South China. We kept ourselves and the three children warm with coal fire burners, using wood when coal ran out as the locals did. It seems impossible now that we celebrated three Christmases and all the birthdays, making and baking birthday and Christmas cakes, decorating Christmas Trees and enjoying Christmas and Birthday parties. The UBA planes brought limited provisions once a week only (weather permitting).

There was a considerable amount of improvisation. Burma had been almost devastated by the Japanese and Allied bombing. But somehow when the recovery came there was no looking back. The other Government Officers were grateful for my school-teacher background; so my three children and those of the DC and other officers had morning school from 9 a.m. to 12 noon.

I must not end without describing another grand experience, though we did not appreciate it at the time. The view from the boundary fence, at the back of the yard, looked onto the China scene of snow-capped mountain ranges, blowing icy cold winds over the tail end of the Himalayas. The few Government Officials stationed in the Kachin State after the war would gather together for Government celebrations and more frequently house parties. Returning from one such evening warmed with much Kachin liquor and Johnny Walker Scotch, we hazily drove through what next morning we discovered had been a blizzard and heavy snow fall. This resulted in the flooding of the Irrawaddy, which had risen considerably during the night. Unfortunately the 'basha' was razed to the ground. The servants had armed themselves with their little circular eating tables on their heads to protect themselves as they ran about collecting hailstones, which fell all night and next morning. We collected enough hailstones to fill our zinc bath tub, and being resourceful we enjoyed that hail-storm for many a day and night with iced lager and wine and good company. After all, there is nothing like a little hardship to bring out the best in us.

1985 - Rangoon - St Andrew's Night — Sue Fenn

One St Andrew's Night in Rangoon we gave a party with all the trimmings - haggis and piper and ode to the haggis, followed by vigorous dancing in the hall. (I had been organising Scottish country dance evenings for several months so there were lots of enthusiastic dancers that evening!) We had a grand time well into the "wee hours"! When the last guest had departed and we turned to go upstairs to bed we saw something sparkling at the foot of the stairway. It was a magnificent diamond ring which we put in the safe overnight.

We were surprised that no-one phoned or came to claim it next day, nor the day after that. On the third day I decided to telephone all our guests to trace the owner - but with whom to begin? I decided that the setting of the ring was Burmese or Thai and ran my mind through my friends who were energetic dancers. Matilda was an obvious candidate.

"Did you lose anything at our party the other night?" I asked her. "Yes. A diamond cluster ring my mother gave me." She described it in every detail. "But why didn't you call to find out if it had been found?"

Then she explained that she'd missed it on the drive home and had wanted to come back at once; but her husband, Ben, had said we would probably be in bed. Next morning he wouldn't let her phone in case it hadn't been found. He reasoned that it if had been found it was safe, and if it hadn't then they mustn't make us go to the trouble of turning the house upside-down searching for it. If it wasn't found even then, the servants would be blamed and everyone would feel miserable. No, they must not say anything.

Well, Matilda wasn't at all happy, especially when the third day dawned and I hadn't called. So she went to her astrologer. He was completely reassuring. "Your ring is in a very safe place and will be returned to you very soon".

"So" she concluded "to save you any more trouble, shall I come round right away to collect it?"

Which she did.

1920s AND 1930s

Stella

The Diocesan Girls High School in Rangoon was enormous. In the middle of the day, servants would arrive with our lunch. My favourite meal was "Pish Pash" a chicken and rice stew. Although I loved jelly we could only eat that at home as the jelly melted in the heat. We always had lots of fruit but I can't remember having many sweets. I suppose this was because there were no small areas of shops as we have here in England and it was not easy to pop around the corner to buy them.

Rangoon was divided by the railway line. The best residential area around the Shwe Dagon Pagoda was on one side and the commercial and poorer area and the Sule Pagoda was on the other side, with the river. A visit to the Burra bazaar was an exciting expedition - one could buy almost anything there - and the smell of fruit and spices hung over the huge covered corridors with cave-like rooms from which were sold cloth or utensils or vegetables or fruit or lacquer-ware or leather goods or brass, gold or silver. As one stepped out of a car or a Tikka gharry (a kind of horse drawn carriage) the native people would run forward to be hired to carry one's shopping in baskets balanced on their heads. Here we bought mangoes by the hundred, or custard apples, marrions (small plum-like fruit) pineapples, lychees, papayas (pawpaws) and other exotic fruit. Oranges had loose skins and were sweet. The saddest sight there were beggars all pleading for baksheesh. Sadly one learnt to be hard-hearted and say *"masheeboo"* (haven't got). But just before driving off we would give them one or two cents or rupees.

Street vendors carried their wares in baskets hanging from either end of a pole slung on the shoulder. If it was hot food a charcoal brazier would be in one basket - hot food was mostly Chinese. Ice-cream *"Koorfie burraf"* was served from aluminium cones, kept cold surrounded by rock salt until the "Stop me and Buy One" choc ices arrived. One saw sugar cane juice pushed out of long stalks and sold straight from the cane. Also ice shaved off a block, shaped round and flavoured and coloured - lolly ices. At night there were the street stalls lining Mogul Street. Here one could buy the most delicious curry and also paratas and other delicacies that I can still taste and smell but can't name. Then there were the "Box Wallas". Two men, one in front, the boss, followed by a native with a black tin box on his head. They came right to the house and spread their wares out on the balcony to tempt one. Chinese men carried their own bundle containing beautiful hand-embroidered silk garments, table linen and lace - "Nice Lice Ladies" was their opening gambit. At nightfall two bamboo sticks knocked together rhythmically and the cry *"Eeabaysala"* (hot roasted peanuts) which could be measured out in tiny, thimble sized china cups and were often eaten when playing bridge in the evenings. Much nicer than any sold now. There was another delicious little edible salted pea called *"patanie"*, popular with Bridge or Mah Jong players like my Mother. A Box Wallah that I remember from very early days was a Jewess named "Sadie". In her tin trunk she sold clothes, braid, buttons, laces and other treasures. We liked the Chinese men best and they seemed to come around on Sunday morning.

1930 **Evelyn**

The school at Kalaw had beautiful gardens as it was a great interest of the Principal's and she tried to import plants from the USA. I heard they did manage to grow avocados after the war. All the fruit and vegetables were grown there and we children had our own little plots to tend as we wished. I grew peanuts and kohl rabi. The Vice-Principal taught the cooks to make lovely cakes and bread and the aroma of baking bread always recalls school days; also a dish of endives cooked with crispy bacon which I discovered years later when I was in the USA was a German-American recipe. We had a choice of tea, coffee or cocoa and could choose brown or white bread and as many slices as we wanted, spread with home-churned butter. I took all this for granted and realised only later that this was not common in all boarding schools.

1921-22 **Stella**

When the then Prince of Wales visited the Far East it was a time for grand festivities. On the residential side of Rangoon there was a beautiful lake "the Royal Lake". Many years later we lived by it. On this occasion all the trees around it were garlanded with lights and bands played and there were firework displays. My parents knew someone who had a House-boat on the lake and we visited them and enjoyed the excitement even more. We were invited to visit them on this special night and I can remember the slap slap of the wavelets under the floor boards and the delicious box of chocolates that was passed around. Boxes for chocolates were actually made of tin in those days. My young brother John was too small to be out at that time of night and I remember secreting half of my chocolate in my hanky for him. (I have always enjoyed things more when I share them and my elder brother Eric also has this characteristic.) On this night there was a wonderful firework display but I kept falling asleep. I can also remember seeing the Prince play polo and overhearing snippets of gossip about him. Another time my father phoned to say Lady Elizabeth Bowes Lyon was about to drive past the house. So we got out our flags and stood by the gate and waved frantically when her car drove past. When abroad we felt so cut off from Britain that these Royal visits were possibly greeted out of all proportion.

The Prince of Wales arriving in Rangoon in 1922.

Stella

(This photo shows her aged 23)

We belonged to many clubs. The Gymkhana Club being the most prestigious. The Golf Club, The Boat Club (on the Royal Lakes) and Swimming Club. It was not easy to be accepted in these clubs - one had to "be put up" by a member then voted in. There were dances nearly every weekend at the Gymkhana or the Boat Club and at Christmas and New Year there were Balls, sometimes Masked Balls and Fancy Dress; Concerts and Plays were held in the Gymkhana - known as "The Gym".

The dances at night were very romantic. There were also dances and Bowls (skittles) in the afternoon. Sunday evenings the Band played and one sat on the balcony drinking, chatting and eating thick crisps with tomato sauce. While the poor hard-working men were at their offices, we spoilt females shopped, visited, played Mah Jong or bridge, sewed dresses and perhaps baked cakes. Two of the houses we lived in had tennis courts and so we held tennis parties and were invited back to other tennis parties which always included outdoor tea.

The Garden Parties and Balls at Government House were very grand affairs. When my Father was a young man he had joined the Volunteer Defence Brigade and gradually climbed the ranks ladder to become Colonel, then Lieutenant Colonel and Honorary ADC to the Viceroy of India - a very exalted position. This meant if the Viceroy visited Burma, my Father would have been his right hand man. This opened the doors of Government House to us, after duly signing the "Calling Book" at the gate. This was in the days of Lord and Lady Stephenson. In time we received invitations to Garden Parties and Balls and Swimming Parties. I liked the Garden Parties best. Marquees were set out on the manicured green lawns - and there were little round tables and chairs. Dainty sandwiches and cakes were served by smartly dressed servants. Military bands played the latest dance music while Lord and Lady Stephenson and other big wigs wandered about greeting people - then everyone wandered around meeting friends and "being seen"! We wore long pretty dresses, large rimmed hats and long, elbow length gloves. Long white gloves were worn at most Balls. Daddy wore his uniform and looked very smart and I was so proud of him. I am sad now that I took it all for granted and my right. The Balls too were on a grand scale. No dancing until the Governor and his Lady entered - then a path was cleared for them through the ballroom and we bowed our heads and those who had been presented at Court curtsied. Then the bands played - one military band and one civilian. All around the room potted ferns and chairs were positioned, and in the grounds, fairy lights

Garden party in the grounds of Government House, early 1930s.

twinkled in the bushes and trees. As we arrived at the front entrance we were presented with our little dance programmes. After ascending the grand staircase to the ladies room to leave our cloaks we came down again and hopefully filled our programmes with the names of dance partners. It was fine if one was booked for every dance but rather miserable if there were one or two blanks. Then one went upstairs again, fiddled with hair and waited for the next dance. This happened to me on one occasion when to oblige some friends to make up their numbers I attended twice one week and did not know many people the second time - was I miserable! The first time I went with my parents I wore a long white satin dress with a low, full tulle skirt; it was lovely. My brother Eric was with us and that was nice as I could always depend on him for a partner.

The swimming parties were for young people and the Governor did not attend. One of the stunts was to place a chair backwards on the diving platform and tip us young ladies over - not too nice! A feature at the Balls was the supper - laid out on long tables and consisting of every conceivable goody. Eating it was not easy - long gloves, with the finger part rolled back and tucked in, an evening bag and programme dangling from one's wrist, a glass of something and one's plate and at the same time trying to make polite conversation - there were never enough chairs for everyone. Lovely iced champagne was served on arrival. All in all I must have attended six balls. Other grand occasions were being entertained to cocktails on Navy Warships. Once it was the German Navy! Launches collected us from the jetty and we were ferried across in style. Bands played and all was very ship shape and Bristol fashion. It seemed very posh.

Noel Holmes

I was born in Maymyo in 1931 and for the next ten years lived almost 100% of the time in this delightful hill station. Both my parents were devout Catholics and religion played a significant part in everyday life. I was the last of nine in my family and by the time that I 'appeared' my father had retired from the Excise Department. Apart from his pension he rented out four houses in Maymyo and had some small other investments. For those familiar with Maymyo, I was christened in the church of the Immaculate Conception and went to St Joseph's Convent until we were evacuated ahead of the sweeping Japanese invasion in 1942. The things I remembered at the time were

(a) My first day at school and the very strict nuns. Discipline was, perhaps, the main feature of my early education.

(b) The Burmese generally were regarded as 'second-class' citizens. As a whole they did not seem to want to speak English - unlike the Indians, many of whom were Christians - and they played their own games, never wanting to participate in

The governor, Sir Archibald Cochrane, in residence at Maymyo, with Lady Cochrane.

soccer or cricket. Indian servants, rather than Burmese, were considered better.

(c) My first film - *Snow White and the Seven Dwarfs* - at the Regal cinema in the town centre.

(d) Learning to ride a bicycle - and owning my first one.

(e) Picnics at the old "Hampshire Falls".

(g) The railway station where we used to meet or say farewell to my brothers and sisters.

(h) Rides in gharries, legal or otherwise!

I mention all these factors because when I returned to Maymyo over 50 years later I was able, to a certain extent, to compare my childhood memories with the present.

For Maymyo, at any rate, nothing has changed. The nuns and convent are still there even though the school is now secular. Religion is taught separately. I was delighted to find that the four houses my father had rented out were still in use. The Burmese were most hospitable and friendly even though I was regarded as a "foreigner". The cinema is still functioning though, of course, no longer showing English films. Cycles are very much the main form of transport especially for children. Picnics are still enjoyed at Pwe Kauk (Hampshire) falls and this area has been developed and looked after. The railway station has not changed and still 'exports' the fruit and vegetables always associated with Maymyo. Gharries are still the main form of hired transport.

So overall Maymyo has not changed to any significant degree. We spent three and two days in Rangoon and Mandalay respectively and overall they are very like the other Asian cities we have visited - crowded, dusty and bustling. I am, of course, unable to compare them to the pre-war days.

"Paddy boat" in the 1920s.

1947 **Glyn Court**

who came into Burma with the Allied forces in 1945

I suspect that after a much longer residence in Burma than my three years the unending exotic beauty might have made its strangeness felt to my English soul and the absence of the changing seasons might have left me ill at ease and longing for them. I shall never know, of course. But the people, not the climate or the beauty of nature, make a country, and of knowing the people I should never tire.

As foreigners to Burma we were warned, "Take care: they are the Irish of the East: humorous and easy-going, but prone to outbursts of passion and capable of violence!" - which last seemed not too inaccurate a description of ourselves! But one soldier, and many others who looked for themselves, found so much more to warm to and feel unexpectedly at home with: the absence of the caste system which infected the life of India; the independence of Burmese women and their social equality with men - in some ways, superiority; their attention to cleanliness of body and neatness of dress; their love of children; their response to any approach by us foreigners; the generally beneficent influence of their Buddhist faith, and the generosity they showed while seeking to acquire 'merit'; and as for the violence, many a night I walked alone through the darkness in Rangoon to broadcast on Forces' Radio, and no one gave me cause for uneasiness or disquiet.

1941 **Sylvia**

Among many varied tasks my husband was qualified to do in Burma was the job of magistrate. Our tour took us to a village called Loipyi. The day before we arrived, Pat received a report that a man in this village had shot his wife through the leg. On the evening of our arrival my husband visited the injured woman who the *duwa* (headman) said was being cured with local medicines. He came back for me, as it was obvious she was not being cured in any way. I had never seen such a horrible sight before. In the front of her thigh was a gunshot wound about one and a half inches across, which was all septic, and the thigh was terribly swollen. A poor young thing of seventeen, she was lying in a mess of filthy rags, and the smell from the wound was frightful. I bathed the wound with a solution of potassium permanganate and dressed it with Chinese plaster; this is a dark coloured paste which heated and applied to wounds - we have found it most effective in drawing out the poison. With great difficulty we turned the girl over on to her side and in the back of her thigh was a great hole about three inches across where the bullet had come out. I cleaned up the green pus and the dirty stuff which had been applied and we bandaged the leg. It appeared that the thigh was broken, as the villagers said the bullet had shot out pieces of bone. I got some of the men to make splints from the ever useful bamboo, which was also used in making the stretcher. Next morning she was sent off to Namtu hospital, which was a walk of about three hours for the bearers. The girl had lain like this for seven days; if we had not arrived at this time she would have died and no one would have received a report as to the cause of death. We discovered later that the accused man was the adopted son of the *duwa*, who, being the chief, ought to have sent her immediately to hospital. This young man sat with her in the hut holding her hand and looking sorrowful. He said he was unconscious of doing the deed till afterwards, a very unlikely story unless he suffered a fit of madness. The shot was fired in the presence of another girl of seventeen. We did not hear the end of the case, as we left the district soon afterwards, but later heard that just when the injured girl appeared to be returning to health, she suddenly died. It was a sad story, but not so uncommon in a country of savage emotions.

1987 Derek Brooke-Wavell

In 1987 I arrived in Rangoon for three weeks of learning conversational Burmese, determined to shun all English speakers. Two or three hours each day would be spent studying in the Institute of Foreign Languages; and at least another hour roaming the streets, striking up conversations with whomever I could.

But just before the flight to Burma, someone claimed it was now against the law for Burmese to speak to foreigners. And on my first day, the heedless bustle of Rangoon streets was disheartening. So I walked off my jet-lag by myself in the sun - around the shores of the Royal Lake.

On the map the lake looks small enough, but the tour took two hours - mostly through deserted parkland, with the golden spire of the Shwe Dagon shining above green waters and toddy palms.

Half-way round I met someone who, as he got closer, looked more and more like my first Burmese problem. He wore a brown longyi; he and his mate took up the whole pathway, and ignored my "*mingalaba*" greeting. With coarse features and protruding lip, he stared intently as he approached. Before I could think of a suitable Burmese phrase, he was planted in front of me. Very seriously, he said a Burmese sentence. "*Ba agu ani bei ya ma lay?*" The meaning took a moment to sink in. My goodness - it was "What help can I give you?". Anxious moment over -

I politely declined, and they went on their way.

But there was something not quite right with my translation of the Burmese. Playing back his words through my head, I stuck on the *"ya"* - "must". It was "What help **must** I give you?" And that was something that had never sunk in before. A Burmese **must** give help to a stranger who asks for it - it is part of their culture.

That thought put my stay on a new footing. You don't need to win or buy the friendship of the Burmese. Anybody will give it freely. In that crowd of heedless strangers in a Rangoon street, I could go up to literally anyone, and ask some simple question - "Which way is the Sule Pagoda?" Not only were they pleased to show me the way; they would ply me with further offers of help. If I accepted, they'd be only too glad to invite me to their house - and would have put me up for the duration of my stay, had the regulations permitted.

What a difference from London! And yet the British too are generous at heart - we give regularly to charities, and even animals come in for our love. But for some reason we feel ashamed of our good impulses. Going to Burma, one sees that a different way is possible - and that can be both a happy and a humbling experience.

1940 **Sylvia**

I started to learn Burmese as soon as I had settled down. I can still remember the first complete sentence that my husband Pat taught me to recite parrot-fashion: "*Budda yone go thwa bidaw parseh ta toke u geh ba*" (go to the railway-station and bring back a parcel). In this way I learnt Burmese by ear only, picking up enough vocabulary to instruct our *lugale* (butler) and converse with villagers. I found Burmese one of the prettiest and more expressive languages I have ever heard. It seems characteristic of its people who are petite and dainty and very polite. There are in the language special words inserted only as a polite addition to speech. Though I gave my servant orders I always had to use a polite way of asking him to do them. My husband Pat, being master, wasn't obliged to use these terms. We were addressed by our Burmese servants as "*Thakin*" (Lord) and "*Thakinma*" (Lady). A party of nationalist Burmese called themselves "Thakins" by way of revolting against British rule. I never found any hostility against us in the Shan States. The people seemed very fond of us. They preferred British rule to that of the previous Burmese kings who treated the Shan princes as underlings and made concubines of the Shan princesses.

1962

Sue Fenn

It was three o'clock in the morning of 2 March 1962, and I was in the Prome Road Nursing Home. I was woken by my five-week old son - or perhaps by strange noises outside. As I sat nursing my baby I was aware of loud rumbling sounds from the Prome Road. Then there were scufflings, footsteps and whisperings below my window. I looked out - nothing. Yet, carrying my infant son, I went to the night nurse and announced "The army has taken over". Naturally she put my delusion down to my fever and tried to soothe me back to bed!

Then the doorbell rang loud and long, and I followed the nurse down the wide marble stairs into the spacious entrance hall. Through the grill across the doorway six or seven bayonets were pointing at us. The nurse calmly asked their business. I then discovered that the only other patient was the Sawbwa of Kengtung, Saw Sai Long - known since schooldays as Shorty. The men had been sent to arrest him at his home. Coming on here they were behind schedule and in a hurry. The nurse declared firmly that she had no authority to release a patient but that she was willing to telephone the doctor for guidance. It was only then that we learned that the telephone service had been disabled. So she let the men in and went to wake up Matron.

There was I, with my baby, face to face with perhaps ten embarrassed and worried soldiers, thwarted from carrying out orders by a calm pint-sized young Karen woman in a starched uniform. Nothing was said; but, as I stood there smiling a trifle anxiously at them, I suddenly remembered how I had observed, during our year in Mandalay studying the language, how fond Burmese men of all ages were of children. On an impulse I asked them if they'd like to hold my son. Immediately the guns were stacked against the walls and Robert was passed from arm to arm. When I told them in my very limited Burmese that we had also given him the name Aung Kyaw there was added interest and approval. (The young man Aung Kyaw is revered as the first martyr in the independence struggle against the British!).

When Matron and nurse returned to the hall the atmosphere was relaxed and cheerful. But the men had been given orders and there was no way we three women could stop them. Shorty - blissfully unaware of our situation! - was woken and wrapped in a regal silk dressing gown. Matron insisted he be carried out in a carrying chair and his departure seemed almost triumphant. Twenty years later he told me that he had planned to go home the next day anyway and that the soldiers had treated him with grave courtesy - but he had been locked up without trial for over six years. As he had assured me, as he was being carried down the stairs: "Don't worry, this is just one of those things! " Next morning a member of his family came to pay the nursing home bill!

As soon as the telephones were reconnected, I phoned my husband. It was seven o'clock and I woke him up! I told him not to worry about us: Robert and I were fine. He was puzzled - "Why shouldn't we be all right"? I told him that the army had taken over during the night. "Look out of the window if you don't believe me!" He rang off and phoned his Ambassador. So that is how the British Embassy was the first to report the Burmese revolution.

Most foreigners thought that someone was shooting a war film! The local people, in their thousands, spent much of the day praying at the great Shwedagon Pagoda.

This was the Army coup of March, 1962

1937 - Village Life

Maureen

In school holidays I could leave the convent and go to my mother's village. It would be hard to say just what the people of Sat-thwa did for a living. There must have been about five hundred people in the village all selling foodstuffs and firewood to each other, or building houses for one another. There was a school two or three doors away from our house and a monastery (*phongyi kyaung*) on the outskirts. Even in those days there was a relatively high rate of literacy, for monastic schools were generally available in almost every village throughout the country and open to all Buddhist youths or boys, who went there for a period of one or two years to learn the rudiments of their faith and receive an education. Girls also had a basic schooling in Burmese. Private fee-paying mission schools taught only in English, and these afforded the easiest entrance to colleges.

The better-off villagers drove bullock-carts, one or two had a horse and cart which plied to and from Taungdwingyi, some cut sugar-cane, but there were no paddy-fields or cultivation of ground-nuts. Nor do I remember any shops. But there was a market every five days, when ear-piercing and tattooing took place. People carried out their chores in leisurely, unhurried fashion. There was always a great deal of activity at the village's four wells and fetching water consumed the greater part of the day. Always performed by the young girls and women, with pots balanced gracefully on their heads on coils of cloth, it gave ample opportunity for mild flirtation with the young gallants who hung around hoping for just such an opportunity. Almost every day as night fell the plaintive calls of mothers rose from their verandahs, as they waited impatiently for the return of their dallying daughters.

1965 John Okell

For a time I tried hard to learn to play the Burmese oboe (*hne*). Competently played, the *hne* can carry its listeners away in a torrent of trills and scales and arpeggios, but in the hands of a novice it makes embarrassing squawks. I was so ashamed of my efforts that I used to walk miles into the rice fields to get out of anyone's hearing before I started my practice.

Then one day I noticed that Ko Tin Hla, who was also learning, didn't suffer at all from my sensitivities. He sat in the middle of his family home, with all and sundry coming and going, and made his dreadful noises unabashed. He was a beginner and as such didn't expect to play well. His family knew he was a beginner and they didn't expect him to play well either. So why was I so anxious about people hearing me? That was one lesson.

At about the same time we went one evening to a *pwe* where we listened to a master musician performing marvels on the tuned drums (*pat-waing*). When the performance was over I plucked up the courage to go and tell him how well I thought he had played. A British player would have been a little embarrassed, or pretended to be, and many would have pointed out some real or imagined shortcoming in their playing. The Burmese *hsaing-hsaya* just smiled and said: "Yes." He knew he was good: why pretend he wasn't? That was another lesson.

1925 - Raft

Stella is the "pioneer" on the far right.

1946 - Lorry

Philip Plumb

In November 1946 an Indian driver was taking me into Rangoon in a truck when an ancient car, driven by a Burman, shot out of a side road and hit us on the driver's side. We exchanged details and heard no more until a summons was received to attend the Law Courts. The 7th Additional Magistrate, an elderly Burman, was sitting in a small room at an office table. In front of him was a portable typewriter on which he was taking down the evidence with two fingers of the case he was currently hearing. His clerk, with a big revolver strapped to him, sat beside him. We were allowed to see the evidence which seemed to put all the blame on my driver for being rammed by the other vehicle. However, the prosecution witnesses were missing so we went away and heard no more.

1926 - Tikka Gharry

Stella

We owned two black horses and a carriage at this time. The larger horse was named "Shaitan" (devil) and he certainly was one. We eventually sold both horses and carriage and then had to hire "tikka gharries" when we wanted to go out. A servant would be sent to find one - they were like wooden boxes on four hard wheels. There were two bench-like seats inside facing each other and there was a large mirror behind one seat.

Windows beside each bench and the doors opened on to a step. The driver sat perched on top and the whole thing was drawn by a thin pony. A long whip kept the poor horse alert. One afternoon my Mother was taking me to the Dentist - as we crossed the railway bridge, something frightened the horse and it bolted - cyclists and pedestrians scattered as we approached and we narrowly missed the tram at the bottom of the hill. The gharry toppled over but my Mother had wrapped her arms around me and we emerged safe. I wonder what happened to the driver! Visits to the dentist were dreaded. He used to put a small amount of quicksilver into my hand and I would play with this, pressing on it until smaller balls of it would spread out and rejoin again until eventually there was nothing left. This was to distract me from the sound of the drill and the pain. A couple of years ago I heard how dangerous contact with Mercury is.

Another time when we owned a horse and carriage again, Gwen, my sister and I were waiting for my Father outside his Mess. It was dusk, and once again this horse bolted - it careered down the road, across a wide pavement and ended in a deep ditch. Once again we escaped unhurt. But it took a long time and a plank to get the horse out.

1930s - Paddle Steamer, Canoe etc. **Evelyn**

Home was the far-flung Frontier areas. Father, to give him his full style and title, was Deputy Commissioner, District and Sessions judge, also B.A. and Barrister-at-law. In the course of his work he had lived halfway up Mt. Victoria (10,000 ft) in the Chin Hills and had hundreds of miles of the Irrawaddy and Chindwin rivers under his jurisdiction. On the Chindwin there was no rail or road link, so he was provided with a Burma Government Launch known locally as the "Bhail Gharry" or bullock-cart as it was so slow - it was the *Mandalay,* a paddle steamer. We all piled in - servants, dog and all, and spent many days on the river. On one occasion I remember we went as far north as we could on the *Mandalay,* then transferred to a smaller and faster paddle steamer, the *Chindwin,* which belonged to the BBTC (Bombay Burmah Trading Corporation) and went as far as that would go, then travelled the rest of the way by *longdwin,* the local sort of dug-out canoe until we got to the rocks and rapids rushing over and could go no further. What all this was in aid of, I do not know. We were brought up never to query what our elders did and we hardly knew our parents anyway as we saw them so seldom - they could even leave us at home alone for days with the servants, presided over by a uniformed butler.

1926 - Car **Stella**

When we lived in Kandawglay, Mother heard of some one who wanted to sell their car, an open top two seater large enough for two or three adults with a canvas folding roof. Mother and Father were tempted - great excitement and suitably dressed for driving - veil over one's hat, etc; they got in and off they went. We waited eagerly for their return and verdict. The car ran well and the deal was finalised. Mother was going to be taught to drive. So our friend Bob Hall was enlisted. He cranked the handle and nothing happened; cranked again - twiddled knobs - cranked again - poppings like pistol shots then silence. More twiddling of knobs and cranking of handle - at last sputterings and rumblings and the car started - Hurrah! But what was that? Smoke issuing from under the high bonnet? Followed by flames. The car had caught fire. Mother and Father hopped out just in time. Sadly that was the end of our first car. It was years before my Father bought our "Tin Lizzie" and we had a chauffeur to drive and maintain it.

Stella's in-laws, the Watsons, were rich, and here they are with their Armstrong-Siddeley. The dress was obligatory for motoring in the 1920s.

1931 - Aeroplane **Stella**

Another really great excitement was our first view of an aeroplane. Somehow my father always knew approximately at what time these events were to happen and we took up suitable positions - and there was the miracle of this unbelievable huge bird-like structure moving across the sky. Later one of our relatives was to buy his own aeroplane but died in an air crash. All very sad.

1954 - Flight to Mandalay
from the diary of Anna Allott

Jan 8th 1954 The four of us had an excellent dinner at the Strand - steaks and plaice - and dropped me home to Inya Hall by ten. On the way home the subject of passports came up. Angus Carnegie (ICI rep) realised for me that I had done a dreadful thing - I had never gone to the immigration office and had been here for two months with no visa - I could be arrested and prosecuted. Complete panic - I couldn't sleep for two hours.

Jan 9th Sat Got up at 6 - packed all my things and went round and got Dr Htin Aung out of bed and threw myself into his hands - he rang U Ba Saing, controller of immigration, who was grim and said proceedings had probably started. U Maung Maung Gyi came - we went to the airport, transferred my flight to Tuesday, back to Htin Aung to collect a very strong letter of recommendation and into the Immigration office - U Ba Saing still grim - till my thick file of papers was brought in and he saw that proceedings hadn't yet been started - so he gave me a visa till 9th August 1954 (cost K25/-) and regularised everything. I got off completely freely. I am really a most extraordinarily lucky person - always lucky - air passage shifted, insurance shifted - no fine, no prosecution. Back for lunch to Carnegies - afternoon dropped a message of thanks to Dr Htin Aung - visited the Sule Pagoda.

Jan 11th Mon We had been talking about air crashes and comets last night and this morning's news of the Comet that crashed into the Mediterranean was a bit of a shock - Chester

Wilmot killed - after just writing to Tony that I might fly - I think I'll go by sea after all. Collected my passport with visa from Immig. Office. My coloured film may well be on the Comet.

Jan 12th Tue A little apprehensive about my first plane flight for 15 years. U MM Gyi came to fetch me. Glad to be leaving Rangoon.

A very smooth comfortable, if noisy, flight of 2 hours by Dakota, clear sky, could see the ground all the time, we seemed to go so slowly. Hundreds and hundreds of little squarish and roundish paddy fields, trees, sparkling white pagodas, and dried up yellowish streams. The Eastern Yomas away to the right. As we circled over Mandalay saw the Irrawaddy and the broken Ava Bridge and Sagaing on the other side. Flew in over Mandalay University building. Met by Ma Khin Shwe (Anne) and Ma Ma Gyi in a jeep - two of the three unmarried Tokegale sisters with whom I am going to stay in Mandalay.

1922 - Train **Stella**

We were fortunate - as my Father worked for a shipping firm we were able to travel first class but pay second (even on railway). Maymyo was the biggest hill station. The Government went there in the hot weather. I think we went there two or three times. Once we rented a house and took our own servants and another time we boarded.

I remember going up to Maymyo through the mountains - with one train pulling, and another at the back pushing. Then when we reached the hair pin bends the roles would be reversed and the rear engine would pull. Gradually the air became cooler and then pine scented. But first, setting out:

At the station - such excitement, the platform would be crowded, passengers with their bundles and children, vendors selling all manner of foodstuffs and drinks. Porters carrying our trunks and bedding. Our servants getting us settled in and opening our bedding - carried in envelope-type canvas holdalls and spread on the opened out seats which converted to bunks at night. There were no passenger cars; people hung on to the outside of the train as one sees in travel films of India. After much clanking, several bumps and false starts the whistle blew and we slowly started on our way.

The trains were noisy and dirty, with coal dust everywhere. The windows were covered with mesh but still the coal dust entered.

There was so much to see from the train. As we gradually left Rangoon and its shunting yards and sheds and then the outskirts with scattered houses, small pagodas and monasteries, darkness swiftly descended. We always left in the evening and traversed the plains at night when it was cooler. We undressed and got into our bunks - then I liked looking out at the night - the stars and the dried out paddy fields with tiny shacks in the distance and here and there a small fire where a paddy field was on fire.

And then glorious morning - a servant would appear with a tray with a clean white cloth, on which was hot tea and toast and fruit. The hot water for tea came from the engine and the train always stopped at the small way side station long enough for us to finish breakfast.

The long day journey was hot and dusty and very, very noisy. The rhythm of the train changed when we went over a dried up stream. Small villages, pagodas and monasteries and small stations out of which would come a vendor selling water, these broke the monotony. I think we ordered tiffin in Rangoon and it would be ready for us at one of the bigger station waiting rooms - but I am a little hazy about this - I do clearly remember one occasion but that was another time. Another night on the train and next morning we started to climb the foothills and Maymyo was eventually reached. After settling in we were enrolled in the Church Of England Convent for a few weeks. At weekends, though, we had picnics and good times.

Stella's photo of the Goteik Gorge.

On the way to Maymyo, as we left the plains and started to climb the hills the train went through many tunnels, when we would be plunged into darkness. The hillsides were covered with dense forests and we climbed very slowly. Eventually we came to a deep gorge - quite famous: it was the "Goteik Gorge" I think that is the spelling but it was pronounced Gotake. I enclose a photograph - you will see how small the train looks and also, apart from small jutting out platforms for the men working on the line to get out of the way of the train (one track), there was no protecting barrier. The train crawled over and we were told to sit very still or the train would rock and tip over. I suppose we were told this to give my Mother a little peace - probably we were restless and bored by the long journey. At the bottom of the gorge a stream meandered - but when the rains started it was turned into a raging torrent.

1934 - Car **Stella**

I forgot to mention something very important and wonderful. A short while before leaving 12, Park Road my parents bought me a second hand Baby Austin. The vendor agreed to teach me to drive. When applying for a driving licence I was told to go to the garage and satisfy the owner that I could drive. Jack's brother, Willie Watson owned a large car sale room and garage and he gave me a licence - just like that! ! ! Life was almost perfect! Now I could drive my Father to work in the morning - with the chauffeur sitting in the back just in case anything went wrong.

1941 - Car **Sylvia**

The "Burma Road" went on for 700 miles, and we met hundreds of lorries carrying supplies into China.

We travelled in our 12-year-old Essex tourer via Lashio, headquarters of the Northern Shan States, which was where the Burma Road to China began. Between Lashio and Kutkai we climbed two thousand feet, the road being very steep and winding. We had wonderful views of the plains as we climbed; the bare cliffs were very different from the wooded hills of Burma. I have always loved this kind of mountain scenery; one can see the shapes and structure better than if covered by trees. All along the road we met lorries either going to, or coming from, China. At Lashio we had seen thousands of them, many of them American and of the latest design. On the Burma road there was hardly room for two lorries to pass and in one of the steepest parts we found two jammed together. This was on a corner overlooking a precipice.

After Kutkai the route is even more precipitous and winding. We travelled round and round one mountain, down to a valley and up again; this went on continuously. The scenery was the grandest I had yet seen, fold upon fold of mountains opening before my eyes, those in the distance of deep blue. Many of the mountains were bare with only short grass. The road was cut into the mountains with a sheer precipice at one side.

Some of the lorry drivers were very careless and the road dangerous; I imagine the drivers were always in a hurry. We saw a lorry which had dropped over the precipice and hung about twenty feet below. Another lorry on the road was attached to it by ropes in an effort to lift it. We saw two more damaged lorries. On our way back we saw another one over the side. On another occasion on our way from China we saw a man asleep in a lorry which had its back wheels hanging over the side. He was quite unconcerned, but if any vehicle had hit that lorry it would have gone completely over the edge. We took great care and blew the horn continuously.

It was most exciting to arrive in Kyukok, the last town on the Burma frontier, and look across into China. At several points this side of the frontier there were large white crosses on the ground to show Japanese planes that they were over Burma. The reason for our visit to this place was to investigate the possibility of building a refugee camp in Burma for the Chinese who would flee over the border if the Japs attacked in this part of China. In the evening we walked into China with an official well known to the Chinese authorities in Wanting, the Chinese town.

Next day we set off for another Shan town near the frontier, Namkhan, ten miles from which was the only Chinese aeroplane factory at Loiwing. The Japanese had attempted to bomb this factory, but had dropped their bomb two seconds too soon. One bomb thus landed accidentally near Namkhan on the Burmese side. The heads of the Loiwing factory were American.

WHEN WE WERE VERY YOUNG

1930s **Amy Forbes-Mitchell**

My younger sister Anne must have been about three years old when my grandmother decided to take us to the Rangoon Zoo. I had been before. My grandmother thought for a treat she would also invite my friend Betty, six months younger than my sister, and Betty's grandmother, "GaMa". We had a very enjoyable day at the Zoo. It was getting dark, and we hurried along to see the elephants near the EXIT. The elephant-keeper had trained the elephants to trumpet "salaam" (thank you) when they were given any sugarcane. This also encouraged the public to buy the sugarcane. My sister Anne was probably getting tired by the end of the day. So when the keeper said to the elephant to say "Salaam", Anne turned to my grandmother and said, "Come on Granny, Jumbo says goodnight Anne."

1930s **Maureen**

In my mother's village of Sat-thwa I spent some of the happiest times of my life. Nothing in the way of chores was required of me, although I longed to be allowed to fetch water from the well. But my mother was a bit of a snob in her own way. She liked the homage paid to her as the wife of a foreign official, setting her apart from the rest of the village.

So I played all day long with the village children who, unlike me, had more than a few chores to get on with, and who often came to play with babies almost as big as themselves strapped on their backs. When the games became more demanding, the babies would be unstrapped and allowed to roam freely amongst the pigs and hens, to be hastily strapped back when we heard a particular child's name being called by its parent. No sooner had one child been called back than another would appear, complete with baby sister or brother strapped on her back. At first I was rather perplexed by the names given to some of my playmates, such as Kwe-Ma, literally Bitch or worse. But I came to understand that these were protective names designed to disguise the fact that the parents hoped the girls, in particular, would grown up into raving beauties or have untold good fortune in later years.

1930 onwards — Tony Foucar

My memories of Burma go back to my early childhood and the dramatic events of 1930. On the evening of 5 May when my sister and I were in bed in our family home in Rangoon, we were suddenly awakened when the glasses and ornaments on the dressing table started to rattle and jump, then our beds careered across the room towards the window, the fan smashed against the ceiling and the whole house was plunged into darkness. Our parents rushed into the room to see if we were safe, but fortunately, the danger had quickly passed, and Rangoon had escaped the worst effects of the earthquake which had almost totally destroyed Pegu.

We children were very aware of the later events of that year - the racial riots and uprising in Rangoon jail so well described by Maurice Collis in *Trials in Burma* - but for us the real excitement was the night of the earthquake.

I move onto 1940: in that year when England was under the threat of invasion, my sister and I were evacuated from our boarding schools in Southern England, to join our parents in what was then seen as the safety of Burma. After a sea voyage of seven weeks round the Cape in one of Paddy Henderson's rather older ships - I believe she was the *Kemmendine* - we eventually arrived in Rangoon. As we were driving from the docks to our family home at 90, Campbell Road near the Royal Lakes, my sister and I smiled at each other as we knew that we were home to the sights, sounds and smells we had nearly forgotten. It was indeed a very happy family reunion.

Although we did not know it at the time, we were of course living in a fool's paradise which was violently destroyed by the Japanese in December 1941. The happy lives we had been leading in Rangoon with visits to Kalaw came to an abrupt end, culminating in the loss of our home and possessions.

While the rest of the family had to make their escape from the advancing Japanese overland to India with all the hardships that entailed, I had the good fortune to travel to India by sea aboard the troopship *President Doomar* carrying only a handful of passengers. It was a melancholy evening in January 1942 when my family came to the docks to say their farewells. Rangoon after the air raids was a much subdued city whose population was nervous and fearful of its uncertain future. For security reasons the blacked-out ship sailed at night, but there was still enough light in the sky for me to stand on deck and bid farewell to the Shwedagon as we moved slowly down the river. Some months were to elapse before the family was to be reunited in India.

I move ahead to a happier time - 1945 and the closing stages of the war with Japan when I was once again back in Rangoon. As soon as I could after my arrival, I returned to our family home in Campbell Road. It was a sorry sight: the garden was overgrown and the gates had been removed; the Japanese, who had used the house as an officers' mess during the occupation, had built an air raid shelter under the tennis court, apparently scorning the slit trench we had dug in 1940 as affording inadequate protection against the allied air attacks; and in the house, doors and many of the fittings had been removed. I had hoped that I might find some evidence of the family's earlier occupation somewhere in the house or garden, but sadly there was none.

Houses have a habit of living in one's memory, so after an absence from Burma of fifty years and with encouragement from my wife on her first visit to Burma, we went back to 90, Campbell Road. This time we were agreeably surprised to find that the house, albeit not restored to its former elegance, was at least being lived in as some sort of nursing home or hospital. The garden, while uncared for, was no longer overgrown and wild. I walked a little way back down the road past the reclining Buddha towards the Royal Lakes, to remind myself of the many evenings I had walked that same road with my father before the war with Japan had changed all our lives.

Large Buddha at Hlegu, on the road to Pegu.

1962 **Nick Fenn**

Everyone told us that we should not employ in the same household a Burman Buddhist houseboy and an Indian Catholic cook. We engaged Aung Hla because he was recommended by the local church. We employed Simon because his wife was the best teller of Burmese ghost stories that we had encountered. In due course Simon tried to murder Aung Hla with the kitchen knife - but that is another story.

One day there appeared in our kitchen a Banded Krait, so named after the black and gold bands across its body. It is by reputation the most deadly snake in the world: if you are bitten, you die. But it does not attack humans intentionally: only if you step on it by mistake in the dark. And it lives on other snakes. So some Burmans keep them in their compounds because then at least they know that they have only one snake to fear.

The question arose which of our two staff should deal with the Banded Krait. To Aung Hla it seemed obvious: as a Buddhist he was not permitted to kill; as a Catholic, Simon not only killed animals but ate them; the kitchen was Simon's empire and the snake was in the kitchen. Simon took a different view: he was the senior servant; he had instructed Aung Hla to kill the snake and Aung Hla was guilty of insubordination. Eventually Aung Hla lost his temper, seized a broom and killed the snake. Immediately the Catholic rounded upon the Buddhist and pointing a quavering finger declared "Mr Buddha will be very angry with you."

The next morning at breakfast Aung Hla was nowhere to be seen. Simon said with a triumphant smile that Mr Buddha was very angry with Aung Hla. Aung Hla was in bed with a temperature of 105°. Sheer terror. At least that was my wife's diagnosis. She gave him an aspirin, bathed his head in cold water and sent him back to work. She might have killed him. But mercifully her diagnosis was accurate and Aung Hla was fine. Until Simon attacked him with the kitchen knife - but that, as I say, is another story.

1940 Sylvia

When we were in Kutkai, we had an extra servant, a watchman or *durwan*. As he had very little work to do we asked him to help with the washing up, but being a higher caste Hindu he refused to touch dishes which had been used for beef. To the Hindu the cow is sacred. However he was willing to wash dishes which had contained mutton. Such are the paradoxes of life in the East.

1962 Nick Fenn

On the walls of our dining room in Kent hangs a *paya-ka*. It is the front of a chest in which the scriptures used to be kept, crudely framed in teak with the nails sticking out. It is a Burmese strip cartoon made in relief with three kinds of lacquer and adorned with gold leaf. It depicts the Buddha as prince going out in his chariot and encountering the old man, the sick man and the monk, the experience which converted him. Then you see him in his palace saying goodbye to his sleeping wife with the babe suckling at her breast. Then he mounts his horse and leaves through the palace gates accompanied by his famous servant Myin Swe Maung San. The spirits of the forest lift the hooves of his horse lest they should wake his wife. He canters off into history on the next panel and of course on the lid would be depicted cross-legged under the Bo tree in his moment of enlightenment. It is a priceless possession.

I found it in a pigsty. We were visiting friends in Momeik, a village 20 miles south of Mandalay. My friend was a pig farmer. Having made a lamentable failure of his academic career at the University of Mandalay, he had conned the Australian government into giving him three Australian sows and one boar under the Colombo Plan. He was cross-breeding these animals with local pigs to his enormous financial advantage. The smell was memorable.

As we walked amongst the sties, he caught me with my head on one side examining a curious piece of wood which formed part of one of the walls. "Oh yes" he said, "that's rather interesting. It's a *paya-ka*. Would you like it?". I said I would. "OK" he said "you can have it on two conditions. First, find another piece of wood to fill that hole; and second, take it to my aunt in Mandalay to have it restored."

I did as I was told. And the *paya-ka* now hangs in our dining room.

1961 Sue Fenn

We had had more stomach problems than usual and I was sure that the drinking water was not being boiled long enough - if at all! But, I reasoned, why should the servants bother if no one explained why it was necessary? So, one afternoon, I called our three to the living room for a lecture. I tried to explain scientifically about germs and microbes and amoebae, and the blank faces stared back respectfully. I tried again in simpler language and again in words of one syllable, but all in vain.

Then suddenly light dawned in Margaret's eyes and she turned to her husband, Simon, and the houseboy, Aung Hla, and, in a torrent of words and gestures, described the evil work of these demons in our water who could only be driven out by long boiling. Soon all three were promising to boil the water for hours.

After the two men left I thanked Margaret for her assistance. She, who had spent two years at a convent school and described herself as a Christian, beamed in triumph.

"Well," she said, "I certainly convinced them about the water *Nats*. They'll boil them all out now. But as for us, we're Christians, so we don't have to believe in germs."

1941 Sylvia

On the way to Hsampu we had a most dramatic view of clouds below us veiling the lower ranges; making us feel that we were really on top of the world. On arrival at Hsampu we found that there had been a death recently. When a Kachin dies he is buried soon afterwards but the funeral ceremony is postponed until it can be held in style with the sacrifice of a bullock, and other rites. Until then there is dancing every evening in the house of the dead man. In Hsampu this had gone on for a month. We were invited to see the dance (called *Gebung*) one night. The reason for the dance is to keep the dead man and his relatives happy as if it were a wedding. Everybody gets very tipsy. To propitiate the *Nats* a fire is kept continually burning beside a bamboo shrine made for the *Nats*.

The villagers were pleased when we went to see the dance. They said that Pat was the first Assistant Superintendent to do so. A Kachin house is made of wood and bamboo and consists of two very long rooms divided by a bamboo partition. One of these is the 'lounge' while the other is further subdivided into bedrooms. In this funeral dance the men and women do a sort of 'conga' down the whole length of the 'lounge' then disappear into the bedrooms behind and out again into the living room to carry on dancing. Our clerk who was with us told Pat that from time to time dancing couples would dally in the bedrooms for a spot of unashamed sex before rejoining the conga. I had noticed that most of the men looked listless. No wonder! The conga had become a tired shuffle, but it had to go on non-stop or the dead man would be offended. We didn't stay long. The dance was dreary and the dum, dum, dum of the single drum was very monotonous. Both Pat and I had taken a sip of the drink that was passed round in a lacquered bamboo bowl. It was made from boiled fermented rice, and was very powerful, like gin.

In its origins this dance was supposed to mimic the daily life and actions of the dead man, walking to his *taungya* (hillside cultivation), clearing jungle, cutting down bamboo, stalking deer and wild pig, and so on. The dance is instigated by the dead man himself. Before it starts, his relatives throw a piece of bamboo on the fire of the living room. The bamboo bursts and little hairs or splinters burst out of it. If they are numerous it means that the dead man wishes them to dance.

On the whole these Kachins lead a hard and dull life, and it is not surprising that they make the most of the three important events in their lives (births, marriages and deaths) and invest them with extended ceremonies to give them a bit of fun from time to time. By introducing them to Christianity the American Baptist Missionaries have done a lot to broaden their lives and expand their interests.

1940s — Elizabeth Shepherd

I arrived in Burma as a new born in 1936.

My parents, Rev. Vincent and Mrs Nora Shepherd, were missionaries with the Methodist Church, stationed in the Upper Burma District. My first home was in Pakokku, and later we moved to the mission house in Mandalay. The relations between Burmese Christians and the missionary families were warm and close. It was a far more exotic and comfortable life in many ways than that of a minister's family in a "home" church in England where we would have been housed in a manse provided, often draughty and rather drab in those days. In Burma I had an ayah to look after me, Mary - her husband, David, was the cook - and there were other servants for our needs. Large rooms cooled by fans, wide verandas, mimosa and mangoes in the garden, and retreats to the hill stations at Kalaw or Maymyo when sun gave way to rains.

We left on furlough just before the Japanese invasion, so did not have to escape by trekking over the Himalayan foothills like others. We should have returned later but for a twist of fate.

My father was in Calcutta in 1943 organising the re-entry of missionaries when he discovered he had contracted leprosy. He had been particularly drawn to the sufferings of patients at the Methodist Leper Home in Mandalay, and spent much time with them. He had opened his heart so fully, combating with God's love the stigma of this disease, and perhaps that was why he was then chosen by God to bear witness of that love from within the disease itself. He certainly accepted his illness as part of his mission. He remained in South India for treatment, and was eventually cured. But both he and my mother always missed Burma, and spoke lovingly of their personal ties there.

When I returned to Burma in 1996, it was obvious how mutual those ties remain. I was welcomed into the Methodist communities with open arms, as if I was coming home. The missionaries brought us "the good news", they said joyfully. When I visited the leprosy hospital at Mandalay, now run by the authorities and moved way out of town, I met several patients who had been in the children's ward, Hope Ward, in my father's time.

"How he loved us," they said.

I am told the story of a statue that had stood in the old Leper Home, of Jesus holding out his hands to heal the lepers in the Bible. When missionaries returned the statue was smashed, by the patients themselves.

"Why?!!"

"The statue was a lie'" they replied, "Jesus would have **touched** them."

I believe they learned that from my father . He touched them. A legacy of love.

1923 **Stella**

Then came the day when my sister Gwen and I had to leave for school in Mussoorie. Sadness mixed with excitement. I think we were on a cargo boat but it may have been a small passenger boat as there were, as far as I can remember, seven passengers. Across the Bay Of Bengal and up to Calcutta. It took several days and it was rough and not as much fun as when we were with my Father. Once again we had to wait for the pilot as the Hoogly is a dangerous river with shifting sand banks.

Most of the time I was in Mussoorie I felt off par due to the altitude and homesickness. Also the food was not particularly good. I used to stand on the Mall and look down at the plains stretching away in the distance and wish I could jump down and run home. The rest of the day would be spent in the usual school routine. The senior dormitories were much nicer; they had curtained cubicles and were cosier. We went for the usual crocodile walks all over the town and hill and to the parks.

I shudder to think now that my particular age group of girls used to jockey for the right to quickly follow one of the teachers into her cubicle and use her cooler, soap scented water before the servant could tip it away! And the toilets - in the school proper - a long shed attached to the building - wooden cubicles, wooden shelves with holes cut in them, and the pots were removed from the outside back - I was always terrified that they would come to remove the pot while I was on it. And when it was dark in the evening with only the dim oil lamps, it was a place of terror as we were convinced that it was haunted. This was an expensive school - what would the Social Services these days have to say about even their problem cases having to put up with these conditions? My parents had no idea what it was like as they had trusted the judgement of Mrs Murray - and perhaps that was the norm for boarding schools in the hills at the time. Always in the distance we could see the beautiful perpetual snows - one felt one could reach them quite easily.

1940 Maureen

After two years in the convent's kindergarten, aged about seven, I was put in the first standard. This was in the charge of Sister Seraphina, the most dreaded of all the nuns in the convent. Never in my life had I come across anything or anyone quite as terrifying as her. Totally possessed by some demoniac force, she made effective use of cane, ruler and her right hand. And all because I could not speak English! Not understanding the language and therefore unable to do what was required of me sent her into a rage. In desperation I would throw out the odd word in English that I had retained through the holidays - most often the wrong word. This would so infuriate Sister Seraphina that she would lash out at me with her fists, hitting me with such force that it sometimes threw me to the other end of the room, making me temporarily deaf. I was not her only victim, but I was certainly the most favoured. Unable to stand up for myself and consumed with fear and misery, I did not attain even the minimal academic standard required.

1925 Stella

During the holidays one afternoon a car drove up and two Head Mistresses stepped out. They had come to persuade Mother to send me to school at the Methodist Episcopal School at Thandaung, 200 miles north of Rangoon, run by an American Mission, and also to engage Gwen as a teacher for a couple of months till the new teachers had finished their training at the Teachers' Training College. So it was all arranged. I needed new clothes and they had to do for nine months - so excitement took over - I can still remember the smell of a pair of brown leather sandals that were part of my equipment and that I thought were wonderful after the lace-up boots I had to have in Mussoorie! Once more out came our trunk and the day arrived for us to leave. I remember my younger brother John whistling away while I was in tears. Having Gwen with us did help.

Back to the railway station, with our trunks, to the noise and bustle. We travelled in relays as transport up the mountain was limited. There were probably eight or ten girls of my age in my carriage. Next morning we reached Toungoo - the small town at the foot of the hills where the train was dismantled and our carriages were shunted into a siding while the rest of the train travelled on. I suppose we had breakfast there. A lorry with wooden benches along each side was waiting for us - there may have been more than one - I can't remember - anyway we took our seats and the long uphill climb began - through the small streets of Toungoo which we gradually left behind and the bamboo forests became thick jungle with the narrow road winding up and up with many hair-pin bends and the branches overhanging the road. The road had been carved through the mountain so that one side there was a steep embankment and on the other a deep drop. Very frightening. As we got to the top of the mountain we passed one small shack shop, then nothing till we came to the road leading to the school, with a grassy field and a small stream running through one side of it.

The road up to Thandaung.

This field used to get rather wet but when it was dry we played rounders and football on it. The school was co-educational with boys in one wing and girls in the other. As it was before the so-called permissive society of today, there was never any misbehaving. A few love bites or a bar of chocolate was all. I was in the junior dormitory with about twenty young girls - the matron had a room at the end and the "flush" toilets were at the other. There were even shower cubicles. It was a roomy dormitory quite different to Mussoorie.

Downstairs there were the classrooms - and the Head Mistresses' rooms. And a very large dining hall with long tables and benches. The teachers had a table to themselves and so did the Head Mistresses. For a few months my parents paid extra and we sat with the Head Mistresses eating their superior food! This did not improve my relations with the other girls - though the food was excellent !

1930s — Evelyn

Only two English-speaking schools were run by the government - these were boys' schools in Rangoon and Maymyo. All the other English-speaking schools were run by the churches: Anglican, Roman Catholic, Methodists, Baptists etc. They were all fee-paying, so were not available to everyone. The exams were in English, so if you had been to an Anglo-Vernacular day school where English, if taught at all, was a second language, you had very little hope of going to University. The Buddhist monasteries gave a very good education from time immemorial but not in English. This I thought was a very unfair system - U Thant, Secretary-General of the UN, didn't get to University because of this.

1926 — Stella

The photo was taken at Thandaung.
Stella (aged 12) is sitting on the right, next to the French teacher.

There was a school car and the Headmistresses used to go down to Toungoo from time to time driven by one of the *hlooglays*. That school could have been paradise - can you imagine it? I can see it so clearly I will try to let you see it too. Miles from people - the tops of mountains, long, winding, forest-clad roads, sparkling streams cascading over boulders into shallow depressions just deep enough to swim in, steep climbs up to the top of the mountains from where we could see the plains spread out below and it was all ours to wander about, over and in.

We all carried butterfly nets when we left the school and in fact even in the play grounds for our chief hobby was collecting butterflies and beetles. There were so many beautiful varieties. The Headmistresses had glass cases full of them - all lined up with pins through their middles. It sounds so cruel now - but then the hunting bug got into one and as there were so many around, conservation did not seem important - and the beetles all colours - iridescent greens and blues and rose coloured - the wings that jewellery is made from.

After "Homework", if we didn't have a sing-song, out would come the big old gramophone and we would all sit around in a special classroom and listen and sometimes sing all the old favourites. Old war songs, twenties favourites and novelty numbers like *The Laughing Policeman* - a great favourite. But never any dancing. Nevertheless we did dance up in our dormitory - there I learned to do the Charleston. We had to sing or hum the music. Also the Hawaiian Hula.

At weekends and holidays we went for tremendous climbs up the mountains. These had to be started at the crack of dawn - and the servants carried the food - easily the favourite was chicken curry and rice followed by fruit. It could be really frightening at times and we were glad of the helping hands of the servants.

If we didn't go up we went down. When we came to a stream, the boys would go up-stream and we would go down, remove our dresses and lie under the cool small waterfalls or slide down with the water over the smooth rocks. It did not take long to dry off again. One of my

School bathing party near Thazi.

friends found a tree with lovely velvety green leaves, she picked one and smoothed it over her face.

By the time we got back to school her face was covered with small pimples ! For all the time I knew her she was never able to be cured. Dermatitis I suppose. Once, coming back we heard rustling in the undergrowth. "Elephants!" someone called out and we all scrambled wildly for safety - very difficult as the forest came right down to the road on the safe side - thankfully, as the elephants came up we saw that they had chains on their legs and were working elephants belonging to the Forestry Commission.

1946 Nancy Larmour

When my husband, Nick Larmour, got a job in the Civil Service in Rangoon it was Ruth Donnison, wife of the then Chief Secretary, who suggested that I (who had just arrived and had never taught anything before) might help out by teaching English and history at a local school. This was *Mrs Hla Oung Memorial Buddhist School*, behind the Rangoon General Hospital. The Headmistress, Daw Mya Sein, was to set off in a few days as the Burma delegate to the opening session of - I think - UNESCO, in Paris; and I had agreed to help out in her absence.

There were no schoolbooks of course in 1946, except a borrowed copy of a Burmese history book in English, vintage 1910 or thereabouts. So at home in Windermere Park I would read ten pages or so, summarize, and then, next day, expound to the class. Then I wrote my summary on the board, and they copied it, whereupon they all protested - in quite orderly form and excellent English - that it was all wrong. After much discussion and variant readings of the history, I told them all to go home and ask their parents, friends, *phongyis,* to give them a short summary of the relevant Burmese history, and bring it as homework to the next class. The accounts included much myth and legend, as well, probably, as history, and the discussions continued amicably, till each time I ended by saying, "So you must all just grow up, go to Rangoon University, and then write your own history." I learned a lot, but I often wondered what their parents thought of it all.

1953 Anna Allott

In 1953, Anna came to Burma for the first time, to study at Rangoon University - and was thrilled to be allowed to stay in the girls' hostel in Inya Hall. This is her first letter back to her husband Tony.

c/o Daw Thein Nyunt
Inya Hall
University College
Rangoon
10th October 1953

My darling Tony,

I am here, safe and sound on Burmese soil, dripping with sweat but confident and cheerful about what is to come. The customs officials etc, came on board us this morning about 7 a.m. By 9 a.m. we had waved goodbye to the *Worcestershire* - moored out in mid-stream - and come ashore by tender. A colourful crowd of Burmans greeted us - waving black umbrellas over their heads to keep the sun off. I was almost immediately found by U Htin Aung's official representative - who told me transport would arrive in half an hour. Both Merrells and Carnegies were fuming because there was no-one there to meet them. As well as arriving 24 hours early, we had got ashore earlier than expected. I was through the customs and ready by about 10. They have taken my tape-recorder to the Customs house - I may have to pay duty on it. I shall get it on Monday.

The chief item of news is that I could hardly have timed my arrival better, or worse. Rangoon University students are on strike - as we drove in, compound and house gates had to be unlocked for us and the whole place seemed very quiet and deserted. The students have struck, it seems, for longer holidays. They want the holiday which starts on Oct 7th extended from 2 to 4 weeks. Students and police came to blows on Oct 2nd. Last Weds they were still holding fire engines and ambulances in readiness. Now it seems a lot of the students have gone home and will stay away next week, thus taking their extra holiday. Inya Hall should hold 100; 350 girls have been crammed into it. Luckily for me, all but a 100 or so have gone home for the next 3 weeks so I have been put into what used to be the assistant warden's rooms. Before, 6 girls slept where I now am. I have a bedroom, another room and a room as large as our sitting room, the "parlour", just out on the veranda is my own bath and lavatory room. It could be palatial, at the moment it is just liveable-in. The warden had to get everything ready for me in a hurry. (Birds fly in and out of my room - little Burmese girls clip-clop along the verandas peering in - the heat and lack of sleep last night have made me very sleepy - but I must write this.) When I first saw my room, my heart sank a bit - it was so bare - but a miracle has been wrought.

I have unpacked, hung my clothes up, made my bed (which will be hard!), contrived to drape the mosquito net over the bed - a bit tricky because the wire is too high. It seems I am advised to sleep with all doors and windows shut because of marauding burglars. The warden does so herself - she is Daw Thein Nyunt - c/o on my address. That will be almost as bad as the Red Sea because there is no fan. I don't think I shall get myself a fan, because I shan't be staying here for more than 3 weeks more.

They are all terribly concerned that I shan't be able to eat the hostel food. After some of the poisonously hot curries from the boat I am not scared. If the food gets me down I can go and eat with the British Council pair Mr and Mrs Morgan. But I think if I can stick it, the experience of staying in the hostel with all those young girls will be exciting and very valuable. They do talk Burmese among themselves, I am relieved to hear. They chatter away - I can catch occasional words. So many of them seem to me to be so breathtakingly beautiful, I feel large and awkward and ungraceful. No fan and having to sleep with closed windows may get me down - but it should be getting cooler and although I perspire and the heat doesn't appear to worry me. Daw Thin Kyi is taking me out to supper tonight with 2 American women - it should be interesting. At the moment I am starving - as I had a minute breakfast at 7 a.m. in the excitement and of course by the time I got here it was 11.30 - rice and curry "breakfast" having been over by 10. I had coffee and a coconut "pattie" for lunch and the next meal will be about 6.30 I suppose - that will taste good. It is now Saturday afternoon - I will try and post this as soon as I can.

All is well - a new big adventure is beginning - all my love - Anna.

EAST MEETS WEST

1961 — Sue Fenn

Early in 1961 there were anti-American riots all over Burma. Mandalay was no exception. We were living on the University Estate, south of the city, because we were teaching Spoken English to the final year students.

One afternoon when Nick was in town - being abused as an American! - I was languishing in bed with flu. I was woken by the roar and chanting of a crowd outside my window, and sent the houseboy Aung Hla to find out what was happening. He returned, very excited, with the information that the students wanted to set fire to the house. I sent him back to ask why. "Because you're American." I sent the luckless lad back to assure them that no Americans live in our house. There was a worrying silence and I feared that it might be discovered that our neighbours were a Ford Foundation zoology teacher and his wife, an expert in the Burmese harp, both distinguished, white-haired and not at all "ugly" Americans. So I was astonished to learn that they had decided to burn down the garage instead! My next message to them said that they were welcome to burn it, it belonged to the University and was empty.

Eventually, with renewed shouting of slogans, the crowd moved away and I sank back gratefully onto my bed. Aung Hla's cool behaviour had probably saved not only our house but probably our neighbours' as well. I sometimes wonder if those hot-heads - some of my own students perhaps - would have ever carried out their threat. I doubt it. But if their aim was to frighten us they certainly succeeded!

1986 — Nick Fenn

My wife and I were on our valedictory tour of Upper Burma in 1986, driving west of the Chindwin where foreigners were seldom seen. We came into a village square. The children crowded around the Landrover, curious about the double cooling fan. I got out.

"Beka lathelay?" they asked - the opening courtesy of a conversation, meaning literally "where do you come from?" Just for fun, I asked them where they thought I came from, and pointed to the flag on the car. Consternation. "Japan? - oh, no no no!.. Germany?"

There was old man standing in the shade of a tree, leaning on a stick. He hobbled over, shaking his stick at the children, exclaiming "You don't know that flag? You should know that flag. It's the British flag. We'll be all right now, they're back!"

What does the British Ambassador say then?

1942 **Sylvia**

We heard that the Prime Minister of Burma, U Saw was under arrest for having contact with the Japanese after the beginning of the war with Japan; he was in Britain at the time. He hoped by league with the Japanese to get independence for Burma, but he was foolish to trust the Japs. I did not condemn him entirely. I felt his attitude was influenced by the behaviour of a large class of English people in Burma. There was much snobbery there, especially in Rangoon among the trading class of English people there. There were clubs in Rangoon barred to Burmese people, which I felt to be quite wrong. This attitude was not as a rule found among the civil servants, who wished to help and co-operate with the people. The civil service was open to Burmese as well as English.

1961 **John Okell**

I wanted to see something of the life of rice farmers in a small village, so a kind friend arranged for me to stay in Kon-de, way off the beaten track beyond Shwebo. My host was a kindly old farmer who never stopped marvelling at the fact that someone should have travelled 8,000 miles and ended up not just in his wholly undistinguished village, but in his very own house. I am still moved when I remember the way he turned to me one day and said affectionately "You know, the only explanation is that you and I must have been brothers in a previous life."

1939 Maureen

It was a shock to find that the religious instruction given to us in such large doses at the convent school dwelt so long on Heaven and Hell, and specifically the damnation to Hell of all non-Catholics, and the obligatory prayers for their conversion before this fate overtook them It was not long before the school bullies, mostly European children, goaded me into admitting that my mother, being brown and Buddhist, would go to Hell. Fiercely protective of her, I never failed to take the bait, and their derision only served to make me hit out in a blind rage. So once more I would be led away by the supervising nun, hands tied behind my back, to be locked up in a classroom or dormitory.

There was definitely a desire among some of the Burmese to be like the British in appearance and manners. After all, were not the ruling races British and Europeans? In her village my mother had accepted a sort of star status as her due for marrying a British man. But not everyone thought of such a marriage as an honour. Some, like the head teacher in Sat-thwa, even despised her for marrying a foreigner, and every time this woman saw us her hard eyes raked us with positive dislike. The club in Kalaw was not open to Burmese or Indians, no matter how well connected or educated they were. Prejudices and bigotry were rife and complicated. People of mixed race were looked down on by both Europeans and natives and preferred to be called Anglo-Indians or Anglo-Burmans rather than Eurasian. Even the nuns were not totally free of such ingrained colour prejudice, exhorting us not to go out in the hot sun without our topees, otherwise we would become as brown as the natives!

1941 Sylvia

While in Pangyan we visited the Sawbwa's mother, an ancient woman about 100 years old and a Wa. She lived in a dark sort of den much like the Sawbwa's palace and we could not see her as we entered. She was more interesting than the Sawbwa, who seemed much less intelligent. She remembered the Scott expedition; we asked her if she liked Scott, who was the first Englishman to go to the Wa States and she answered that she was afraid of him. Strange when one thinks that those Englishmen must have been very afraid of the Wa "head-hunters". She told us that the Wa's, not knowing the Assistant Superintendents' names, used to give them nicknames. One Assistant Superintendent was called by them the dwarf Assistant Superintendent, another the toothless Assistant Superintendent, a friend of ours called Rossiter was called the mad Assistant Superintendent, and I felt they were not far wrong, while Roy Ogden, another friend, was known as the handsome Assistant Superintendent, again an accurate description; he was very tall dark and handsome. When I asked my husband's nickname, she said it was the "broken toothed Assistant Superintendent". He had a small piece off one of his front teeth and they had spotted it.

THE SHAN STATES WERE SPECIAL

What is now Burma's largest and most ethnically-diverse state used to be a cluster of smaller states. The Shan plateau was cool and not too far from Mandalay and Rangoon - so the "hill stations" built there were top holiday destinations for Europeans, and the workings of Government moved there all summer. But this was a land of hill tribes, mountains and forests too.

When officers of the Frontier Services - like Sylvia's husband and Maureen's father - travelled in wild country, they normally took an escort of Indian Sepoys.

1940 **Sylvia**

Under British rule each Shan prince, like an Indian rajah, ruled a large area and was known as a Sawbwa. My husband's job was to act as adviser to the Sawbwa, and whatever may be said of British imperialism, the British officers really loved the country and tried to improve the conditions of the people.

We were naturally involved with the lives of all our servants, who were, as it were, our family, and this is what made life in Burma so interesting for me, because I wanted to learn the customs of this very delightful and strange country. Thaw Ma announced that he was about to get married, but could not make up his mind which of two women he should marry. The deciding factor was that in one case he would have to pay 50 or 60 rupees for his bride as she was a virgin, whereas the other, who was a widow, would cost him nothing and bring him a house and property besides. The two possibilities were sisters and Thaw Ma finally decided in favour of the better financial proposition, the widow. He eloped with her in the customary Burmese fashion; when the bride and groom cannot afford a large celebration they arrange (usually with the knowledge of all the relations) to elope secretly. The girl simply disappears from her home and lives with her man. Afterwards they hold a small tea-party, at which the runaway couple are formally forgiven.

We were invited to this tea-party which was quite a brilliant scene. The floor of the bamboo bungalow was covered with highly coloured rugs and all the Shan ladies and men were seated on the floor eating some curious concoction. The women were segregated from the men, but they were nevertheless very lively. Most of them had lovely sprays of flowers in their glossy black hair,

"Lugale" - this is Sylvia's sketch of her lugale in Mongyai,

a Burmese custom I learnt to copy. The Burmese women use a white liquid to make their skins whiter. This liquid is a mixture of water and a white powder called *thanakha,* which is obtained by rubbing the bark of a tree on a stone with another piece of stone, rather like a pestle and mortar. This powder, which I tried, has an astringent effect on the pores.

At the tea-party, Pat and I were given chairs to sit on, being Europeans. In the course of the ceremony a large basket of fruit, rice and other foodstuffs was held at the door by some Shan maidens. They demanded a price of ten rupees for this offering (15 shillings) and the money was to be collected from the company present. All but two rupees was collected and it was hinted that we should contribute this amount. Unfortunately, being ignorant of this custom, we had brought no money with us, but our cook's wife Mary generously lent us two rupees to give as our wedding present. When the basket was brought into the room, prayers were said over it. Thus did Ma Shin become part of our establishment.

I was the only white woman in Kyaukme and I must confess that I quite enjoyed the esteem in which I was held and the fuss made of me. I was quite pleased to hear the bazaar sellers say in Burmese, "*Hladabè!*" (How pretty she is!) When I was interested in buying a sunshade they insisted on my having a lavender coloured one as they said it suited me. I wanted to learn more and more of the Burmese language so that I could converse freely with these charming people. I could equally well have said, "How pretty they are!", with their dainty figures and soft creamy complexions, their lustrous jet hair and fascinating slant eyes. The Burmese and Shans are so clean and fresh looking, and their clothes are spotless.

1922 **Stella**

When I was nine, we went from Maymyo by bullock cart to see the Inle Lake. A dusty, dirt track miles long led to it. It was huge and probably shallow - for the whole bed of the lake was covered with frondy weeds, waving about in the current. As the weeds died they floated to the surface where they massed together and formed floating islands, some small and some large enough to be cultivated.

We spent the night in a *Dak* bungalow, a wooden house supplied by the government for travellers. We had to take our own bedding and book in advance. There was generally a *Durwan* (watch man) in charge. Again no flush toilets (general away from Rangoon.)

Very early next morning we walked down to the shore of the lake to find the boats that had been ordered - they were like long punts with a part roof of broad leaves. The seats along each side were level or below water level - and I could see the reeds looking like a smooth lawn just below the water level. I can't remember how many Shans rowed the boats. The method of rowing was unusual and clever and suited the lake. The rower stood with one foot right along the edge of the boat, the other leg was wound around a long, pole-like oar and he punted along and when an island floated near he just pushed it out of the way, very casually. I was warned to sit very still, as if I fell overboard the reeds would wind themselves around me and I would not be able to be dragged out and would drown. It seems I was always being warned to sit still but I don't think I was particularly naughty or jittery! Sometimes we saw water snakes slithering through the reeds.

A leg-rowing race on Inle Lake.

Leading to the village on the far side were channels of clear water with tall reeds on either side - I do not know how the rowers knew which channel to follow. Wooden walkways helped us to reach land. It was only a small village and we soon saw all the sights (nothing much) but the head man let us sit under cover on his veranda where we ate the lunch we had brought with us. I can't remember the return journey across the lake. I think we had to spend another night in the Dak bungalow and piled into bullock carts next morning. There was always lots of singing when travelling - it helped to forget the bumpy, dusty, creaking ride.

A Dak bungalow.

These hill stations had one excitement every week - that was "Shandy Day" - market day. Villagers from miles around brought their produce to sell - vegetables that could not be grown down on the plains - lovely small peas, cauliflowers, egg plants (brinjals), strawberries, damsons and blackberries - and many others that I can't recall. They also brought carved items, jade and alabaster and wood. And woven articles too - baskets of course and Shan bags - oblong bags with a broad head band as that was the way they were carried. One time Gwen and her friends with me tagging along managed to escape vigilance and have a Chinese meal - this I remember was called *Panthay Kaukswe* and was thick, yellow noodles and delicious. People from China could be found all over Burma - China was over the hills and mountains and they walked for miles and miles.

On the train journey back from Maymyo to Rangoon the monsoons had broken and the scene was quite different. The paddy fields were covered with water and women were attending to them. Water buffaloes plodded along and large white birds almost like gulls or herons sat about - they were called paddy birds.

1946 (soon after the War ended) **Lewis Shaw**

I only had a brief look around before pushing on up the winding road to Maymyo, in the hills at about 3500 feet. It was only forty-two miles, but seemed like twice that with all the hairpin bends. Maymyo is an old Hill Station, established a hundred years ago to get the military and government staff up out of the heat of the plains in the hot season. It appeared that the Japs had hardly damaged Maymyo, which was still a very pleasant Colonial town. I stayed in the Officers' Leave Hostel, which was run by the WVS (Women's Voluntary Service), and it was an unusual experience to spend the evening with a book in front of a log fire.

Although not on my direct route to Loikaw, I decided to go N.E. about 110 miles up to Lashio, a remote town in the mountains on the road to China, and the Admin centre of the Northern Shan States. The hillsides were grassy, but there was plenty of jungle and forest too, all making for magnificent scenery. The most impressive part of that day's journey was negotiating the Goteik Gorge, a river valley with almost vertical sides, where there is a spectacular iron lattice bridge, built in 1900, and set 800 feet above the water. The town of Lashio itself held nothing of interest, though I was glad to have made the journey through the rugged countryside, to see the famous viaduct and to find myself only a hundred miles from China.

Our route from now on was due south, and we still had almost three hundred miles to go to Loikaw. The road was really no better than a farm track, though we passed several gangs of men repairing it and no other traffic for miles. The scenery was still mostly thick jungle, and the few villages were many miles apart. I did wonder if we would meet any dacoits, but being so sparsely populated it probably wasn't worth their while. Nevertheless Mafooz had a rifle and I had my pistol to give us some comfort. It was impossible to do the whole distance in one day, so after about 120 miles we stopped at a convenient PWD (Public Works Dept) bungalow, near

Mong Kung. Looking at the map, I had the odd feeling that I may well have been the only white man for a hundred miles in any direction. We were in the Shan States here, where the locals speak the Shan dialect, so even Mari with his Burmese was unable to communicate without difficulty.

1941 **Sylvia**

At the next village we got an even better reception than usual, being met by all the villagers outside of the village. They were playing drums and cymbals and all walked in front of the car as we moved slowly on. I must confess I felt somewhat like the Queen of England. We were handed water to drink as a sign of hospitality. One must take a sip to show friendship and hope it is not typhoid infected. I was given a bouquet of roses, for these charming people always say it with flowers. The house prepared for us was carpeted with rugs, and a magnificent Burmese embroidered screen hung on the wall opposite us as we entered. This told the story of a nobleman and a *bilu*, a fabulous creature which could change its shape.

Opposite the screen the villagers had placed a table decorated with vases of flowers and eatables which included bananas, Chinese biscuits and buffalo butter, which was always given to us in a bottle; it puzzled me as to how one would get it out - only by melting it, I imagine. One young man brought me an offering of orchids to plant and another a freak bamboo which tapered to a point and in which the sections were in a spiral shape. By request from us the villagers entertained us that evening with a *pwe.* It was thrilling to hear the rhythm of the drums, gongs and cymbals, and to watch the men dancing with great agility and balance. Two men danced with *dahs* (knives) in both hands, swinging them around their heads and bodies most daringly. They had stripped themselves to the waist and tucked up their trousers and they finished this dance with an imitation of killing an animal. The dances are, like most tribal dances, based on events in the lives of the people.

From the next village came Palaung girls to dance to us, a simple rhythmic dance in a circle. Their dress was strikingly different from the Shans. Their striped skirts, mostly in black and red, were girdled around the waist with steel rings. One of these girls knelt before me and very sweetly offered me Palaung woven bags and orchids.

1932 - Visit to a Padaung Village **Stella**

Our neighbours were American missionaries, Mr and Mrs. Jones. A middle aged couple and they asked if I would like to motor up to the Shan States with them and two other women, each paying a share of expenses. And so, very early at the crack of dawn to avoid the extreme heat, and loaded down to the gunnels we set off in their Tin Lizzie. We were a happy and friendly group. This was a different way to see Burma. The road was in fair condition, though dusty. About midday we reached a village. All the rest of the party were teachers and one had taught the daughter of the Head-Man. His was the biggest house, built on stilts, but a good, strong house of wood with wooden stairs leading to the main floor. I think the reason for the house being raised was to keep it from getting flooded in the wet season.

Early next morning we were on our way again. Our destination was Taunggyi. A cluster of stone houses and bungalows around the tennis court and club house met our eyes, looking a bit like a Cotswold village. One of the bungalows was to be ours. It belonged to the mission and was fully and comfortably furnished - with a Shan cook and house boy and sweeper to look after us. It only had two bedrooms so the married couple had one and the three of us ladies shared the other. There was plenty of room and in any case we were out more often than in. There was tennis to play but we preferred the walks up and around the nearby hills. Shandy day was once a week and we loved wandering around the stalls. Our cook was very clever, he had been taught many American dishes - my first Strawberry Short Cake was his creation, with almost clotted cream. One of the snaps show two of us with our harvest of yellow raspberries. Delicious with soft pips. We also gathered blackberries.

One trip was to some caves. We had to have guides - and when we went to the small town to meet them, they were still asleep and no one would wake them up - as their souls were not in their bodies and they would be harmed if they were wakened! (a good excuse). We drove for several hours and at last found the cave. It was fairly large and very dark and inhabited by bats. No doubt an interesting cave for anthropologists. After a picnic lunch we drove on, making arrangements to pick up our guides again to take us to a Padaung village. The village of the giraffe-necked women. We had to leave the car and climb up the mountain (we were already in mountains). It wasn't a forested climb but scrubby with clumps of bamboo and dry grass, hot and dusty. At last we reached the bamboo fence surrounding the village and were greeted in a friendly way by the Head man - who placed his own house at our disposal as it was getting dark by this time. We were just as much a curiosity to the villagers as they were to us - they had never seen white people before and the women kept feeling the stockings on our legs. At puberty the girls have brass rings wound around their necks and legs and arms to prevent them from running away. The rings around their necks cannot be removed as the neck would collapse. Their heads appeared to be small at the top of these long necks.

We were tired so spread our bedding on the bamboo floor being aware of eyes observing us through chinks in the bamboo walling. The usual pariah dogs barked and babies cried but I must have soon fallen asleep without any fear for the next thing I heard was cocks crowing and it was time to get up, boil a kettle and wash. We did not fully undress that night. There was so much

A "giraffe-necked" Padaung woman, smoking a cheroot, is embraced by a missionary!

to see before we returned that we did not waste time. Outside the villagers were getting ready for their day. The women with their spades (for they were the workers - no wonder the men did not want them to run away) were going out over the fence to their vegetable plots. The crop seemed to be poppies. The men brought out their prized possession, a nose flute and played and danced for us. The dance was very sedate - just gentle knee bending as they moved around in a circle. They willingly sold the flute to Mr Jones before we left. There was nothing else we could buy by way of souvenir. We scrambled back down the dusty paths and found the car safe and sound where we had left it. That was a really memorable visit - I often wish that I had had a camera of my own - but I am lucky to have the snaps I am giving into your care.

1946 **Lewis Shaw**

I stopped for lunch next day at Loilem, which was the prettiest town I came across, with pine trees and cherry blossom everywhere, in a setting surrounded by mountains.

From there on I calculated that although we had 110 miles to go, I must reach Loikaw by dark, to catch up with my programme. But it took longer than I thought, and we finished up driving with full headlights with scary jungle closing in on both sides, arriving at Torry's house about 7 o'clock, an hour after dark.

Torry's job was as a Government representative for the Karenni people, the chief of whom was the *Mahadevi* (Queen). He took me to meet her in her *Haw* (palace), the largest building in the town, though sadly in need of repair. There was a wooden throne, badly in need of re-gilding, but as the *Mahadevi* was in everyday dress, we sat round a table in the throne room, while Torry acted as interpreter for a short chat.

The highlight of the whole holiday was a trip thirty miles further up into the beautiful hill country to a village called Hwariku, in the area of the country occupied by the Padaung tribe, famous for their giraffe necked women.

Lewis Shaw's 1947 photo of Padaung women building roads at Hwariku..

These women have up to 30 lbs weight of brass rings wound round their necks, the effect of which is to make their necks look very long. In fact it is the shoulders and ribs which are forced down, giving the effect of stretching the neck. In the village we met two Italian Roman Catholic priests who were running a mission church, school and orphanage, and they showed us round the village and introduced us to some of the women. Many of them were working on repairing the road, and others were engaged in various crafts in the compounds outside their houses. The houses were wooden framed, on stilts, with bamboo walls, the space under the house being used for storage. It is interesting that it was the women who were working, and not the men, who were probably in the fields outside the village.

1941 Sylvia

After finishing an exhausting march we rested a day before setting off to Nakao. The journey was very pleasant, the path following a river all the way We had to cross this river several times and did so on horseback. After travelling along the banks of this large river for some miles, we came to another river which we crossed more than twenty times.

When we were about two miles from our destination, a sudden tremendous downpour came on, a cloudburst I thought. In five minutes the ascending track was one stream of rushing water and from the banks above poured fresh streams to add to it. The quiet river became a raging torrent. So it happens in the rainy season in Burma. We were afraid the mules might not get through, but they arrived eventually. Although we had mackintoshes we were pretty wet, but only in the lower half where the water had streamed down the saddle. Pat got into a villager's *bombies* (Shan trousers) and I borrowed a *loongyi* and we quite enjoyed the funny situation.

The fourth march was short on mileage, only four miles, but it took three hours. In that time we climbed 2,300 feet, a very steep ascent all the way, also still a little slippery. Going up to that altitude was cold, but the exercise made us sweat. We arrived at a village where there was no flat space at all. We sat out in the sun to keep warm, at an angle of about 30 degrees. The altitude of this village of Mantam was 4,700 feet and it was icily cold at night; in fact we could not sleep for the feeling of chilliness. The grass hut, of course, let in all the draughts. Our cook had brought only one blanket with him and he got fever the next day. We pushed on higher still to Hsongkye, nearly 7,000 feet in height. The scenery up there was indescribably magnificent. Our path was near the top of a mountain almost bare of jungle with only waving grasses at each side of the road. We looked down on mountain ranges of 4,000 and 1,000 feet, all circled with mist at their base, soft white clouds of mist like snow or a great billowing sea with islands jutting out. There was a lovely fresh breeze and in shady parts it was unpleasantly cold.

1941 Sylvia again

We were met by Lahus singing a hymn. The women wore most beautiful costumes. Over a *Loongyi* (skirt) of brilliant colour (usually scarlet patterned material) they wore a straight navy blue dress with slits at the sides so that the colour of the *loongyi* made a stunning contrast. On the navy dress a border pattern of bright colours was stitched along the slit end and on the sleeves were bands of bright colours. They carried beautiful shoulder bags in shape like Kachin bags but different in pattern.

The Lahu marriage custom is very interesting. At their New Year, about February, the boys and girls, in separate groups, sing love songs. The young men sing of the imaginary difficulties they have experienced to reach the 'land of the virgins' and the girls console them in their reply. One of the obstacles was a rock some thirty miles around, so that the young men had to get a chisel and tunnel their way through it. At the end of the story-telling the boys and girls who are attracted to each other exchange turbans, and if the proposal is serious, the lover sends a go-between to arrange a marriage.

While at Pangyan I did an oil painting of two Lahus, a boy and a girl. Their costumes were the best I had seen in Burma and would be hard to beat in the costume of any nation. The boy's was similar to the girl's which I have described before, being navy with strips of colour on the jacket and bordering the trouser bottoms. On the dark navy were bands of decoration made of silver plaques, buttons and tassels, looking very bright against the dark background. I started the picture with the boy playing a kind of flute made from a gourd and bamboo pipes. Being rather romantic in those days, I wished to make it a love scene, but this was not perceived by the models or I doubt whether I should have got them to pose, because they are very shy people. I also did a sketch of a muleteer playing that peculiar fiddle the Chinese make out of a bamboo trunk section . [*See facing page - Ed*]

That I still have some of these sketches in spite of being chased out of Burma by the Japanese and leaving everything behind, is due to the care taken of them by the Shan-Indian doctor of Mongyai. He preserved them for me during the Japanese occupation. The painting of the two Lahus was never recovered.

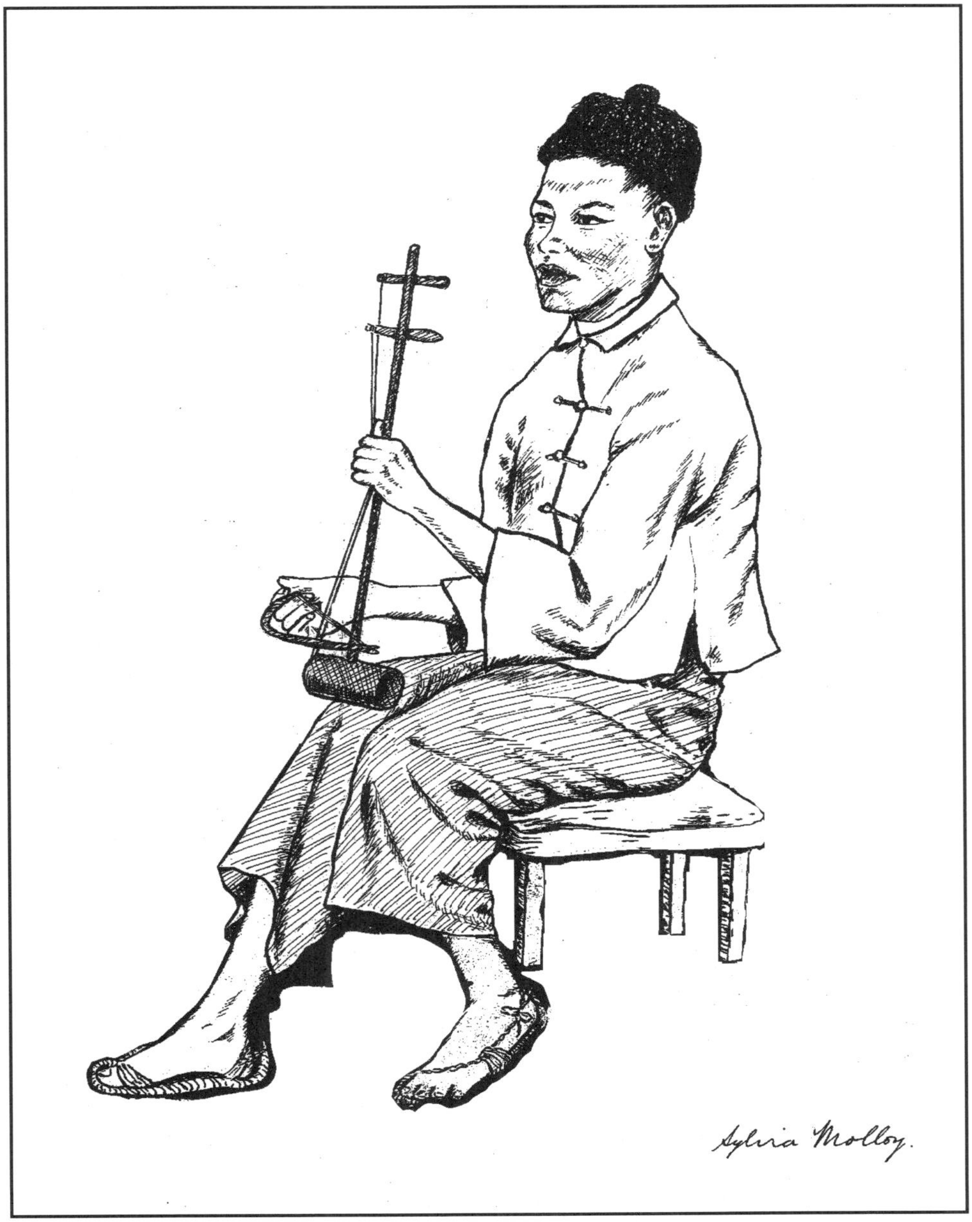

Chinese muleteer with fiddle - a sketch by Sylvia Molly.

1941 Sylvia

During our last evening in Hsungling, the people of the village, Lahus and Wa's, gave us a dancing display. The Wa's danced the most peculiar dance I have ever seen, it was more like an acrobatic feat than a dance. Three couples sitting opposite each other banged together pieces of bamboo trunks or rice pounding sticks, while the dancer had to leap between the sticks with great agility to avoid being caught in them. The couples beat the sticks to rhythm and if the dancer kept perfect time, he could just manage it.

* * *

Originally it was our intention to visit a district where another Assistant Superintendent lived. Pat wrote announcing our coming, and received a very strange reply. The Assistant invited us to stay at his home for the days we spent there and pointed out the amenities of living in a proper house once more, but he said there was one feature of his household which might prevent us going there. He told us that he had a pleasant little Shan girl living with him who shared his bed, his table, and in fact the whole of his life. He said he had no intention of marrying her. He also added that if we refused to stay with him for this reason he would understand but would not approve. One could not but admire his candour, as many men kept Burmese girls, but out of sight. Actually we did not wish to stay with him or anyone else, as we had our own habits of living and took our meals at different times from the customary Burma meal times. We felt it now very awkward to refuse, however, because whatever our reason he would suppose it to be due to our prudishness. Fortunately in the end we found no need to go.

His way of life was not uncommon among men who led lonely lives on the frontier, but few were open about it. We knew one man who eventually married a Burmese woman after she had had two children. In addition to the wife, he had a Shan girl who went on tour with him while he left his wife at home. In fact he had become Burmanised in having more than one wife to comfort him. This man was a heavy drinker (as were quite a number of the officers) due once again I think to loneliness. He had been at one time Assistant Superintendent in Mongyai, and there we heard of a queer episode connected with him. He left his Burmese wife in Mongyai with an ayah (nurse to children). They had not been long in the house he had chosen when the ayah became possessed by a spirit, said to be the spirit of a former Sawbwa. She went quite mad and told people truths that only the former Sawbwa could know. Her frenzy rose to a climax when, old as she was, she leapt on a bicycle and sped down the road. The Burmese wife fled from Mongyai, and the old ayah was perfectly sane as soon as she had left this house, though she still continued to live in Mongyai.

Strange doings, though not of a supernatural kind, had also occurred in our house in Mongyai. One Assistant Superintendent who lived there had a Burmese wife. He was a man of violent temper. His wife had a fondness for a Shan lad of the village; when the Assistant Superintendent was out, clandestine meetings used to take place between the two lovers. One day as her husband went out, the wife admitted the young man from the back door. Unfortunately for her, her husband returned almost immediately as he had cut his finger. She smuggled the lover into the wardrobe (which still stood in our bedroom) and tried to carry on a normal conversation with her husband. She managed to get rid of him before he discovered anything, and let the man out of the wardrobe. I myself tried standing in the wardrobe just to see how it felt to be in such a romantic situation, and it was not too comfortable. Later, however, the Assistant Superintendent discovered the affair, which was of course well known to all the servants; in a blind fury he drove his car to the lad's house and tied him up in a sack. He then proceeded to the Sawbwa's palace and informed him that he was going to throw the bundle in the lake. Fortunately for him and the youth the Sawbwa intervened and saved the young man's life. The Assistant Superintendent left his wife and married another.

* * *

In Mongyai we had a Sawbwa living in a palace with the *Mahadevi* or chief wife, and several other wives, and many children including two grown up daughters called Kitty and Nancy, who were educated at Maymyo convent so that they spoke English. These girls were not children of the *Mahadevi* (who had no children), but she adopted a loving maternal attitude to all the children. I looked forward to making friends with Kitty and Nancy. Both were attractive and Nancy was particularly pretty.

The Sawbwa was in many ways a very interesting old man. It is true that he had twelve wives and numerous progeny, but his main interest was in carpentry and tinsmithing. He could copy any design of furniture and mended my revolving bookcase, which had got damaged on the way from England.

The Sawbwa's *Haw* or palace was a large wooden building on the top of a hill. While practising driving I had great difficulty after climbing the hill to drive between the house and the pillars of the entrance. Around the palace was a large verandah and the rooms were tremendously spacious. The occasion of our visit was a farewell dinner given to U Tu Aung, Pat's predecessor in Mongyai, who was leaving there to go to Falam. The local doctor was also invited to the party. We were the only English people there, but the conversation was mostly in English, as all but the Sawbwa and Mahadevi spoke English. This included even the Sawbwa's

"Kachin Girl" - a 1941 sketch by Sylvia Molloy.

ministers. We had a proper Burmese dinner though I personally preferred my own cook's curries. At a Burmese dinner all the dishes are set on the table at once, many different kinds of curries, meat, vegetable, and fish curries, spices, pickles, and chutneys. I like eating this way because of the pleasant variety of tastes on one's palate.

1941 Sylvia

The Sawbwa was a great "do it yourself" man. Although invited to the wedding of the new Governor's daughter, he did not intend to go. Apart from the fact that he felt it would cost him too much money, he was not keen on social life. He preferred to stay at home in his carpentry shop, where he was busy all day. One day Pat admired a lovely ivory penknife being made by the carpenter and immediately the Sawbwa offered it to him. Some of the bamboo knitting needles he made were very beautiful with ivory knobs. He also did wonderful metalwork. He was not at all interested in such things as politics.

I taught a lot of cooking to Kitty and Nancy, who were thrilled to make such things as sponge cake and vanilla rings. I also taught them to make guava jelly at the *Haw*. One day their cousin Susan came to visit me with them. She was very charming and had plenty to say. Though Nancy and Kitty knew English very well, having been educated at a convent, they were very shy and it was a long time before I could get them to talk much. Nancy eventually became quite talkative, but Kitty remained very quiet. We wanted Nancy to take up a profession and she thought of going to Namkhan to be trained as a nurse in Dr Seagrave's hospital. He was an American Baptist missionary and a noted doctor.

A 10-month-old baby half-sister of Kitty and Nancy died. They had the same father, the Sawbwa. The baby's mother was the youngest wife, a girl of about twenty-three. The Sawbwa and *Mahadevi* were over 50. The *Mahadevi* used to nurse the sick children with the other nine wives, a kind of situation that the western mind cannot comprehend. One would imagine that the women would be always quarrelling and that they would be intensely jealous of each other, but this was not so. The *Mahadevi* regarded all the children as her own, she herself had none. The other nine wives lived in the old Haw; only the *Mahadevi* lived in the new Haw with the Sawbwa. The two girls Kitty and Nancy called her "mammy", and when Nancy spoke of her real mother she called her "my mother". The *Mahadevi* took an interest in everything they did. When they were making jam, she was there.

Later at the *Haw* an event of importance was to take place, and we were invited to the wedding of Nancy to an Englishman of the Burma Frontier Service, Ronnie Mitchell. The wedding service was performed while Nancy and Ronnie sat on our sofa in the *Haw*. It was a very simple ceremony. Their hands were joined together with a band of cloth. I had always expected Nancy to marry an Englishman and although Mitchell was middle-aged I felt she would be happier than if married to a Shan when she might be only one of several wives. Their happiness was to be very short-lived however. While trying to escape from the Japanese about a month later, Ronnie Mitchell was shot and killed.

1941 Sylvia

We eventually left Mongyai for our tour of Manglung State on 17th March, having had to wait for months to buy opium. The purpose of the tour was to buy all or most of the opium grown in Manglung State. Up to that time it was bought by traders and smuggled into Burma and China. It had been decided that the government should take over sales, but it was a difficult task to stop smuggling and to get all the opium. People would naturally hide it to get a bigger price from the smugglers.

We saw our first opium in the course of a thirteen mile walk (mostly riding for us). There was no colour of poppies because they had all gone to seed. Opium is the juice from the poppy heads which the cultivator extracts and makes into a big bundle by sticking it all together. It is nearly black in colour. This day we arrived at a village where Pat managed with some difficulty to acquire some opium, only 61 ticals (100 ticals equal 1 *viss* which equals three and a half pounds. This measure always amused me as it is pronounced the same way as our "tickle"). The opium was weighed on a villager's scales and the weights were shaped like strange mythical animals.

Next day we were met by the Sawbwa of Manglung State, whose palace was in Pangyan. The Government wanted the Sawbwa to buy up opium on its behalf at 40 rupees a *viss*, of which he would get 10 rupees commission, paying the cultivators 30 rupees.

Opium was sold on bazaar day, when people from neighbouring villages in a great variety of costumes brought their goods to sell. We had sepoys and policemen posted to search suspicious characters who might be carrying opium.

Early in May a caravan of mules arrived on their way to Tangyan. The muleteers were armed with automatic pistols like American gangsters. One of them had his pistol in a neat leather case attached to a cartridge belt. I did not imagine that they used them normally, but it had become a habit to carry them when they carried supplies of opium, which was very valuable.

This caravan had 1,000 rupees in money with them and I suppose they thought they needed protection. Pat made them delay at Pangyan, as he suspected they were intending to buy opium on bazaar day. It was decided that all traders travelling through Manglung State should be disarmed. We were still waiting for the money to pay for the opium; it looked as if we would have to leave Pangyan before it arrived. We were annoyed at the delay, as it was hard for the villagers who had not yet been paid.

But eventually the money arrived and we were able to pay our debts.

The Royal Lake - Stella lived opposite it for a while.

1915-1925 **Stella**

Which of all the sights that come to mind shall I write about first?

Natives pulling a very heavy cart, by rope, with a cheer leader chanting something, to be echoed by the rest of the men in unison, I suppose it could have been "pull, men" followed by "we're pulling". Then funerals - richer ones were led by a "fufu" band. This was composed of a few men (Indian and Burmese) blowing brass instruments and beating drums. Very often trying to play Western music. It did sound strange! Oh - the corpse was carried on a bier covered with a sheet. Chinese funerals were very grand affairs.

Squares of paper with gilt writing on them would be scattered in front of the ornate red and gilt hearse, carried by the Chinese men. Drums and gongs were banged loudly as the procession wended its way to the Chinese Cemetery. Chinese graves were large and ornately carved. The paper money was meant to delay evil spirits who would stop to pick it up and allow the corpse to escape their evil intentions.

Dry cleaners too had their shops. The weekly washing was done by Dhobies. They came to the house, spread out the soiled clothes to be counted and marked up in an account book. Then all would be piled in the centre of a sheet that would be tied by four corners and carried on the head of the native employed by the Dhobie. The next week all would be returned - clean and snowy white and stiffly starched - so stiff sometimes it was hard to separate back from front - and often with most of the buttons missing from shirts - my Father used to say that the buttons were deliberately removed and sold! Once or twice when a garment was needed in a hurry, I was driven to the Dhobie Lines to collect it - I remember long concrete troughs, acres of them, outdoors with men pounding and banging the clothes on blocks - and yards and yards of clothes hanging out to dry. I wonder what they did in the wet season? So many things that I question now but did not bother about then! In the Dhobies' hut, long tables covered with clean sheets and ironing accomplished with heavy brass irons - coal fired. I marvel now that the clothes were so expertly finished with such crude tools. It is only when one has to do these things oneself that one appreciates the difficulty and when I think of the heat that they had to work in! Anyway when the clothes were brought back my Mother with her account book on her knee would go through the list and make sure all linen taken was returned. Amazingly little was lost.

In the town, rickshaws and tikka gharries plied for trade - for a treat on Sunday my Father took my brother John and me for a ride in a rickshaw - the only time I went in one - it was an experience! A little wobbly but on the whole not unpleasant - another Sunday he took us in a tram - this was a long-looked-for treat. The trams ran along the main roads in the town and were like the old fashioned trams in London. There were two large Pagodas in Rangoon as mentioned before. In the town there was the Sule pagoda - a landmark from the river. Unfortunately when driving around it one could not see much of the near area around it as it had hoarding with advertisements. This pagoda divided the bazaar area from the bigger, better shops and the commercial part - the Law Court, Town Hall, Main Post Office, Banks, Shipping Offices, Docks Ware Houses etc. etc. The Shwe Dagon Pagoda was beautiful. It was erected on the last and westernmost small hill of the Pegu Yomas (range of hills). On one side was a park surrounded by grassy land and slopes. Gold leaf was always being applied to the walls and dome and at night it was flood lit. Sule Pagoda had rings of light bulbs around it and also was always covered with gold leaf. Monasteries surrounded the pagodas and saffron robed monks and brightly dressed Burmese people were always around the forecourts and steps leading into each pagoda. I never had the courage to remove my shoes and go into the inner sanctum - though tourists could and did do so. Flower sellers and candle sellers squatted by their baskets on the lower steps. I remember one year near the Shwe Dagon Pagoda there was bamboo scaffolding, thirty or forty feet tall, with a platform at the top for the burning of the body of a very rich man - a great merit for the hereafter. All Burmese boys had to become a monk for a short period.

At one season - I think it must have been after the rains - the Flame of the Forest trees came into bloom. Trees not as tall as Elms or Chestnuts but quite a good size, absolutely covered with bright, flame coloured flowers - a marvellous sight as most of the roads were lined with them. About this time another tree with flowers that, though not exactly pretty, nevertheless had a strong and lovely perfume, came into bloom - and the women loved wearing a spray of the flowers in their hair.

Shwe Dagon at night - 1930.

1921 **Stella**

When I was about eight we moved to another house - upstairs this time and overlooking the Race Course (Maidan). Every Saturday we had a grandstand view of the races! John and I used to fly kites in the middle. My Mother thought I was not getting enough exercise and made me walk all around the course, with a servant to guard me. Every day! I hated it.

From the lower veranda, a louvred door opened onto a wide staircase leading up to our floor. One Sunday I was playing the piano when I heard someone come up - when I looked up I saw a young Chinese woman standing there. She was dressed in a green satin top and trousers and had bound feet. Bits of grass were in her hair so she must have slept out. She was well born to be dressed so well. I called for my Mother and Father. We couldn't talk to her and she couldn't talk to us. However after giving her something to eat and drink - my Father phoned the Chinese Consul and he asked us to bring her to him. I went with my Father as I was very upset and frightened. She was a gentle person and I think she had lost her memory. I never did learn the rest of the story. My parents probably thought it better for me not to know.

Looking back it seems we lived an exciting and busy life. There was always something happening. I remember my Father hiring one of the firm's launches and a party of about twenty or thirty friends and their children went for a day's trip up the Rangoon River, the Irrawaddy River. It was twice as wide as the Thames and very, very, muddy. Logs, dead animals, and flotsam floated on the surface, small boats, some with bamboo covered sleeping areas, some laden with coconuts or other fruit. We took our servants with us and this was the first time that I can remember seeing ice cream being churned - a wooden barrel, with ice, sawdust and salt - rock salt or saltpetre was packed around an aluminium drum in which was the mixture (cream, eggs, sugar etc.) The cover was put on and a servant turned this back and forth till the cream thickened. This in the future was one of my favourite puddings.

1924-26 Stella

There was an enormous lake further out from Rangoon, this was the Kokine Lake and later still we lived within walking distance of part of it. Another person we knew had a wooden bathing cabin on the shores of the Kokine Lake and later we spent many Sundays picnicking there. The cabin consisted of two rooms with a fixed wooden screen dividing the rooms. One for men and the other for women. Wooden steps led right down to the water. Other times we would take our own food and fruit. It was heavenly. It was also near a pineapple plantation - though I don't think we ever had any fruit from it. There were also Mango groves which gave welcome shade. It was quite sandy around the shore and one of the memories indelibly stamped on my mind was the sight of the sand pitted and smelling so fresh after a shower of rain. For we were able to continue swimming and picnicking even in the rain. At this time the whole area was relatively unpopulated. We could wander around at will and not see another soul though we were only a few miles out of Rangoon.

One time far across on the other side of the lake we saw a strange creature emerge from the water. We all looked and couldn't believe our eyes - true, a grey misty rain was falling but unmistakably a large Kangaroo or lizard shaped animal had come out of the water for a few minutes then walked back into the lake and disappeared - this was before the Loch Ness Monster - but it was similar to such descriptions. We were so frightened we never went back. Several people were drowned in strange circumstances in this lake and their bodies were never recovered. After the drowning of one young man, his bereaved father consulted a sooth sayer as he wanted to bury his son's body. The sooth sayer asked for his pillow, made a slit in it, broke an egg and poured it into the slit. They then launched the pillow in the direction where the swimmer had last been seen. The idea was that the pillow would circle the spot and the body would rise. The pillow did circle the spot and then sank...

Two very rich men - one an Indian Broker called Jamal, the other a Chinese named Chin Song, bought land by the Kokine Lake. They outrivalled each other in the houses they built. Jamal built a mansion in the Western style surrounded by gardens. Chin Song was more ambitious - very often we drove past to see how the building was progressing. An enormous tiered Chinese style temple was gradually taking shape with green tiled roofs and carved wood work, windows and doors. Around the enormous gardens, dozens of gardeners laboured fashioning mystical dragons and beasts from the trees. Unfortunately poor Chin Song's ideas were too ambitious and he ran out of money. But he also bought an island on the lake on which he erected another temple. I was rowed over to this island one day and it was sad to wander through the empty rooms and neglected garden with its carved stone Buddhas, lions and dragons. I suppose someone bought Chin Song's Palace as it was called but since then there have been two world wars with the Japanese Occupation and now Burmese Nationalisation with restricted entry requirements to Burma and so it will be a long time before anyone will be likely to go and see Chin Song's Palace for me.

JAPANESE BOMBING - AND THE FLIGHT

Early 1941 — Sylvia

At Mongyin we were sitting reading one night when the cook called us out to see something strange. In the sky we saw a star with a trail of light following it, evidently a comet. The cook said he saw a comet just before King Edward died, and I remembered Shakespeare's lines "The heavens themselves blaze forth the death of princes." I pondered as to who it might be and I hoped it might be the arch enemy of our time, Hitler. The people of Mongyin interpreted it to mean that the war was coming to the East. Events proved them right, though I did not believe it at the time.

Later 1941 — Sylvia

We heard news of the German invasion of Russia. Though it surprised us, it seemed it was expected by Russia. The Russians were doing extremely well so far, and it did not seem by any means certain that Germany would conquer. We felt it would have been ideal if Britain had been ready to invade Germany; our bombers were doing great damage to the Ruhr and munitions factories; the raids on Britain seemed to have lessened, which showed that the Germans could not afford to lose many more planes or pilots. I always felt that my comments on the news would be very stale by the time they reached my mother in England, because the news changed so rapidly, and we were far from events. Our mail was driven by lorry to Lashio, thence by train to Rangoon, and then by air or sea to Europe. We felt at this time that the war was drawing nearer to us and believed that we might soon be at war with the Japanese. If they did attack Burma, it would be through the Shan States and we would be in the front line at Mongyai. Burma was busy preparing for an assault and let the Japanese know it. We fondly imagined that therefore they might not dare to attack.

Japan's surprise attack on Pearl Harbour, in December 1941, was rapidly followed by an attack on Rangoon.

Dec 1941 **Amy Forbes-Mitchell**

The first bombing of Rangoon was on 23rd December 1941. The Japanese planes flew over Syriam, where we lived, to bomb Rangoon, seven miles away across the Irrawaddy River. I was eleven years of age, my sister nine and my brother's fifth birthday was the next day. We rushed out all excited to see the planes as there were so many and they were making such a noise. The planes flew over our farm and we stood and watched them until we noticed "balls of fire" dropping from the planes over Rangoon. We could not hear the bombing as Rangoon was seven miles away. My mother said that the planes must be Japanese and they were bombing Rangoon. She felt that the Japs may not bomb Syriam as the refineries of the Burma Oil Company were just two miles away. As our Air-Raid Shelter was incomplete we stopped in-doors until we could hear no more planes.

Rangoon had been severely bombed, killing and injuring thousands of civilians, mostly Indians. Many people left for the suburbs to stay with relatives. After X'mas my mother visited my father's mother in Rangoon who told her of her lucky escape and of my aunt and her three children, who were visiting her for X'mas. There was an open space behind the street that my grandmother lived on in Rangoon. The residents had thought of building air-raid shelters on the open space. My Granny's air-raid shelter was incomplete. During the first bombing of Rangoon there was no air-raid siren. When my Granny realised Rangoon was being bombed she thought they had better take shelter under her dining-table. My aunt thought they had better rush out to the incomplete shelter. They got as far as the back door and then my Granny stopped. Her air-raid shelter had just been bombed. They returned to the dining-room and sat under the dining-table till the air-raid was over.

My aunt and her family accepted my mother's offer to return with her to Syriam. My Granny packed a few clothes, photos, family mementoes into two trunks and went to live with another aunt who lived in the suburbs of Rangoon hoping to return soon. She never returned. We as a family were evacuated from Burma on 1st April 1942. My father's parents had been in Rangoon since 1910 and my mother's parents since 1896.

Dec 1941 **Evelyn**

I was a student at Rangoon University when Japan struck Pearl Harbour.

The University was immediately closed - I remember a very pretty and popular Japanese student, Lilian, was taken away by the police to be interned. I had a half-sister who lived near the University. "The war will be over in a few weeks" she said, "Come and stay with me and you can return to University when it re-opens!" However, on December 23rd Rangoon was bombed and my sister who was a doctor (obstetrics and gynaecology) at the Dufferin Hospital, the biggest women's hospital in Burma, was ordered to live in at the hospital and I went with her.

Rangoon was bombed again on Christmas Day - it was chaos as the servants' quarters were hit and they fled. I remember one doctor running down the road after a fleeing servant brandishing her stethoscope. Another of my sisters had just had a baby on the 22nd. As the bombs fell, her husband, an Anglican priest in his white cassock, handed me the tiny infant and told me to get under the bed while he spread himself across his wife's bed to protect her as much as he could. I was cured of being terrified of small babies after that! All kinds of people came in to help including VAD nurses and vicars. My sister drove into town to try and get some bread but was offered cake - dozens of Christmas cakes. Christmas dinner, she announced, was "rice and lentils" or "lentils and rice". A helpful vicar was happily adding some tinned sardines he had found to the lentil mixture. Air raid casualties were being brought in by now and one was June Rose, aged 8, whose mother was Princess Bellamy of the Burmese Royal Family. June Rose had shrapnel in her thigh and was very brave indeed, saying, "I'm a Bluebird (Brownie) and I must not cry." Plans to evacuate the hospital to the outskirts of the city and then to Bassein were made and then abandoned and finally it was each for himself - and the devil take the hindmost! We had moved out to Windermere Park to stay with their Uncle - all of us, mother, new baby, vicar and me - incidentally it was the house where Maurice Collis used to live - as their Uncle was the Collector of Rangoon.

11th March 1942 Sylvia

By the 11th March the news was bad, but we still believed the tide would turn soon. The offensive against Japan was said to be almost ready to begin. Although it seemed tragic that our troops were being withdrawn without a fight, I believed it was the best policy, as all our troops would have been encircled and we would have had no forces to fight for us in Upper Burma. We believed the withdrawal to be a triumph over the Japs. (Little did we know the truth!) In North Burma we also had Chinese troops to help us, or so we thought.

All valuable works and buildings in Rangoon had been demolished including the Burma Oil Company. Our friend, Gladys Hooper, had to remain in her job at the Burma Oil Company till the last. We did not know what had happened to her but hoped she had been evacuated. This was a time when one began to lose touch with people, characteristic of the beginning of a war, and many people were lost to each other for months. Our other friend, Molly, had been evacuated with her firm and went to Mandalay by steamer. She had a bad journey on an overcrowded boat. Among the other passengers was an old Chinaman with three wives and seventeen children, who monopolised the bathrooms.

January 1942 Evelyn

I left Rangoon on January 15th to return to the Shan States. In spite of everything, the daily One-Up train left dead on time at 4 p.m. I was dawdling and was flung on to the train by a passing Army Officer. I found I was sharing the compartment (on a non-corridor train) with a couple who had got married that day. As it was an overnight journey they had to share their honeymoon night with me. They lived happily ever after and raised seven children.

I went to my mother's home. My Uncle was a Sawbwa (Shan Prince) and his state was on the Burma road to China.

April 1942 **Sylvia**

The last night before we left Pangyan I saw a larger quantity of gold than ever before. Some Chinese traders were passing though and selling it. There was one viss (three and a half pounds) in gold leaf, small sheets as thin as fine paper, and the rest was in bracelets and rings, all pure gold. If we had had the money to buy it we could have sold it at a good profit in Lashio and perhaps made about 2,000 rupees. People bought gold there as an investment so that if they were in difficulties the gold could be used.

Soon after arriving in Mongyai, on the 24th March 1942, I received a letter from England dated 28th December 1941. My mother had sent a cable which never reached us. Everything was in confusion. Pat wanted me to leave Mongyai and go to Sumprabum in the far north, where my brother was, as it would be fairly easy to get to India from there, but I preferred to await the course of events. Most of the European women had already gone to India; there were special trains and aeroplanes provided, but I still believed there was no danger, and therefore I carried on as usual with the small things of my domestic life - making crumpets from a new cookery book, and commissioning a new easel for my birthday on 27th.

The Shan States were in the world news by now. The Japs were already in the Southern Shan States, but had not advanced very far; I heard that the Chinese had driven them back twenty miles. Government officers had orders to evacuate if the Japanese came to our districts. Our idea for escape was to trek out to Pangyan across the Salween.

However, Pat came back from a trip to Lashio with orders from Mr Porter that we were not to go to Pangyan, but must go north either to Sinlumkaba or Myitkyina. I hate to think now what would have happened to us if we had not had these orders from an older man. My brother John had been transferred from Sumprabum to Myitkyina. The news was a little more heartening. At last Tokyo was being bombed. Yenan-gyaung in Burma, previously in the hands of the Japs, was recaptured by the Chinese.

We were all very calm. The weather was hot and I was wearing my new sunbathing dress every day. My letter to my mother concerning these things was written on the 20th April, 1942. By the 24th April we were fleeing for our lives!

When Lashio and Taunggyi were bombed I knew the invasion of the Shan States would begin. On the 23rd April the Commissioner was evacuated from Taunggyi, Southern Shan States. He came to Mongyai and said he would give orders for me to leave, but said nothing about the urgency of the situation. The next day, a wireless message from Porter came to us. Fortunately the RAF had just set up a wireless station at Mongyai. The message came in code to them, and as Pat decoded it we read, "Enemy taken Loilem use your own discretion leave Mongyai." We heard in Mongyai that the Japs were in fact in Laica, only sixty miles away and of course they were motorised.

While I was frantically packing, Pat was rushing around getting money from the treasury to pay everybody advances of wages. We had two lorries, which Pat with great foresight had requisitioned before, and fortunately we had plenty of petrol. We set off at about 1 p.m. with the cook and his wife and children, also Kitty and her mother. We had to leave our faithful and frightened Burmese servants behind. Our cook being Indian naturally did not want to be left to the Japanese. When we reached Lashio, Mr Porter was ready to leave. The Commissioner was there and gave Pat a scrap of paper saying that he was on leave owing to the invasion of his subdivision. And so it was official!

Thank God we had the new car bought at Maymyo. The first day north, we went straight to Kutkai on the Burma road to China. We had terrific rain on the way, though it was early for the rains. For the first time I realised the feelings of the Belgian refugees fleeing from Hitler, for now we too were merely refugees. We drove all day with no food except for a few biscuits and some port wine, which I had thrown into the car at the last minute. At Kutkai, in the Assistant Superintendent's bungalow, we had our first meal since breakfast.

May 1942 — Pat Kelly (aged 9)

There were eight of us: my mother Betty Kelly, Peter Courtenay, a British officer evacuated from Lower Burma away from the fighting on account of his malaria, my seven year old brother Desmond, four native servants, three ponies, a string of mules and myself, aged nine. The date, 6th May 1942.

We were leaving Tiddim where our family had lived for the past three years. My father, Norman Kelly, was Resident and Administrator of a large area of the Chin Hills along the Burma/Assam border with India.

Word had come through the previous night that the Japanese forces were fifty miles away and, with the exception of Father, we were all commanded to evacuate.

There was no railway for hundreds of miles, no airstrip, no metalled road; we were expected to get out as best we could.

Father had already rallied the local tribes to fight a guerrilla war alongside the scattered remnants of the British forces. Armed initially with knives and ancient flintlock rifles, these Chin tribespeople led by Father, helped to hold the hills against the enemy until Allied forces returned. They were later to be known as the Chin Levies. The village of Tiddim found itself on world maps, as headquarters for the famous 17th Indian Division in 1942/43, then of the Japanese. It was eventually bombed to the ground, before it was recaptured in 1944 .

But that May dawn, the monsoon was breaking as we trudged down the narrow slippery track which was to lead us westward across the frontier. The rain, which had been no more than a haze on distant smoke-blue mountains, became a dense mist. My last memory of Tiddim is of shuddering vapour and stark black pines, dripping. At Tuibel, we crossed the mighty fast-flowing Manipur River, by a 300 ft. rope suspension bridge.

1942 **Sylvia**

We eventually reached Hosie, where we made some curry and rice for lunch. A little beyond Hosie we branched off the Burma road to Myitkyina. Much of the traffic went on to China, as there were many Chinese refugees. We had therefore less traffic on our way to Namkhan, where we stayed that night. The road to Namkhan was terrible and part of the way at Musee, we bumped and jolted over huge cobblestones. At Namkhan we were put up in a house by the hospital. In Namkhan we all slept in one room, Kitty and her mother in one bed, Porter in another and Pat and I on the floor. The next day we stayed in Namkhan, a delay we later regretted very much. From Namkhan we wired Mitchell at Sinlumkaba to come down to meet Kitty and her mother at Bhamo, which was on our route.

After sleeping another night at Namkhan, we set off for Bhamo. There we happened to find an empty house and simply occupied it. There was no other accommodation. In one part of the house was a Sikh doctor with his small unit and he told us a sorry story of how he was obliged to retreat and retreat, each time losing more of his equipment until he had practically nothing left. This, he said, was due to the inefficiency and false confidence of the officers, who would not let him leave until the last moment, when he was given half an hour to remove all his patients and equipment. If the story of the Burma war were ever told truthfully it would be a story of shame, inefficiency and cowardice, with not one glory to brighten the picture. This is how it seemed to me, but perhaps all retreats are like this especially when events seemed to take everyone unawares. We heard that in Martaban there was such a state of panic shown by the higher officers who had got themselves safely over the Sittang bridge that they actually blew up the bridge before all the men got across. Those who could swim had a chance, though they were being machine gunned by the Japanese. The fate of those left behind is left to the imagination.

In Bhamo we had three bedrooms, but no beds, and it was a terribly dirty house. Mitchell had sent his car, servants and horses for Kitty and her mother, who were to travel thirteen miles by car and thirteen miles by horse. Mitchell was unable to come. They were terrified to go alone, as they had lived all their lives in the Sawbwa's *haw;* Porter said he would accompany them which meant three days delay. I was very unhappy about it, but those women were just helpless and had no independence at all. Their first day's journey was thirteen miles by car and six on horseback. But that day we heard that Lashio had been captured by the Japs. We were in a panic waiting for Porter and knowing that the Japanese could be in Bhamo as soon as he was. We sent off his driver to find him and bring him back. He returned with Porter in the morning much to our relief and we set off once more for Myitkyina.

This was the beginning of a fearful journey. The road was terrible, neither tarred nor metalled , and nearly all the bridges were broken. There were some bridges where the lorries had to unload before crossing and all the goods had to be carried across separately. Over one such bridge we did not attempt to take our lorry, but the driver drove it through the river. Like all the other lorries it stuck when it reached the steep bank on the other side; the road was all mud and it could not get any grip. After hours of trying to push it out, the men standing waist deep in the water tried jacking it up on logs and after getting it halfway up the bank, another big lorry pulled it up. We slept that night at a little bungalow.

Our greatest trouble was the weather, it rained incessantly and the road was a sea of mud; sometimes it was the lorry and sometimes the cars which stuck in the mud. Each time there was a delay of at least an hour. At one of these places we had to dig dry earth and stones from the hillside to fill up the ruts; at another, the lorry stuck at the top of a very dangerous hill section right on the edge of a precipice. I cannot describe the horror of driving over that hill section on a wet earth road with the sharpest corners I have ever experienced and with only about eight inches between the edge of the car and the precipice. The cars were waltzing all over the road, not once but all the time. Driving behind Mr Porter, we would suddenly see his car swerve at a right angle to the road and ours would probably follow suit. We skidded at every corner, though we were driving at only about two miles an hour.

In addition to these horrors, we had to cross at ferries where one car took from half to one hour to get across. This delay was nerve-wracking, as the Japs were following the same road only about three days behind us. We kept getting news of them as we travelled on. There was dry weather after we had driven the hill section, and that meant that the Japs could easily travel at four times the rate at which we had driven. We covered only twenty miles a day. At a ferry called Gezoo we abandoned the lorry, as no lorries could cross. We also abandoned much of our stores and clothes, leaving trunks just lying on the roadside. Through the good organisation of Mr Crow we waited to cross the ferry only one night and one day. Some people had waited four days to get across. The traffic jam was terrible and panic rife. Mr Crow kept order by brandishing a Tommy gun. That night we slept in our car; it was impossible to get accommodation anywhere.

1942 — Pat Kelly

The day's programme was always the same: up at 6 a.m., with a breakfast usually of burnt scrambled egg and tea made with condensed milk drunk from chipped enamel mugs. Then the day's march would begin. The baggage, which only included, besides food for the animals and ourselves, two small suitcases and two rolls of bedding carried by the mules, went ahead with the servants, and we followed. We usually averaged 15 to 20 miles a day, walking and riding.

Clothing was simple: khaki shorts and shirts, socks and sandals. We each carried a rucksack; among other things mine held a tin of bull's-eye sweets into which rain invariably leaked. They tasted strongly of the tin. Peter, related to aristocracy, carried a quantity of treasury notes, and slept with them under his pillow with a revolver. His Army stories were fascinating and so was his language; he would entertain Des and me with both as we skidded down steep, glass-hard muddy roads, while black gleaming leeches crawled unnoticed up our legs.

They dropped unfelt from trees and sucked blood until, too satiated to withdraw, they had to be burnt off with salt and tobacco juice.

In spite of leeches, our travelling through the green steaming jungles, crags and ravines which loomed in the mist, and the incessant whisper of raindrops on sodden leaves, were forgotten. Des and I adored Peter. Soon after we left Tiddim, however, he had another attack of malaria, so severe that he had to be carried on a litter, delirious. Mother, nearly frantic with worry, now kept the revolver herself. To make matters worse, the bamboo huts in which we camped were not ideal for a malarial patient; rain seeped in at every crack, spiders, snakes and squirrels infested them, the weather was depressing.

The day came when we eventually waded across the Tyao River between Burma and India, into Assam. I remember the clear water of it, glinting with the colour of wild honey under the tropic sun. I also remember sleek black water snakes sliding among stones on the river bed. Des remembers looking back for the last time at Burma, and thinking this is where I was born; one day I will come back. He did, in 1986.

Then one day we reached an oasis in the wilderness of jungle. Aijal was one of the main towns of Assam and there we stayed a day or two with the British Resident and his wife. What luxury that was - to sleep on a bed and not the floor, to bath in a tub and not in a river, to eat fresh food and to see a well cared-for garden. With the McCalls we left some of our glass and plate, family wedding mementoes, hoping to retrieve it when the war was over. We never did.

1942 — Sylvia

Somewhere behind us was an RAF convoy of sixty lorries and we tried to keep ahead of them. It seemed to me at the time that all they cared about was their own safety and thought they had a right to pass any car which had been waiting days to cross a ferry. Perhaps they had their orders, but in that situation it had to be "first come, first served". The selfishness which we met with on that road was incredible. Only in moments of extremity does one discover the true character of a man. A civilian in a high position would drive up and expect to have priority over all the other cars, not caring about women and children waiting to get across. But we treated everyone alike and refused to allow them to pass in front of us. I had to brandish our pistol at a Chinese driving a car and trying to pass us, with some excuse about repairing the bridge; he soon stopped when I pointed the Sawbwa's very large revolver at his head and said "This is loaded", which it was. We were in desperate circumstances and had to use desperate means.

We finally reached Wymaw, where we had to cross the River Irrawaddy to reach Myitkyina. Unluckily we did not get into the ferry queue that night and in the morning had to take a back place. There was a passenger launch, but only one ferry for cars. Two ferries had been sunk because some RAF ground crew had insisted on driving their huge five ton lorries onto them. They were also instrumental in breaking some of the bridges the same way.

Mr Porter crossed the river by launch and contacted my brother John who was in Myitkyina on the other side of the Irrawaddy. They were frantic to get us across. The situation was really desperate by then; the Japanese had taken Bhamo and were on their way to Myitkyina. Finally we packed our goods in a country boat, a long dugout, and had to look for a crew ourselves.

We left one man, a chance acquaintance, Lecky Thompson, to bring the goods across, and Pat and I crossed by launch. We reached Myitkyina only to be told that my sister-in-law, Iris, and her mother (also Pat's mother) and the children had left that morning on the last plane to India, and that there would be no more planes. I felt awful (after our eleven day's journey - only 300 miles in all that time) at the thought of walking to India.

That night my brother and I packed for the trek. We intended to drive near Sumprabum by car and then trek into Assam. Our car and Porter's car were still at Wymaw with Porter's driver. Pat went down to the ferry and only at 2 a.m. did he get Porter's car over. Our own car, being behind, had to be abandoned. By that time it was too late to set off for Sumprabum and we went to bed. Early in the morning John made more enquires and found there were to be more planes. When we heard the sound of a plane, Pat rushed me down to the aerodrome, but that plane took off as we arrived. Then we remembered in our mad dash that we had forgotten to bring the cook's wife, Mary and the children, and Pat raced back for them. We were waiting for an American plane, but two RAF planes came in and we ran up to them. I had a *phar* (box made of plaited straw) packed with only 33 pounds, but as I got on the plane I was told "no baggage at all" and so I went to India in a pair of dirty shorts and a blouse, with not even a toothbrush. I could not even say goodbye to Pat except from the window of the plane. If I had not jumped in, I would have lost my place. The pilot looked askance at my black Mary and her two children, but I said they were mine and pushed them in. I had no money as it was in my *phar*. Fortunately Mr Porter came with me and I would be able to borrow from him. He was over fifty; men under fifty had to walk to India.

And so my husband and brother were left to trek to India. Heaven alone knew whether they would ever reach their destination. It was a desolate feeling as the aeroplane lifted off the ground and I watched Pat's lonely figure slowly recede into the distance.

As it happens, Pat Molloy was to join up with our next author, Edward Rossiter - who is none other than our own Maureen's mysterious father, who had married that beautiful Burmese girl from the cheroot factory twelve years before. Edward Rossiter was to complete the harrowing journey into India and send the following letter to his mother in Ireland before dying in Calcutta. Pat Molloy survived, and was able to join up with Sylvia in India.

1942 **Edward Rossiter**

My dear Mother,

This begins where it ought to start, i.e. with an account of my wanderings and adventures since early May, 1942.

Early in May Capt. Kingdon Ward (the botanist) came to Fort Hertz (or Putao), bringing me the latest available news and although Mandalay, as a result of Japanese bombing had been wiped out, he did not seem to think any early collapse was imminent. Fortunately I had made certain preparations in case of need and these preparations turned out to be most valuable. It had been my intention in case of need to go to China and not India. The road to China was comparatively easy and from various places in China I could have flown to India. There was no route at all to India, there was, it is true, a path marked on maps but this was through a deep jungle and at the very best of times required 6 weeks and no villages at all existed, this means no food was obtainable en route. All would have to be carried by coolies and food for the coolies would have to be carried also and so on.

Maureen with her father - Eddy Rossiter, the author of this account.

Anyway on evening of 9th May I received a special runner with a note from Leyden (in Sumprabum 8 days south) saying Myitkyina had been entered by the Japanese, that all the Myitkyina officials had cleared away (by another route) and that he was coming to meet us and we both had been ordered by Govt to proceed to India. He said India had promised to send a party to meet us at the Chaukan Pass (the boundary) and were sending up food supplies. It was only because of this assurance that I agreed to go at all. I had prepared to disregard the orders and go to China as starvation along the India route seemed more than probable. Anyway since Burma Government had been in WT communication with Assam and received an answer that we would be met, the risk seemed considerably reduced.

So after carrying out various acts of destruction at Fort Hertz I left and met Leyden 2 days out. We had at this time huge amounts of rice and stores, tea, coffee, tinned milk etc, sugar, flour. We had 300 coolies and had no trouble in reaching the boundary, Chaukan Pass, 8,000 feet in 10 days although we got drenched in rain and soaked through having to wade through various rivers etc. At the pass all our troubles started, all the coolies declined to go forward. We paid them off and decided to wait at the pass till the Assam party came to meet us, we had enough food for 3 to 4 months provided we remained sitting at the Pass, but as we had no coolies we could not move forward. At the pass we remained 5 days and then a party of Indian soldiers came along, they were really an undisciplined rabble and had run away from the Japanese, they had no food for several days and were starving. We minded them with food and they agreed to accompany us on - we estimated it was 20 days on to the nearest village. Anyway we started off - no road or even a path, we had to cut the jungle down as we progressed. We continued around mountain spurs, crossing many small mountain torrents and all the time in pouring rain. After two days we reached a large river which we had been searching for as we had to have some landmark to find our way and to follow - else we should have penetrated into mountains and probably reached nowhere. The going along the river was awful, at times we were up to our chests in deep fast water, at times rocks stopped us - huge boulders - and we had to climb up the banks over the rocks, at times we would go up 500 or more feet to get to the other side of the rock - down the same height to the water again. At times huge landslides caused us to make wide detours. Anyway on 11th June we arrived at a place where on account of a river further progress became impossible. I should have mentioned our party was increased by a few odd Europeans and this total was 12. Here trying to cross the river one European was carried away and drowned. Another died later of fever - several Indians too died from various causes. Anyway we were forced to halt and managed to erect a small shelter of grass and banana leaves. We weighed and measured out our food and found we had enough rice to last us 25 days at rate of a quarter cigarette tin per head per day. We had some coffee - no tea, milk, sugar, flour etc. We were all in a weak condition and our boots were in pieces - none of us was in a condition to move onwards - apart from the difficulty of the route.

1942

Pat Kelly

Leaving Aijal, the last and worst part of our journey followed. For three days and nights we travelled northwards downstream by native boat on the Dhaleswari and Katakhal Rivers.

And those boats were terrible. Shaped like long canoes, shelter was provided by a piece of bamboo matting bent over the craft like a tunnel. Inside, these were so dark one had to grope one's way around, but so cramped there was no space in which to grope and so stuffy that the only hope of survival was in crawling out and sitting on boards by the stem or bows, where the native boatmen who punted ran up and down. Their bare brown feet provided most of the view as one sat in the tunnel, so it was worth the risk of being trodden on to dangle one's hands in the river and watch the jungle slip past on banks of rubbery grey mud, and to stare at the stork-like birds wading in the shallows on their red sticks of legs.

That river was full of rapids. The agony of sitting in the tunnel of matting, seeing bright

The route taken by Pat Kelly and her family (see Tiddim and Kalewa at top left of main map).

sheets of water rising over the sides of the boat, towering up before us and dropping away with a sickening thud, of feeling stones grating along the bottom and seeing the sweat of concentration on the men's brows, was unbearable. But shooting rapids during the day was as bad as sleeping at night. Then the boatmen ate garlic and smoked rank tobacco - opium too - and the fumes drifting into the blackness of the tunnel, mingling with the sweet smell of fresh bamboo, was suffocating.

It was far more restful to stumble out into the clean night air away from them and listen to the waters and the ceaseless hum of cicadas, in the jungle.

Then one daybreak, as light was just beginning to steal along the River, we looked out - to see a dim line of grey humps above the high bank. Elephants, I thought. But I was wrong. After 19 days' travel through tropical forests we had found the first tentacle of civilisation: the railhead at Lalaghat and the Bengal and Assam Railway. We left for Calcutta on 24th May.

Odd that I didn't consider it important at the time, which may indicate how much more intense were those other memories, but my legs were covered with boils and infected insect bites, for which there was absolutely no treatment except applying salt or neat peroxide.

1942 Edward Rossiter

The river went down a bit and we pooled some of our food, subsequently sending two of the strongest on with a letter explaining our conditions and saying our food would last 25 days. We spent 21 days starving - a quarter cigarette tin of rice per day plus what leaves and roots we could collect - no wild fruit was to be found. During that 21 days my bowels never moved once. On 1st July we heard the sound of an aeroplane engine and later a plane came, it circled overhead many times and we knew we were located. The plane dropped nothing - not even a message, but we expected it would return with food supplies the next day. This proved to be so and bags of rice, atta, sugar, raisins as well as tins of milk, butter, sausages, beef etc were dropped but no message. The plane again came on several days and dropped more supplies. We now had a huge store of rice, over 2,000 pounds as well as atta, sugar, tea etc and as we were all frightfully weak we started to get somewhat stronger - prior to the arrival of the food some of us were unable to walk. Then on 25 July we got a message saying on no account to move - that a relief party was on its way to us. The message also said that coolies previously sent to rescue us had after a certain distance turned back and run away.

As I had waited from 25th July to 29th August and no rescue party had come nor had the aeroplane returned I decided to set out myself along with a few Indians. It was a very great risk, a huge risk for we were all so weak we could only carry food for 10 days and we did not know how long we might not be held up by rivers and rain etc. I will not bore you with details of that journey. We were extremely fortunate to meet a relief party with elephants on the 9th day. We learnt that the officer in charge of the previous relief party for which we had waited had shot himself on which his coolies had run away. After one day on elephants we reached a camp, where I had the first decent meal I had for almost 4 months. What pleased me most was a pot of home made vegetable marrow jam made just as you made it. I ate all this jam with water biscuits. I also had some chicken.

On the next four days I went by elephant as I was unable to walk, swollen feet and ankles as well as beri-beri (more about that later). After 4 days I arrived at Miao where two tea planters had a base camp, here I halted for two days, got some clothes, some more food too. Then for three days, by boat to Marguerita in Assam, here is the railway and a small European community. I was still unable to walk alone and unaided, I had to go between two coolies with my arms around their shoulders. I stayed a very comfortable night, had an excellent meal, fish and a bread pudding, the latter was so good that I still remember it, also had a warm bath - the first for four months. The next morning I was taken to hospital at Digboi - the hospital of the Assam Oil Company - there I remained for 15 days and then went to Calcutta.

Beri-beri is a disease due to lack of vitamins and nourishment. It first reveals its presence in the extremities, i.e. finger and toe tips etc, a tingling sensation is present, something like pins and needles, later the part affected becomes numb. Numbness leads to inability to use the affected limb. One of the reasons why I decided to set out from the camp and risk arriving at safety on 29 Aug was because I felt beri-beri coming on, to remain would I know have been safer but I decided to risk going, things turned out well however. After all on 29 Aug it was almost 3 months during which time I had not had an egg, any fresh vegetables, meat, milk, bread, fruit etc and in addition I was on a very reduced diet of rice only. Beri-beri is however not serious - all that is required to cure it is good food and a suitable diet containing plenty of green vegetables, milk, fruit etc. The tingling, pins and needles etc has almost vanished from my fingers and very little remains in my feet. I have not been troubled with it elsewhere.

I don't think there is anything else of interest I can record. We were just over four months on the journey and fortunately the days seemed to pass quickly. Two Europeans of the party were lost and a few Indians - no Burmans accompanied us. Otherwise nothing to report about the journey.

I think I told you Fogarty was dead, he died as a result of an air crash in China. On a route through Kamaing thousands travelled - after the fall of Mandalay it was the only route - 40 days. Owing to cholera thousands perished and hundreds were drowned crossing the many rivers. Thousands are reported to be still isolated as till the rains are over the wide rivers are uncrossable.

Best wishes to yourself and Patricia
Eddy

Pat Kelly

Fifty years on and empathising with my mother's intense anxiety, I feel nothing but admiration for her. Here she was, fleeing with strangers to an unknown future with two young and vulnerable children, possibly never to see her man again. Later on, she was to make an unauthorised and equally dangerous trip back to visit him - behind the Japanese lines.

Father was a distant memory. The enemy had a price on his head of one thousand rupees and many of his men died speechless at their hands rather than betray his whereabouts to the Japanese. For over a year Mother had no word of him; he was with his tribes in guerrilla warfare, harassing the Japanese. Swoops down to the plains; raids; fading back silently into the jungled hills again.

In May 1942, Father was made a Lt. Col. in the famous 17th Indian Division which won more Victoria Crosses (7) than any other Division in the British Army. From the seat of his Jeep, he killed with his revolver the Japanese commander in Kalemyo. His conscience racked him even on his deathbed. This time I was privileged to care for his last few months of life 30 years later - it was I who took the confession and absolved him.

And arriving in a cold distant land; alien culture; freezing winters; rationing; English boarding schools; loneliness, isolation. The war in the Far East was not much regarded by a nation bombed by Hitler just over the water - so one locked up experience and silently mourned the loss.

Radio spoke a few hours a day and here again were the chimes of Big Ben at 9 o'clock as we'd heard them years before in the Tiddim bungalow, our radio run off a generator powered by Father or our gardener pedalling a stationary bicycle on the verandah.

But no hurricane lamp smoking and guttering in the wind; no pet monkey on my arm; no

Siamese cat on my bed; no imaginary tiger under Desmond's; no Wendy house in the grassy garden or mud village built and peopled with clay around puddles beneath the pines.

No vistas over range after range of distant green-blue mountains; no cosmos flowers in birdsong clearings; no - well, who wanted to know?

Here was instead the British boarding school toughly outfacing the brown North Sea.

After the ordeals of the British defeat and the flight from the advancing Japanese soldiers, there was some time to recuperate and regroup. Many of those who did so were to wait in India for four years until the tide of war brought the British back, however briefly, into Burma. So perhaps there is time to spend a few last minutes with a previous friend, before we rush on with the story of the War and Independence. Stella McGregor, you remember, was the girl with the gibbon; born in Rangoon in 1913, she left Burma some time before the arrival of the Japanese and lived to a ripe age in the UK, so this is our goodbye to her. She has recorded the tapestry of life in Burma in the 1920s with remarkable observation. We have already heard about her early years; Rangoon itself; her schooldays in Mussoorie and then Thandaung; her trip in a Tin Lizzie to see the "giraffe women" of Shan State; her own little Austin, and her participation as a young adult in the social whirl of the early 1920s. Let us now fill in a few of the gaps. First, the period immediately after her return from school in Mussoorie - which was another part of British India, though not of Burma - she must have been 11 years old.

1924 **Stella**

Those nine long months finally came to an end and there were my parents and my younger brother John waiting on the wharf to meet us and then back to another different house on the outskirts of Rangoon - Boundary Road - a wonderful home for us children. It was in an acre of ground, backing on to a golf course and it had a tennis court. Most of the land was uncultivated but it had a small flower garden in the front and in this garden there was a cashew nut tree. The nut actually grows from the bottom of the fruit not in the middle giving rise to the legend that this was the forbidden fruit. We had three particular friends at this time and many happy times were spent playing tennis or Red Indians and Cow Boys all over the golf course, where we wandered freely. And we were nearer the swimming club. We had a car now. Oh happy days.

One fifth of November we had a fireworks party around the tennis court and lots of friends were present. The grown-ups danced in the open after John and I went to bed. We were woken by my Mother and hustled into her room with our feet well off the ground. The little puppy that we had recently acquired was having fits and it could be rabies. He had to be shot! It was not positive that it was rabies but the whole family had to be inoculated. Every day we had to go to the Pasteur Institute and bare our tummies and have a jab on alternate sides. I forget how many we had - thirteen or fourteen on each side, I think. Our rabbits too had to be destroyed.

Now more on the "paradise" schooldays in Thandaung - 200 miles north of Rangoon - and the abundant wildlife of that period:

Stella's sketch of villagers.

The villagers one year brought a magnificent Tiger that they had shot for us to see. The poor beast was strung up by its legs with its head lolling down. Although it was very dead, nevertheless it filled us with fear - for it is known that an animal's mate will follow it. Another time a long snake was killed and brought for us to admire. Strangely enough, although we wandered through the jungle and undergrowth I can't ever remember seeing a snake in the wild. Mangoes did not grow in these higher altitudes, but when it was mango season, we would eat baskets of them outdoors. Mangoes are very, very juicy and about as long as a banana. Burmese mangoes are not the roundish variety sold here, those are either from the Caribbean or India and I think the Burmese variety are far superior. Another fruit with a dubious name is the Durian (not sure of many spellings, please excuse). It is a large fruit rather like a marrow in shape, with a prickly skin and it grows at the base of the tree. It has to be split and inside are yellow, soft, delicious pods, about the size of a large plum. People say they do not like the smell but if you never have the notion that the smell is unpleasant it is truly delicious. My Father used to be given a large tin of Durian preserve every year by one of the Insurance Brokers. Although the pods were yellow, when the pulp was preserved it was black and thick enough to cut.

Back to Thandaung - I was at this school - off and on - for three years. As we became more senior we were allowed greater freedom to wander farther afield and I remember finding a tall tree about the size of an oak and underneath were dozens of nuts - like hazel nuts and they tasted like them too. I never saw another tree like it. I wonder we were not poisoned as we wandered and tasted! We always had fresh milk so I suppose there must have been a village with cows nearby - but in my memory we had the mountains to ourselves. And always our ears and eyes were on the alert - a shimmer of gauzy wings could be a rare beetle or just a large dragon fly or butterfly or a disappointing repulsive dung beetle. They were quite large and fat, four or five inches long. If it was a slow green flight it was a cicada (not suitable for collecting). And LEECHES!! LEECHES, awful blood-sucking leeches. They spoilt many an outing or activity. We were not supposed to pull them off but to either drop salt on them or wait till they had gorged themselves and fell off naturally - ugh! They penetrated any vulnerable space, even under elastic and we did not actually feel them till one saw the slimy black creatures, upended on their back portion with their bodies stretched out and weaving around looking for an uncovered section of skin. A slight itch was felt if they had already had a meal - ugh again! It was difficult not to scratch the many different "bites" we had.

The next year, for some reason I can't remember now, John and I missed the general leaving and went up with Mother a few weeks before school started - and the following year again we did not travel up with the school but with a friend who was going that way on business. Well, when we arrived in Toungoo in the early hours of the morning, Bobby Hall, our Scottish friend, got out of the carriage and went off to attend to something leaving us to finish dressing. We remembered that the carriages were dismantled and the rest of the train went on - so we took our time and were in the middle of a pillow fight when the train started moving. Wild shouts from the platform, Bobby Hall tearing madly beside the train calling us to throw everything out and jump out ourselves! Well it was a scramble and fortunately the train started very slowly, but we did manage. After picking up all our belongings and having a slight scolding from Bobby Hall who knew we were not entirely to blame, we had a nice breakfast in the station waiting room before being handed over to the school driver.

In 1927 - when Stella was 14 - various events were to make a deep impression on her...

My elder sister Gwen's wedding (Gwendoline Louisa Edith McGregor) was a very big affair with hundreds of guests and wedding presents - silver, cut glass and enough linen to start a shop. Her fiancé was John Vernon Watson known as Jack. Jack's family had a big house in the suburb of Rangoon called "Mount Vernon" with a tennis court and a full size billiard room. The

"Mount Vernon"

presents completely covered the table and several side tables. The reception was held in this house and garden. I was a Bridesmaid. My life also changed then. John and I spent many weeks with Gwen in her new home while my parents looked for a new home. Then it was decided that as Jack and Gwen were coming to England for Jack's leave - I would accompany them and John would go to school in Darjeeling - a famous hill station in the Himalayas - not as far from Burma as Mussoorie and within sight of Mt. Everest. Gradually the great day approached. Clothes

were bought and a new trunk to put them in. I was excited yet sad for this time I would not see John or my parents for three years and all the good old happy days were over.

My parents and John and our friends came on board to see Gwen and me off to England. Daddy knew the captain and we were put in his care - it's sad saying goodbye, for in one way the time drags and in another the time flies - soon the call - "All ashore who are going ashore - all ashore who are going ashore" and it was time for the last kisses and instructions - one of them was "Keep out of draughts". I hadn't the faintest clue what a draught was! Down the gang plank they went and were on the wharf waving us goodbye. We pulled away from the shore, the siren sounded and we were soon in the muddy river with eddies of water curling around us. We passed Monkey Point where we had many picnics. Gradually the banks grew wider apart and it was time to go down to my cabin and unpack. Naturally Gwen and Jack had a cabin to themselves and I was put with another lady.

Arriving in London, the sight of all the narrow streets lined with rows and rows of houses and smoky chimneys were somehow what I expected to see though they must have seemed so crowded - and the trains so fast.

1930-31

The day came at last for the journey home to Burma. The taxi was ordered to take us to London where we were to entrain for Liverpool. It was sad saying goodbye to Gwen and Jack and little Peter who was a beautiful baby but I was eager to grow up and wear my new clothes, throw away my brown uniform and travel again.

We were a few of the first passengers and were able to watch our fellow travellers come on board. Once more at long last we were in the muddy waters of the Gulf of Martaban then up the Rangoon river and the thick ropes were thrown across to the wharf and gang planks were lowered by my elder brother

Eric and several friends who came aboard to welcome us. We sat around with drinks for a little until our luggage was taken ashore and we said goodbye to fellow passengers, some we would never see again and some that we would see at various functions. Many went up country to oil stations or mines or timber plantations.

Waves of nostalgia wash over me as I see and feel and smell again those hours, days and weeks of returning. Eric drove us through the wharf side streets, through the commercial part. Past public parks with green lawns and shady trees, past the Sule Pagoda, which had been our land mark for many hours when steaming up the river - over the railway bridge and out to the more affluent residential area. Now the Royal Lake looking lovely; we turned right and the road skirted the edge of the lake. It was an avenue with palm trees growing down the middle and along the grass verges. Oh so beautiful - then the Boat Club, broad and spreading with its open balcony, wide and inviting, over the lake.

While I had been away my parents had moved again and I was longing to see the house. It surpassed my imagining - there it was - on top of a low green hill with a winding drive of red gravel with red canna plants at intervals on each side - a long, large white bungalow surrounded by flowering plants and Bouganvillea. White pillars supported the porch under which we drove. Two dogs bounded barking down the wide front steps that led to a long veranda and two servants in white with happy smiles salaamed us. The dogs belonged to two men friends who had lodged with my brother while my parents were away - they stayed with us for several more months as paying guests till they found accommodation. I can't begin to tell you how wonderful it was to be with my parents in my own home - and what a beautiful home it was - overlooking, the lakes, with just a road between us and Shwe Dagon Pagoda on the not too distant horizon. The sunsets though brief were breathtaking over the Pagoda. Everything seemed spacious and shining - polished floors and wooden furniture (cooler than upholstered), whirling electric fans and bamboo furniture on the veranda with its ever-changing view. The house was surrounded by a couple of acres of waste land - later we were able to practise golf around this land. Actually this house was so large that they had divided it down the middle. The veranda had a wooden dividing screen and our neighbours had their own entrance on the other side of the veranda. Once more food of many varieties and fruit that I had only dreamed of! With servants ready to please.

1933

The rains soon broke after our return to Rangoon from the trip to Taunggyi and cool weather, though too wet for tennis, was appreciated. One day my Father brought home a darling puppy. Very like a West Highland White, but with drooping ears and she stole our hearts. We called her Betsy Prigg and she was my dear companion on many walks around the lake and through the gardens of the lake. She would sit for hours watching the small white lizards that crawled over the walls. She always hoped to catch one but they never came down and in any case were extremely quick but harmless.

Another day my Father came home with a dear little gibbon on the end of a string. It is sad but the only way gibbons could be captured was by killing the mother of the baby, I know this now. So Jacko had been brought from Malaya by one of the Sea Captains. Jacko arrived about a week before my Father's annual leave was due and this time we were going by ship to Penang and Singapore. This was entirely new territory for Mother and I and we looked forward eagerly to our departure. I was trying to make friends with Jacko who was still a baby and wild. We kept him on a lead fastened to the veranda railings - I was coaxing him with a banana and had progressed enough to take him in my arms when he bit my arm, fortunately through my sleeve. The bite came up like a large blister. Any bite by an animal in the Tropics has to be taken seriously and we were to sail in a couple of days. I went to the Pasteur Institute expecting to have to stay behind, but fortunately the skin had not been broken so I was told to report if I felt at all unwell and could go ahead with the holiday. What a relief !

Stella with Jacko, and Betsy Prigg hiding behind her skirt

Then on to Penang. The sea at night was miraculous with the ship's wash sparkling with fluorescence. During the day we saw shoals of flying fish trying to keep up with the ship, but we did not see them often. Another phenomenon to be seen in those waters were 'water spouts', but really they were the reverse of water spouts as what we could see was clouds hovering low over the sea and grey funnel-like appendages reaching down to siphon up water! An awe inspiring and rather frightening sight. Penang was beautiful. Absolutely beautiful! Clean sandy beaches, palm and coconut trees in profusion. I had never seen so many clustered together and the roads wide and clean.

When we arrived back at l2 Park Road the dogs went wild with joy. By this time we had another dog (thanks to my Father). It was so pretty like a small toy, but not very friendly. It might have been ill treated before we got him. Poor Jacko looked miserable, thin and droopy. He had caught a cold. A friend of my Father (a German married to a Burmese lady) kept a small private zoo - so we consulted him. The advice was to put Jacko on a cane seat with a towel and underneath a bowl of steaming hot water in which was a liberal dose of Friar's Balsam (useful for humans too). After a couple of days of this treatment Jacko was well and TAME. He was an interesting and fun pet to own and very mischievous!! When we let him off his lead he would run and then have a long slide on the polished floors, or else he would leap up to the electric lights and swing then let go and the lights would swing back and smash on the ceiling - so we had to stop that game. He also loved to leap on to the top of the mosquito nets. Beds were like four posters with nets hung on them forming a canopy - these made a lovely bouncy platform for him. Sometimes he would grab a dog's tail. There came a time when he started to lose his hair and look miserable again. Once more we consulted the German vet and this time he said that Jacko was missing the small grubs and insects he would normally find and eat on a tree - so as we had a small tree near the house we tied a long piece of string to the collar he wore around the lower part of his middle and stood around while he joyfully scrambled up. We were all so happy to see his capers till we realised that he had become hopelessly tangled in the branches. We should have foreseen this but we didn't! So the sweeper (who came every day to sweep the house and attend to the animals) and who was used to handling Jacko, climbed up and undid the knot around his waist. He still needed the freedom of the trees so we just let him loose and waited around till he was tired, then lured him down with a banana.

1935 Stella again

I thought this wonderful life would continue for years and years but alas one evening a lady friend came to visit and when she got into her car to drive away she could not get the car to move. My dear Father did his best to shift it - till the silly woman discovered that the brake was still on! Next day we were invited to the Adjutant's house for tea. While there my Father felt unwell and complained of a pain in his left arm. An American friend was spending a short holiday with us (we travelled with her attractive sister on our return journey from Singapore. She was on a world tour). This friend said she did not like the sound of it as a friend of hers had suffered the same sort of pain and it was Angina. I am sorry to say this conveyed nothing to us. We had been invited next door to a celebration of the Landlord whose son had reached an age when all

Burmese boys became monks for a short while. They have their heads shaved and don saffron robes and live in a monastery. A grand feast is put on to mark the occasion. An outdoor stage was erected in the front garden and musicians and guests arrived. We had to decline the invitation as my Father felt so unwell. Then the music started!!! Very loud and foreign, with gongs banging and xylophones plonking. The dancers and singers on the stage were doing their stuff and the audience was laughing loudly. We had to ask them to please try to be a little quieter - which they did try, but it was difficult for them. Anyway we sent for our Doctor who confirmed that it was Angina and Daddy had to go to Hospital. He was there for six weeks - Christmas came and went and he said he felt well enough to come home but the doctors said "no" and there in great pain, with us spending nights at the Hospital my kind, good Father died.

He had retired from the Civil Defence Force a short time before so did not have a full military funeral. Even so it was a partial military funeral and the Cathedral was full to overflowing. He is buried in Rangoon in the Kimendine Cemetery.

The morning came at last for us to leave. Friends came to wave us goodbye and one of the sights I shall long remember was our chauffeur lying, crying on the wharf... So much for the native population wanting the British to leave ! !

There is a legend that if one looks back at the Pagoda when leaving and sailing down the river, one will return. At that time I was glad to leave and would not look back. I wish now I had!

1935

The ocean journey back to England was full of event, and if my Father had been alive and with us, this voyage would have been truly great.

We missed him so much. Shortly after his death I recall a vivid dream where we were in this beautiful, bright garden. He came to me and said "Stella, always follow the Radiant Star". I have always been puzzled by these instructions and for a long time even though I do not follow horse racing, I looked for a horse named "Radiant Star" that I could back as I am sure it would be a winner!! However now that I am in my latter years, Pauline tells me perhaps I have been taking the instructions too literally. She says maybe he referred to my name, Stella, (meaning Star) and that the instructions meant that I should be true to myself and my own conscience. Well, he taught me lessons that have not been forgotten and have served me through my life in the difficult times that followed. I hope my children and my grandchildren and their children's children will always carry these words in their hearts...

My wonderful, old life was over and a new, more ordinary life about to begin.

Perhaps you Pauline will recount the following years; getting married, the Second World War and the lives of my three children of whom I am so proud.

Stella McGregor , who eventually became Mrs Stella Prothero, died in England in 1995.

Her daughter Pauline Currien plans to publish an autobiography of her early life, from which these extracts were taken, along with many of the photographs in the collection of Mrs Caroline Donachie née Watson, her cousin. It will appear under the title "Radiant Star".

UNDER JAPANESE RULE

1942 Maureen

One of the first things the nuns did on our return to the convent was to lay a hurried plan for our safety in case we were invaded or bombed by the Japanese, for by now their low-flying planes were dropping leaflets in English informing us that we would soon be liberated from the "imperialist" British. The large red rising sun blazed down on us from the underside of the aeroplane wings, threatening us with their display of confident strength. The safest place for us all, the nuns decided, was the space beneath the large chapel where it was possible to stand upright to a good distance from the door. No light whatsoever penetrated the space, it could not be reached through the floor of the chapel but only through a door build into the stonework. All in all it seemed the soundest idea in case of a bomb attack.

We children knew that we were supposed to be afraid, and we acted the part in the presence of the nuns, but truth to tell it was so very exciting that it was difficult to keep up the pretence when on our own. In fact we vied with each other to see who would spy the Japanese first.

Soon we caught our first sight of the conquerors, a long line of soldiers, three or four abreast, clad in khaki, flaps hanging down from their caps, bayonets glinting in the sun. It was a compelling sight and we were unable to tear ourselves away, until the nuns, seeing them as well, half pushed, half dragged us to the underground space. Mother Superior and Sister Erminia, having made sure we were all safely locked up, hurried up to the chapel itself and barricaded themselves in the sacristy above. In an uncharacteristic display of fear and panic the nuns sent up loud prayers for our deliverance which must have been heard by anyone outside the wall. Soon the soldiers could be heard marching up the gravel drive to the accompaniment of loud guttural orders. In no time our door was battered in and before our terrified gaze Mother Superior was pushed at bayonet-point into our midst. Now we were really scared - for behind the bayonets were round yellow faces with narrow slit eyes full of menace and hate, snapping orders we didn't understand. The same bayonets pushed us out into the sunshine and we were surrounded.

An officer speaking English asked Mother Superior, "You English?" It took some time to establish that most of our community were Italian. Relaxing a little, for the Italians were their allies, but still keeping us in a group, the soldiers ordered a search of the entire convent. Satisfied that we were not harbouring any British or Chinese and leaving sentries at the gates, the soldiers formed up and marched away, having given us to understand that we were all to report to the Kalaw Hotel the next day.

On the day, after a long wait, Sister Erminia explained that my father was Irish, not English. This explanation seemed to satisfy the officer and, after relaying this to his superior, we were allowed to go.

On the walk back to the convent everyone was quiet. Things had gone better than we had feared and we had escaped lightly, but we had seen enough of the methods of interrogation by the Japanese to convince ourselves that now we were an occupied country. Seeing harmless, innocent people being hit on the head with rifle butts was a terrifying and sobering lesson and we knew that there would now be a great deal of change. It must have required an enormous amount of courage for Sister Erminia to respond to the interrogation in that calm, dignified way of hers, and we were greatly impressed and filled with a silent gratitude, for we had seen some of the other children in that gathering not so lightly treated.

1942 — Evelyn

After the bombing of Rangoon, I went to my mother's family home. My Uncle was a Sawbwa (Shan Prince) and his state was right on the Burma road to China. He was a Colonel in the Burma Rifles but was told not to retreat to India but stay with his people. He was told to camp off the road. We could hear explosions, not petrol drums as we thought but the rapidly advancing Japanese Army. There were also a lot of Chinese soldiers retreating through the village on their way, hopefully, back to China. The Japanese later dropped leaflets and ordered us to go back into town and carry on as normal. They gave us safe conduct arm bands and passes for the cars. I think they thought we were more important than we were. We discovered later that the only other women with these armbands were prostitutes. They were pink cotton and I never found out what they actually said. Father was lucky as he did not meet a single Japanese on the way back into town. As an obviously non-Shan man in a large American car - it was a situation of shoot first and ask questions afterwards - no-one was going to come up and see what was on the notice on the windscreen. We were in another car with grandmother who had had a stroke, and met Japanese soldiers about five times who shouted and gesticulated, but stopped when they saw the notice and the armbands. One of them looked about 15 years old and asked for a cigarette.

To complicate matters we had our Chinese cousin with us - she had come to visit Grandmother and couldn't get back. Her father was one of Chiang Kai-shek's generals. However this matter was not brought up until near the end of the war when we were arrested and interrogated and we thought they did not know! We were allowed to live in the Old Palace which was a huge building with tiered roofs like a monastery - it had 400 solid teak pillars supporting it each from a single tree - built by our grandfather at the turn of the century. The several wings provided enough room for us all. The Japanese took over the New Palace on one of the foothills - this was brick-built and had electricity and plumbing. In 1945 both palaces were bombed by the Allies in their 'scorched earth' policy - the Old Palace (all that teak!) burned for three days and nights and caused a fire-storm. There was a 7,000 ft mountain backdrop to the foothills - Loi Hsam-Hsip - the 30 hills we called them - it was a beautiful view taken for granted. I only appreciated it when our driver (before the war) asked if he could bring his wife on one of our trips from Maymyo and he was excitedly pointing out the view- the caves, the waterfalls etc.

We spent most of the war in the palace - life was not too harsh; there was plenty of food and we had our servants with us. We also observed all the strict protocol that exists in that kind of family - that helped to keep our morale up.

1943 **Maureen**

Having no access to a radio or newspapers, we were totally unaware of the world situation. Indeed, anyone found with a radio was shot on the spot, and now and again terrible stories reached us of Japanese atrocities, particularly against any Chinese sheltering in the village. Suspects were strung up between two trees tensioned with ropes, which were then split asunder, and people suspected of withholding information from the Japanese had boiling water poured down their throats. We understood that we were being treated comparatively leniently because Italy was on the same side as Germany. Frequently we were gathered together when a Japanese officer appeared, immaculate in his highly polished boots, pistol and sword for all to see. In perfect English he would shout at us, telling us what great things were being done by his race, how the English had been disgraced and that the Nipponese were now our masters.

1943 **Evelyn**

Even when we were finally arrested we were allowed to take three maidservants with us. The Sawbwas were being flown out by the American Force 101 and we couldn't reach the air-strip in time. Our head-servant who was an intelligent and educated man and had been a monk for seven years was arrested and tortured by the Japanese. He blamed us for this and never forgave us and left our service though he had been with three generations of the family. We were interrogated by the Kempeitai but not ill-treated.

I asked the lieutenant who was in charge of us why it was necessary to send thirteen armed men to arrest us - one old man and the rest women and children. "Ah," he said, "We have a proverb - you can hang a man with the hair of a woman and drown in a woman's tears." He spoke English as many of the Kempeitai did. Throughout the war we had a Japanese sentry posted at one of the four palace gates.

1943-44 **Maureen**

Because Mary and I were more European-looking than Burmese the nuns sometimes feared for our safety. It was on this account that whenever a Japanese appeared in our midst Mary and I were hidden away and Lucy would be paraded as a token pupil. Only if the visitor was deemed safe were Mary and I brought out of hiding to be presented as part of the community also. Our piano-playing proved to be very useful as a diversionary tactic on these occasions. For, as times worsened, the Japanese would often send soldiers in search of whatever could be had to take away by force, such as chickens and ducks. Hastily, we would be summoned, cleaned up and plonked on the piano stools in the front room with the Japanese soldier, while the nuns chased the chickens and ducks into the jungle.

One day we were in for a surprise. A soldier came and was seated as usual and after a certain amount of quarrelling about what to play we settled down to perform our set pieces. Curious to see what effect our playing was having on him, I turned around to have a peep. I was flabbergasted. There he sat, a rough-looking chap, tears flowing silently down his face, while he gazed at a snapshot cradled in his yellow palms.

Nudging Mary with my elbow I hissed, "Tell Lucy he's crying!"

To which she hissed back, "Don't be stupid." Nevertheless she also turned round to see for herself.

"What shall we do? Shall we stop?" asked Mary.

"No," said Lucy, "keep going."

But it was difficult to do so and our playing soon trickled to a stop. The soldier beckoned to us and we stood cautiously on either side of his chair. Pointing a stubby finger at the photograph, he showed us a formal picture of a Japanese woman and two children, a boy and a girl standing stiffly beside her - his family? Without saying a word, he returned the photograph to his breast pocket and, patting each of us on the head, left quietly.

This was a side of the Japanese I had not seen before and it made me wonder whether they were not so different from other people after all.

In the evenings they would sing as they marched in long columns past our house and we would watch them while their voices rang out, repeating each line twice. They had quite a repertoire, the tunes were easy and, despite their guttural voices, very catchy. What were they singing about, I wondered, finding it easy to put myself in their place, so far away from home and family. About two years ago at a dinner party I recounted this memory to a couple of Japanese guests, a father and teenage son, humming part of one of the marching songs. To them it was instantly recognisable and with a smile they told me that it was a well-known nursery rhyme! Of course we don't know what words the soldiers sang to the tune.

1945 — Evelyn

We lost most of our possessions and came through the war relatively unscathed. My father suffered the most and, as a government official and a practising barrister when the war came to Burma, he was always suspect. He returned to Maymyo and resumed his practice and was busy until the day he died in 1950.

I left the country in 1946 go to an American university and have never returned. I would love to see the mountains again in our home state but I believe tourists are not allowed in that area.

1945 Lewis Shaw

"Two or three years ago I came across an old shoe box full of letters I had written to my parents from India and Burma between 1944 and 1947. I found another box containing pocket diaries. The following account is based on these sources."

Having crossed the River Brahmaputra on 1st January 1945 with the advance party of N° 123 Indian Infantry Workshop Company, I reached Dimapur the next day. This is where the main road starts, going south through Assam into Burma, about 180 miles away. The border in the mountains to the east was only 100 miles away, and earlier in 1944, the Japanese had crossed into Assam from there in their attempt to take India. Our troops held them at Kohima (4500 ft), in one of the fiercest battles of the campaign, and since then had driven them south back across the border. My job was as a REME Officer with the N° 123 Indian Infantry Workshop Company, looking after the maintenance needs of various units of the 17th Indian Division in the push south.

We crossed into Burma at the border town of Tamu, between Palel and Kalewa, and were from then on classed as being 'On Active Service'. This, I believe, made us much more aware of our situation, and the fact that it would not be long before we had to face up to the Japs. There were compensations though, in an increase in our pay, a weekly rum ration, and the privilege of sending letters home without stamps. The road surface now became very dusty. What had been muddy ruts in the rainy season had become gouges inches deep in dust, so that the convoy became lost in a cloud, so bad that we were all issued with cloth face masks and goggles.

1945 — Glyn Court

For 990 out of a thousand soldiers of the Fourteenth Army fifty years ago, Burma meant misery compounded of mephitic mud, pitiless rain, steaming heat, the elusive but ever-present Jap, leeches, cobras, jungle sores, mutinous mules, 'mozzies', dysentery and several unimaginable diseases. For the other ten, the one per cent, Burma had one meaning more : mud, rain and heat, naturally, Jap, leeches, cobras, jungle sores, mules, mozzies, dysentery and disease - but with them the storing up of memories to be cherished for ever after.

Of course we were the happy few, the uniquely favoured one per cent, for we came into Burma in 1945, when Kohima was living legend but the way down to the Chindwin lay clear. The jungle had released its hold on the army and we drove south 'unvexed' to Kalewa and the central plains.

And the revelation! The four hundred miles from Manipur Road, through Kohima, Imphal, Palel and Tamu to Kalewa, had not prepared us for this. Our East African drivers brought us down through the teak jungle, shaking us nearly every yard by plunges into deep potholes in the unmetalled track; but they pressed on with inexhaustible patience for five days until suddenly, one bright morning, they brought us into the dazzling light of the river plain; and moments later gave us our first sight of the majestic Chindwin, spanned there by the longest Bailey bridge in the world.

From then on the oldest of soldiers' old friends, Corporal Leftfoot and Sergeant Right, took over the transport, and our twenty miles or more a day with digging in at the end of it left no time for diaries such as were kept by the trench soldiers of 1914-1918. It is a tribute to the uniqueness and beauty of Burma that even after fifty years those memories shine bright and clear.

1945 **Lewis Shaw**

One day all Officers and NCO's were gathered together in a clearing and told the plan of action. We were to be part of a 'Hammer and Anvil' manoeuvre, and our objective was Meiktila, an important Jap base in mid Burma some 80 miles south of Mandalay.

33 Corps, consisting of three Infantry Divisions plus a tank Brigade, would take Mandalay, and flush the Japs southwards to 4 Corps, which was us, who were to take Meiktila. That meant we were about to set off into Jap-held territory, first of all crossing the river Irrawaddy, a distance of 330 miles from Tamu, and then to carry on to Meiktila, a further 75 miles to the south east. And all this was to be done as secretly as possible, to confuse the Japs who would be expecting us to be making for Mandalay. With all the dust, we could not hide ourselves, but at least we could stop them seeing us from the air by keeping their planes away. The RAF did an excellent job there, because I did not see a single Japanese plane during the whole of that journey.

My unit arrived at the bridgehead at Nyaung U, on the outskirts of Pagan, the ancient Burmese capital with its thousands of pagodas, which had been taken a few days before by our forward troops. We were ferried across in small flat-bottomed boats, an alarming process as we were loaded to the gunnels, the fast flowing river was over 1000 yards wide, and we could not be sure there were no snipers about. The country between Pagan and Meiktila is open and flat scrub with occasional small villages of what had been neat timber houses, but which were now burnt-out shells, leaving an unforgettable smell, quite unlike any fires I had smelled in the blitz at home. The small outposts of Japs in our way were easily dealt with by our forward tanks and infantry, and the transport convoy followed. One day, even with just a few vehicles to attend to, I got well behind, for the main column did not wait for me. However, I had been given an armoured scout car as protection, and, fortunately one of the vehicles which broke down was a water cart! Although I didn't fear an attack, there was always the possibility of a Jap sniper left behind in a tree.

Quoting from a letter home, "We would advance by day and consolidate in a box in the evening. We put wire around the perimeter some 20 or 30 yards beyond the infantry posts. Then in the morning, the armoured cars would come out of their box and a few tanks out of theirs (we may not all have been in the same box) and go off down the road, followed by the infantry in their trucks. It was all right until we came to a spot of trouble from the Japs. Then we would call on the RAF 'cab rank' to come in, and we sat back and watched. The cab rank was a few planes cruising about all day waiting to be told where to drop their 'eggs', or to do a spot of strafing! Then we'd carry on the advance."

The battle for Meiktila started on 28th February, and after fierce fighting, the main part of the town was occupied on 3rd March. For several nights the Japs coming down from Mandalay and various outlying towns, made suicidal attacks on our perimeter, but every night they were slaughtered. The Infantry made excursions out each day, supported by the tanks, to search out and dispose of the enemy, and again they sustained heavy losses. We of course, were on the receiving end of a variety of shells, mortar bombs and machine gun fire, but our losses were remarkably few. One of my friends, a Signals officer, was killed by a sniper while out repairing a line, and another day, two Indians who had been sleeping under their tank, were run over by it when it started off unexpectedly. It was not until the end of March that the Japs were finally cleared out of the area. During this time, we were cut off from our supply route by road, but the RAF provided us with everything we needed. No wonder our morale was sky high, and we had great confidence that Rangoon, another 337 miles on, would soon be ours.

1945 — U Khin

who at the time was a civilian under Japanese control

It was during the month of March 1945 when the Japanese Army in Burma was trying to stem the onslaught of the British and Indian Armies in Central Burma. A group of Burmese civilian officers, headed by the Deputy Commissioner, had moved from their headquarters in Meiktila to Thayet-pin village, about fifteen miles to the south. The D.C., U Aung Gyaw, and some of the senior civil service officers were provided with accommodation in the headman's house and nearby houses. I was Treasury Officer and about number five in the hierarchy of the civil administrative officers, but being young and quite mobile compared to the other, older officers was left to find my own accommodation in the village.

On the 24th March, at about 8 p.m., I was asked to attend a meeting at the headman's house. It was an informal meeting chaired by the D.C. U Aung Gyaw and there were U Ohn Gaing, Headquarters Assistant to U Aung Gyaw, U Than Tin, a retired Civilian Officer who had settled down in Meiktila, the Revenue Officer, the Civil Surgeon and the Chief Jailer. We sat in the garden around a pot of plain tea and talked in low voices as we had to be careful of eavesdroppers who might go and report to the Kempeitai, the Japanese military police whose cruel methods of investigation were well know then. We discussed the situation of the war, about our provisions which were running low, and whether it might be safer to move to another village as the shelling of the British army was getting closer.

It was well past 11 o'clock that night when the meeting ended and I came back to the house which was allocated to me. It was some distance from the headman's house where the senior district officers had made their living quarters.

At about midnight, I was awakened by a villager who told me that about half an hour ago, U Aung Gyaw, U Ohn Gaing and U Than Tin, all in their fifties, were seized by some Japanese soldiers and taken away. Before they left, the Japanese searched every room for any Burmese officers whom they might have missed. I immediately sent word to Thakin Shwe Oak, who was a friend of mine, about the capture of senior Burmese officers by the Japanese head of the police in that area. Thakin Shwe Oak, an inspector of police, had connection with Burmese officers in the Burmese Army regiment stationed in Meiktila who were politicians like him. Among them were Captain Thaung Kyi and Lt Than Myaing who were attached to the Japanese Army unit operating in that area.

Thakin Shwe Oak told me later what happened the next day. A Japanese captain, leading a section of Japanese soldiers and another section of Burmese soldiers, led by Captain Thaung Kyi and Lt Than Myaing, was taking U Aung Gyaw, U Ohn Gaing and U Than Tin to a clearing in the jungle where they were to be executed. There were three graves already dug and the captives were ordered to kneel at the top of the graves. The Japanese commander asked the Burmese officers to carry out the execution by shooting them in the back of the head. Captain Thaung Kyi, Lt Than Myaing and a Burmese soldier took their positions, the Burmese officers aimed their revolvers at the captives and the Burmese soldier did the same with his rifle. At the verbal order of the Japanese commander, they were to pull their triggers. When the Japanese officer gave his orders the Burmese officers and the Burmese soldier turned their guns in the direction of the Japanese officers and pulled the triggers. The Burmese soldiers nearby also picked up their guns and opened fire on the Japanese soldiers. According to Thakin Shwe Oak, a little skirmish followed in which most of the Japanese soldiers and their officer were killed while the rest of the Japanese dropped their guns and ran away. This was the first instance of the Burmese soldiers turning against the Japanese. After three days, on the 27th of March, the Burma Army openly launched its armed resistance against the Japanese.

Actually, I did not play a prominent part in this resistance, but I was glad to witness the very beginning of it by being present on the spot.

1945 Glyn Court

Fifty years have not dimmed the associations of certain places: Nyaung-U, north of Pagan, where, just before we went into action, General Slim came and spoke to us - a moment to remember for a lifetime, in the presence of a man of who, more than any I have known, radiated greatness tempered by humaneness and understanding; but also at Nyaung-U, where the sandy bank shelves down to the river, an ox-cart came down, its ungreased axle screaming like a wild hare in a trap, to load or unload one of the few river-boats that remained; and near the river a well, to which a young woman came with a copper water-pot in the early morning, so gracefully that when, months later, I came across these lines by a soldier poet:.

Manipuri maiden to market laden,
Treading as royally as Egypt's queen!

I thought straightway of the young woman of Nyaung-U.

That central plain, in the furnace heat of April, with blistering marches on half-rations of food and water, should have left nothing but a searing memory, but something deeper than the natural reaction of "remembering the good and forgetting the bad" has imprinted happier, or at least more agreeably memorable, scenes on my mind.

I remember the neat villages, pleasant to our eyes after the land we had just left, with their coconut and mango trees and lizards "tuck-too"-ing in the branches - maddeningly at the time, and we set very uncanonical words to their croaking chant.

I remember, too, the little pagodas and shrines scattered over the plain, almost seeming to burn like white-hot, gold-tipped flames; and the chinthes guarding them, baring their teeth to scare off the evil spirits, maybe, but grinning, I thought, amiably enough to us; and still, though faintly, I hear across the years the drowsy tinkling of the little bells on the *hti*s of the pagodas, wakened into music by the evening breeze.

I remember the great woven baskets as tall as we were and three times as wide, filled with ground nuts from the fields around; and could never, never forget the rich and 'spicy smell' that Kipling forgot to name, the *ngapi*, the ripe river-fish laid out to dry; and I recall as well, in one village, the peacocks, the royal birds of Burma, "from high estate though fallen" like their one-time masters - they merited the epic verse - shedding their eye-feathers like jewels but still maintaining a princely if precarious dignity as they strutted in the dust.

And though I did not wholly understand it at the time, perhaps it was above all the gentle tenor of these villages that won my heart, for although they were half a world away from my homeland of Somerset, in their lack of hurry and fret they were so reminiscent of her quiet ways before the war, nearly sixty years ago.

1945 **Lewis Shaw**

Our usual meals were some form of stew, with curry and rice, plus tinned fruit. This was quickly supplemented from stocks recaptured from the Japs, such as tins of coffee, Horlicks, Nestlés milk and oatmeal. The food we got by air was pushed out in padded bundles (no parachutes), containing a number of packs each sufficient for eight men for one day. There were different packs of course, for Indian and British men. Cooking had to be done under blackout conditions after dark, and as the weather was very hot now, it was no fun for the cooks. As we worked till dark (6.30pm), we usually found ourselves groping in the dark for our food.

I had taken the radio from a damaged armoured car and fitted it up in our mess tent. It kept us in touch with tank operations going on around us, and filled the dark evenings with music and news from All India Radio - provided the Japs left us in peace, that is.

Even before the Meiktila area had finally been cleared, we were given time to relax a little, and especially I remember swimming in one of the lakes. This had been kept for drinking water and so we were given strict instructions to use no soap.

In early April, our forward troops started moving on south, and we still had the objective of taking Rangoon before the monsoon broke in early May. On 12th April I was at Pyawbwe, and on 30th April I reached the large town of Pegu. I wrote in my diary, "Pyawbwe is a pleasant place with plenty of trees, so that it was not difficult to find shade. Pyinmana is another attractive spot. It has a small lake which gives a plentiful water supply. The houses, like the majority around are well built of brick or timber, and if not on a small hillock, are always built up on stilts. The town has a very fine large Golden Pagoda, which is still undamaged. Burma is famous for its pagodas, as you must know, and in fact they are so much an everyday thing that it has not entered my mind to mention them before. They all have their little tinkling bells which blow about in the breeze, and make the place sound quite enchanting. The largest image of the Buddha I have seen is at a village called Kanyutkwin, and is about 70 or 80 feet high. The building housing it is overgrown with creepers, and it must have had a roof on at one time, but right now poor old Buddha is poking his head out of the top!"

Unfortunately it was not for my unit to be in at the fall of Rangoon on 2nd May, for we were still in Pegu. I was not to see Rangoon myself until four weeks later.

On the night of 7th May we heard the PM announce the end of the war in Europe on the radio and we listened to commentaries of the celebrations around Britain. However, as I wrote in a letter home to the UK, it was nice to know that they were safe now, but **we** had to keep in action, and I suggested they save some of the celebrating till we came home!

1945 **Maureen**

Soon we were seeing aircraft flying over us in the daytime, not Japanese because they did not have the red sun emblem painted on the underside of the wings. Quite unafraid, we would run out and count them as they swooped low overhead. We were very excited and wondered what it all meant; only the nuns were cautious, discouraging us from going outside when these planes flew over.

Their caution was not without foundation. Without any warning we received our first bombing, and it was terrifying. The blast took us completely by surprise and in a panic we rushed to the centre of the house. The planes bombed and retreated, then made fresh attacks. All around us furniture crashed and clocks struck crazily...

Now and again we were received news about the Allies' progress from the hill people when they ventured back to barter with us again. At times the news was so exciting it was difficult to contain oneself. When we heard that the British and Americans were only four days away we would be filled with great relief and happiness, but then in two days' time would come the news that they had been pushed back ten days, throwing us into a deep and anxious gloom. But Allied planes were already dropping leaflets announcing their imminent arrival.

1945 **Glyn Court**

I vividly remember a village near an abandoned railway embankment near Kyaukpadaung (the name escapes me and my precious B.O.S. maps went missing twenty years ago). I was sent out with a section patrol to find food and Japs, very preferably in that order, and after my tentative "*J'pun-do shi th' la?*" ("Are there any Japanese around?") to a farmer brought the welcome reply '*M'shi bu*', we went in, to be greeted by a smiling English-speaking headman-schoolmaster. Delicate cups were handed round, and Bermondsey and Battersea did their regiment honour by drinking tea without milk or sugar for the first time in their lives with expressions that fell short of ecstasy but evidently pleased the givers. In a region fought over by armies and stripped of its wealth our search for food to vary our meat-and-veg and K ration chocolate seemed an impertinence, even if we could give sardines and cigarettes to pave the way. But without hesitation the headman said, "We will bring you food in the morning," and we made our way back, only half believing, and bivouacked down for the night.

Morning came and stand-to, and as we resigned ourselves to another day's march and action on half-rations, a procession came down the path from the village bearing bowls of steaming rice, fresh chicken and fruit. The feast got no further than Company HQ and the Officers' Mess ("We feasted right royally," proclaimed the Major), but of course such has been the way of armies since the world began, and it in no way dimmed our appreciation of these Burmese village people who out of their poverty had given riches

1945 Maureen

We were surprised at the appearance of a new type of Japanese soldier who sometimes ventured into our compound when it was dark. For the most part on crutches and maimed, some with bandages on their heads or arms in slings, they would beg for water or rice, extending a metal container and slinking off into the darkness afterwards. They were no longer a cause for alarm, we pitied them and the nuns gave them what they could spare.

June 1945 Maureen

We had been told repeatedly just what to do if any strange people were seen around the compound, and that was to run up to the top floor and lock ourselves out on the verandah next to the chapel, keep our heads down and wait to be called down again. It was 8th June at about noon. Noticing some movement at the foot of the hill, we stood rooted to the spot, completely forgetting our instructions. For we saw crawling up the hill on their stomachs, rifles trained in our direction men not with yellow faces, but bright brick-red ones. Certain that they were British, we threw caution to the winds and beckoned the soldiers on, unable to stop jumping up and down with excitement. We shouted to the nuns that the British had arrived and begged to be allowed downstairs, but they bundled us upstairs where we were still able to peer down at the advancing soldiers through the verandah rails. The soldiers were as cautious as the nuns, edging their way up the hill until they were quite sure that this was friendly territory, and they could enter the house. Now we scrambled downstairs as fast as we could, to see the nuns clasping the hands of the soldiers and praising God and all the saints for our deliverance.

1945 Lewis Shaw

I reached N° 1 Workshop at Toungoo on 14th August, and the surrender of the Japanese was announced the next morning, so I found myself caught up in two nights of partying, with officers from several neighbouring units. The highlight came when the OC fixed our dartboard up to the roof of the mess tent, and we all took shots at it with our pistols! Needless to say the dartboard was not much use for darts after that.

On 1st Oct I travelled with five other officers to Thaton, the one-time capital of Lower Burma. We had to cross the 200-yard-wide Bilin river, on rafts with outboard motors, operated by the Japs. Two interpreters met us on the far bank with large old American saloons, and took us the remaining 25 miles to Thaton. As we passed along the road, Jap soldiers saluted us and villagers gave friendly waves, so at least we knew that we were welcome back.

It was not long before we started to meet the local people. The first formal occasion was a dinner of 'Welcome to the British', put on by the Karen community. The Karens are one of the largest ethnic groups in Burma, most of them are Christians, and very pro-British, and therefore many of them had been living in the jungle to keep out of the way of the Japs. The next night I went to a Victory Dinner provided by the Burmese townsfolk. After the inevitable speeches and a response from our Brigadier, we were entertained by three girls to a display of Burmese dancing, quite strange contortions compared to European dancing.

The Re-establishment of Civil Government was marked on 18th October, by a day's holiday for the Burmese people. As for the military, we put on a football match: Brigade HQ, for whose team I was 'volunteered', against the Indian troops.

1945 Maureen

Early next morning we were up and looking for the promised return of the British, so afraid that it had all been a lovely dream. True to their word, they did not keep us waiting. Soon there was a long line of trucks on the road, and as as we saw one of them turn up to our house, we ran to greet it. The truck stopped outside the kitchen where a beaming Sister Marie-Louise supervised the unloading of sacks of sugar, rice, flour and a drum of cooking oil. Then the soldiers were off again. From now on they called every day.

TRANSITION AND INDEPENDENCE

1945 - Japanese Soldiers — Lewis Shaw

The Japs were still about in Burma of course, now referred to as JSP (Japanese Surrendered Personnel) and they had their own camps outside the town, from where working parties were drawn every day. I had been told that they had a quantity of vehicle spares we could have, and so I went off to Moulmein to find them. This involved a 40 mile journey south from Thaton, to the town of Martaban at the mouth of the River Salween, and then a half-hour trip on a ferry - a barge flanked by two diesel tugs manned by the Japs. Later, I visited the Jap 33 Army Workshops, which much to my surprise was no bigger than the Section I had been running. That was a sure sign of the amount of mechanical transport the Japs had left - they had been using bullock carts instead!

The 25th October was a day of humiliation for the Japs, when, on a large parade ground in Thaton, Lt Gen Honda, Commander of the Jap 33rd Army was paraded with his senior commanders, and made to hand over their ceremonial swords to our General Crowther. I have never seen such dejected faces as theirs. After the senior officers came the junior officers and NCO'S, so that eventually there was a large pile of swords on the ground. Other equipment such as pistols, binoculars, telescopes etc had already been handed in, and was stored on racks in a large stores building.

That evening, we were invited to yet another dinner, this time with the Anti -Fascist Peoples Freedom League (AFPFL), known to us as 'Aff Piffle'. This was the political branch of the Burma National Army, led by General Aung San, which wanted to form a Provisional Government. Very few of them spoke English so there was not much conversation between us.

1945 - Rangoon

Philip Plumb

The city and port of Rangoon, to which I arrived by sea in 1945, had suffered years of bombing and shelling both during the attack by Japan and withdrawal of the British in 1942 and in the process of its recapture in May 1945. Sabotage by the Japanese before their departure and extensive looting by local mobs added to the chaos. When Rangoon was reoccupied by the Allies it was in a state of indescribable filth. The water supply had ceased to function in March on the bombing of the water pipe lines from the Hlawga Lake and all sewers were choked.

Open road-side drains were full of sewage.

Rangoon in 1946 - a postcard

By October the water supply had been replaced and the sewage system was once more functioning. General electricity supplies were not yet possible and local generators were used for vital purposes. Many of the buildings were badly damaged, roofs missing, and girders projecting out of the walls. Thousands of homeless people had erected flimsy bamboo and leaf shanties along the streets in front of ruined buildings and in open spaces. The railway station footbridge was a twisted tangle of metal. One of the spires on the twin towers of the Roman Catholic Cathedral was bent slightly in towards the other. The Anglican Cathedral had been used by the Japanese as a brewery making *saki* and sauces. It had been cleaned up under a service chaplain by a volunteer working party which included one Lieutenant-General, three Brigadiers, two Colonels, four Chaplains and many other troops, all working with pick and shovel with their shirts off.

The Bishop returned in July and held a service of cleansing for the Cathedral and a few days later a service of thanksgiving for victory was celebrated. The electricity supply was not available so twenty jeeps were lined up outside and shone their lamps through the windows. Another jeep was driven into the Cathedral so that the large congregation could read the service sheets in its headlights. Many churches had been defiled in various obnoxious ways and a great programme of cleaning and mending was necessary The Japanese had attempted to eradicate all British influence in Burma, even removing the animals from Rangoon Zoo because they had been introduced under the colonial government. Their greatest vandalism, however, was the deliberate destruction of the fine University Library.

South of the University Boat Club, bordering the Lake, the Japanese general and his staff occupied three bungalows and west of the Lake, in a large isolated house, lived the Japanese ambassador with his offices in Judson College. The Rangoon Gymkhana Club was used as a hotel frequented by Japanese officers and pilots while the Pegu Club was both a club and a brothel for officers. The less comfortable environment of the tramway depot was the brothel for other ranks. Rangoon's pre-war night spot, The Silver Grill, became The New Burma Hall as a general place of entertainment for the Japanese.

1946 - Politics and Elephants **Lewis Shaw**

During September, the country was paralysed by a general strike, originally over pay and conditions of the police, civil servants and oil field workers, but in reality politically inspired. So some of our supplies, which came by train, were held up, until the Japs, who had run the railway during the war, were called in to do it again! During the strike we were ordered to carry arms and not to go about less than two at a time, although in fact we had no trouble in Prome.

One day in November, one of the forestry officers invited me up the Irrawaddy on a gun boat of the Burma Navy. It so happened that his brother was captain of the gun boat, which was patrolling the river to deter dacoits, and coincidentally, Steel Bros. were transporting a number of elephants from one side of the river to the other, a distance of over half a mile. A large raft had been built of teak logs, big enough to take four or five elephants at a time. To prevent the elephants panicking when they stepped on the raft, a 10 foot high wall of bamboo and leaves had been built around the edges. There were 14 adult elephants, who were shackled, and three calves, who were free but stayed close to their mothers. I accompanied one load across, and

waited for the rest to assemble. It was an impressive experience to see all 17 elephants lined up together, and I don't think I have seen such a large number together since. The whole operation was a great success, and we had a relaxing trip back to Prome, especially as the Captain had opened his drinks cabinet!

The day after this outing, 11th November, our OC, Major Jimmy Seddon, handed over the Company to me, while he was packing up ready to set off for repatriation. I was still a Captain however, though the Colonel (in Rangoon), had promised to get authority for my promotion, and it was suggested to me that if I volunteered to stay in Burma an extra six months, it would help the situation. I had no job waiting for me at home, so I volunteered.

On 22nd January I set off early in my Jeep, and headed north, with my driver Mafooz Khan to share the driving, and my orderly Mariappan. I passed through the Yenan-gyaung Oilfields to Meiktila, the scene of the battle in which I had been involved in March 1945. The oilfields were a picture of complete desolation, as no work had been done since our retreating troops destroyed them in 1943. Although there was no large scale extraction, I passed several villagers who were slowly pulling very small amounts by bucket from holes in the ground.

1946 - the Civil Service View — Nick Larmour

In April 1946, when I became the young and very inexperienced Personal Assistant to the Chief Secretary, we were already committed to implementing the proposals for the future of Burma published by the Churchill Government in May 1945. These envisaged three years of direct rule by the Governor, followed by an indefinite period of limited self government, with independence only a distant prospect. This fell very far short of the expectations in 1946 of even moderate Burmese opinion: the offer was instantly condemned and rejected by Aung San, now leader of the most prominent political grouping, the AFPFL (the Anti-Fascist People's Freedom League). Aung San refused any further co-operation with the Governor and immediately stepped up his campaign for early independence. Though many of the older, more conservative Burmans had grave suspicions of the radical Marxism of the AFPFL, and would have preferred to move more slowly, Aung San and his followers undoubtedly enjoyed strong popular support in his demands for independence, and many were already thinking of him and his AFPFL as the provisional government-in-waiting.

Certainly none of the many political groupings now beginning to emerge could match the charisma of Aung San and the power of the AFPFL. They already had an effective political Organisation, backed up by the People's Volunteer Organisation (PVO), their thinly disguised military wing. Their bargaining position, already formidable, was daily growing stronger as they stepped up their efforts to undermine the British administration in the districts, where unrest was growing fast. And everywhere rumours abounded of imminent armed rebellion if no settlement was reached with Aung San.

These danger signs eventually forced the British Labour Government in June 1946 to recall the Governor and replace him by Major-General Sir Hubert Rance, the former head of the Military Government. In Burmese eyes he enjoyed two great advantages: he was untainted by any pre-war Burma connections, and he had played an important part in the dealings with Aung San which had led to the defection of the Burma Defence Army from the Japanese in early 1945. It was hoped that he might succeed where others had failed, in negotiating a reasonable compromise: but he came on the scene too late. In September 1946, the police went on strike, almost certainly at the instigation of the AFPFL, and were followed by most civil servants, University students and key industrial workers. The strike quickly spread and soon paralysed the country. The new Governor had to climb down and appoint a new Executive Council in which the moderates and the ethnic minorities no longer counted and Aung San and the AFPFL took full control. Aung San and his colleagues were technically only Councillors advising the Governor, but they were in effect exercising Ministerial powers and I will refer to them as Ministers from now on.

This was a famous victory and Aung San was now ready to take the next steps towards independence. Only two months later, he presented the Governor with a virtual ultimatum, demanding, among other claims, that a statement should be made by the British Government before the end of January, promising elections for a Constituent Assembly to be held in April 1947, and full independence for Burma within a year. The British Labour Prime Minister, Clement Attlee, recognising the strong head of steam behind these Burmese demands and the potentially disastrous consequences of further delay, immediately invited Aung San and his AFPFL colleagues, as well as other political and ethnic leaders, to talks in London in January.

At these talks, the principle of independence was immediately conceded, the elections were fixed for April, 1947, and most of the other issues amicably settled, with, however, one major exception, the significant issue of the future constitutional status of Burma's "Frontier Areas", inhabited by many non Burmese peoples such as the Karens, the Shans and many others, who had always been under direct British rule and had never been controlled by Burmese politicians. British Ministers and the AFPFL representatives knew perfectly well that this ethnic minority problem (as we would now call it, though the minorities were a very significant proportion of the total population) was an issue which could not be settled before independence, because neither side could publicly give ground. So, it was fudged in the London Agreement and was left, in ambiguous terms, for later settlement, with predictable consequences which have undermined the separate status of the minorities, and still, nearly fifty years later, threaten the stability of the country.

1945-47 - Miscellaneous Philip Plumb

Very stringent censorship had been exercised on the Burmese press during the occupation. The Government Printing Press in Judah Ezekiel Street survived the Japanese only to be threatened by a hooligan mob after the Japanese withdrawal. U Wa Gyi, the Press Superintendent, tried to bluff them by claiming that the Japanese had stored explosives there and the place would blow up if fire broke out. When this failed, his staff held off the attackers with lathis and spears, U Wa Gyi's nephew fired three rounds from a double-barrelled gun into the air and the attackers retreated. Thus most of the machinery and paper stocks were intact on the arrival of the British.

Narayan Nair, with whom I shared a room in I Mess before transferring to RA Mess on the University campus, was a Madrassi. He spoke English and Burmese excellently as well as four Indian languages and progressed from Lieutenant to Major in eighteen months or so. We would often go to the cinema together with a pair of his female friends who might be Indian, Anglo-Indian, Burmese, Parsi-Burmese (twins); there seemed to be an inexhaustible supply. It was not surprising that he found it difficult to chose between two potential brides. He finally made up his mind to marry Leela and I received an invitation to the wedding in July 1948 .

Burma was not a peaceful country in 1945-7. Apart from various private armies, there were gangs of dacoits (armed robbers) at large in many areas. When an Australian academic came on a lecture tour to Burma, I was detailed to escort him round the country. We drove up the Pegu road in a Dodge truck, branching off for Waw, a very dusty track, and came to the Sittang. The only way to cross was by using the tank landing craft which was running an on-demand service. The country from there to Bilin was wild and we nearly hit a tree when the driver took his eye off the road at the sight of a topless Burmese girl who appeared suddenly at the roadside. This would never have happened in Rangoon and the driver must be excused. The river Bilin was crossed by a makeshift ferry of boats lashed together. The journey back from Moulmein was much faster - we caught a Beechcraft plane. As the first sight of the Shwe Dagon from the river was unforgettable, so was this view from the air, circling around the great building before landing at Mingaladon.

1947 - Burmanisation Nick Larmour

The January agreement (in London) in effect decided the future of Burma. The AFPFL would be regarded as the interim Government until the April elections, where they were now concerned to make a good showing, and after their triumph in London they can have had little doubt about the outcome. They were the only party with an effective nationwide organisation and they made full use of this advantage, determined to convince the voters that the British were on the way out. I do not think they were ever accused of serious electoral malpractice: they did not need to resort to that, but they no doubt exerted considerable pressures on the voters which must have strengthened their performance at the polls.

They were also anxious to demonstrate that the British no longer controlled the centres of power, and Burmanisation dramatically accelerated after Aung San and his colleagues took over. Many of them were understandably suspicious of their ICS former rulers, most of whom were considerably older. And some of the former rulers, equally understandably, disliked taking orders from younger Burmese radicals whom they neither trusted nor respected. But the majority of us British in the Service accepted the imminent transfer of power without surprise or bitterness. And before the April elections, almost all the important Secretariat posts in Rangoon and all but one of the senior posts in the districts had already been Burmanised.

The senior posts in the Home department, from the Chief Secretary down, including a new Additional Secretary, had long since been Burmanised and all the holders were hand-picked. Thakin Mya, the new AFPFL Home Minister, one of Aung San's closest friends who had accompanied him to the London talks, was a key figure. I was well pleased to be allowed to stay on as the only "white-faced imperialist" (the usual Burmese press cliché for the British) in this high-powered department and I did my best to adapt to my changed circumstances. The atmosphere was always friendly and I never felt mistrusted or disregarded. I found Thakin Mya invariably warm and approachable, a man of high principles, wise and tolerant with a strong sense of fair play.

With Thakin Mya in charge there was a new sense of urgency. We all realised how much remained to be done by January, 1948, and there was a difference in the way the department was run.

The Home department continued to be responsible for the control of the Burma Police and so, though of course, I had no operational responsibility, I had close dealings with the Deputy Inspector-General about the management of the police budget. Money was tight and our discussions were often fraught. One of these apparently minor matters had serious consequences. The police and the Army were making some progress in securing the surrender of illegally held arms, but it was disappointingly slow. The top policemen became increasingly worried about protecting Ministers, especially while in their Secretariat offices which were always open to the public under British rule. So they proposed to tighten security in the Secretariat by erecting a strong steel gate at the main entrance, manned by armed guards. The cost was insignificant, but the Finance department, short-sighted as always, raised objections. The proposition was supported by the Home Minister and put to the Cabinet. But Ministers turned it down on the grounds that the public right to unrestricted access to their elected leaders must be maintained. The idea of controlling entry to the Secretariat was abandoned: the armed assassins who forced their way into a Cabinet meeting a few weeks later came and went unchallenged.

Not long after this I became involved in another dramatic security incident. The police were seriously short of automatic weapons, which were increasingly being used by criminals and would certainly be used by political extremists mounting an armed rebellion. The British Government had therefore agreed to make over to the police, free of charge, a very large consignment of Bren light machine guns and Sten sub-machine guns. These weapons were to be handed over to the police in June by the 14th Army Ordnance Depot in Rangoon. On the due date, and after the exchange of the formal documentation, the guns were handed over to uniformed Burmans, whom the Depot staff took to be properly authorised members of the Burma Police. But they were not police officers: the arms had in fact been hi-jacked and were now in the hands of an unknown opposition group, who were soon to use them with fatal consequences for Aung San and his Ministers.

The whole country was now on red alert. Though the identity and political orientation of the hijackers were not immediately evident, U Saw, now leader of the opposition Myochit party, was the prime suspect: his contacts in 1941 with the Japanese had led to his internment in Tanganyika during the war. It was soon established that the hi-jacked arms had been hidden in watertight barrels in a lake near his house. Ministers apparently decided not to arrest him there and then, but to keep him and his associates under surveillance in the hope thereby of discovering how and when the stolen arms were to be used.

1947 - Unrest

Philip Plumb

Our dangerous position in Burma in general and Rangoon in particular was never out of mind.

On 16 January 1947 there were no civilians at work including our cooks and four days later Rangoon was put out of bounds. On 21st January, Communists tried to raid the Secretariat but were driven off by fire hoses. Easter that year fell awkwardly as the civilian employees would lose a great deal of money if they had Easter off and then three days for Thingyan, the Water festival, so the C.O.C. decided to cancel the Easter holidays and let the Army have time off during Thingyan. This was not to the liking of the troops as it seemed to be putting Buddhist before Christian festivals.

One of the lecturers brought out to Burma by the British Council was the writer Bernard Newman. On 29th May, 1947 he went to interview U Aung San in the Secretariat building. Newman came back with mixed feelings about the Burmese leader. Compared with many of the world leaders that Newman had met, Aung San had no commanding personality and seemed rather bewildered at the complex burden of responsibilities he was shouldering. Although in his public speeches he talked of a well-equipped army of one million men for independent Burma, in private he was much more realistic and outlined a small but well trained force augmented by local territorial and auxiliary units. Newman believed that Aung San was a great patriot and intended to give a fair deal to the minority races of Burma.

What Aung San lacked in economic or political expertise he thought he could quickly learn from elementary books on the subjects. When a British official had suggested that it was a mistake to send U Tin Tut to London as High Commissioner because U Tin Tut was "the only man that can balance your budget", Aung San replied that he had thought of that and had bought two books on economics. Newman chided Aung San on the lack of security as he had gone straight into his room unchallenged and warned him that the 'love and affection of ordinary people' was no protection against assassination. This proved to be uncannily prophetic.

1946-47 - The Jubilee Hall **Philip Plumb**

The main meeting hall and theatre for Europeans living in Rangoon before the war was the Jubilee Hall, a large, brick, typically Victorian building. The general level of entertainment was not very high, but some of us were privileged to enjoy one of the greatest stage performances of our time. In February, 1946 John Gielgud performed Hamlet in full Elizabethan costume. A few of us were recruited to play small parts and were thus on stage during four unforgettable performances.

Later, when the Hall had been handed back to the municipality, very significant political meetings took place there. On May 19th, 1947, Aung San opened the five day convention of the AFPFL which decided their independence policy that Burma must have complete independence, that no form of monarchy was acceptable, and that the republic would be founded on the principles of socialism and democracy. Today the Jubilee Hall is gone and a Defence Museum stands on its site.

1947 - Labour Problems - and Relaxation **Lewis Shaw**

The biggest headache I was left with was to sort out pay and conditions for our civilian employees, who had been on strike. The directives from Rangoon, in typical army style were not exactly clear! At this time too, throughout the country there were signs of civil unrest, with the AFPFL being very active. Dacoity was common again in parts, and the army had to deploy a Brigade in the Pyinmana area, 200 miles north of Rangoon, to deal with them. One day the

AFPFL had a big rally in Prome, and we were ordered to keep out of the town for the day, in case of trouble. General Aung San, who only three months later was to be assassinated, addressed the meeting, which fortunately was peaceful.

Although I had not been given the rank, I was pleased to find in May that I was given pay as Acting Major, backdated for three months, so my efforts had been rewarded after all! In the middle of May it became our turn to move to Rangoon.

Our new site was on the banks of Victoria Lake, where from the Officers' Mess we looked out along the lake to the beautiful Shwe Dagon Pagoda about a mile away. The lake was of course very inviting for swimming, but we were wary of doing so at first because there were rumours that the Japs had let alligators escape from the nearby zoo, into the water. We were soon able to dismiss that idea though, and I enjoyed a swim directly from the Mess on most afternoons.

Two days after my return, the authority came through for me to put up my crowns, which our tailor very quickly sewed on my epaulettes for me. This called for a celebration, which the IOR's provided in the form of a *burra khana*, and a concert party put on by themselves with the help of two local dancing girls.

1945-48 — Glyn Court

To every coin, every medal, every picture there must be a reverse side, and Burma also created other memories. They were far less delectable, and yet, or perhaps for that very reason, I would not gladly forgo them. I recall the tortured landscape of the oilfields at Chauk and Yenangyaung, with the wrecked oil derricks, the ground polluted with oil, the steep, scrabbly banks of the dried-up chaungs, and the tall cacti that tore at you as you passed by.

I recall the flooded plain and stinking mud of the Sittang Bend under the monsoon, with every track a morass, with dysentery gripping your bowels day and night, and leeches crawling in to get at you through any unwatched opening and at every unguarded moment. I recall the innumerable insect pests - the dozen varieties on the ceiling of the hospital ward, the mosquitoes, the inch-long ants crawling up the trees - the prickly heat which covered you with pustules in the month before the rains came - and at another level, the black day when the news reverberated through Rangoon, Aung San is murdered. These were the dark shadows; but because of them one remembers the beauty of Burma all the more.

1947 - The Assassination of General Aung San — Nick Larmour

While the more sinister undertones of the arms hi-jacking were being investigated, financial propriety required the loss of such a valuable consignment of arms to be formally written off. This was routine for me and my opposite number in the Finance department, my old friend Kyaw Nyun. We were both busy with more urgent affairs and so we decided to meet in the Secretariat on a Saturday when Government offices usually closed. We chose Saturday, 19 July, a tragic date to become significant in modern Burmese history: for Aung San called a special meeting of his Ministers on the same day, a meeting which he and seven of them would not survive.

Kyaw Nyun and I had drafted our report in the Secretariat and were sitting in his office next door to the Cabinet ante-room, speculating about who now held the hi-jacked weapons, when we were startled to hear several long bursts, probably about 200 rounds, of automatic fire coming from the Cabinet room. We threw ourselves to the ground behind our desks, in case the gunmen came after us too. But they had done the job they came to do and quickly left the Secretariat. After a long interval, when all seemed quiet, we cautiously entered the office of the Cabinet Secretary. He was in severe shock and hardly able to speak, but managed to tell us how two gunmen had burst into the Cabinet room and opened fire on Aung San and the other Ministers. He had somehow managed to escape unscathed. Kyaw Nyun comforted him and took him home.

By the time I ventured into the Cabinet room, the Inspector General of Police and his Deputy, who had offices in the Secretariat, were already there, and several doctors and medical staff had also arrived from the General Hospital nearby. I had seen some bloodshed during the war but I was never at the sharp end. The scene of carnage in the Cabinet room was horrific. Aung San and six of his Ministers including my Minister, Thakin Mya, were obviously dead, one other was mortally wounded, all were riddled by bullets fired at point blank range, their clothing soaked in blood, their sandals lying where they had been kicked off. There was still a strong smell of cordite, and spent cartridge cases were being collected and examined by the police. Though I write from memory of events nearly fifty years ago, this terrible sight remains fresh and vivid in my mind.

I tried repeatedly but unsuccessfully that morning, with the help of my colleague, Patrick Rathbone, to contact the Chief Secretary and other Home Department officers. Probably all of them, having heard on the radio what had happened and not knowing what was behind it, were lying low in fear for their own lives. There was confusion everywhere. Many Burmans were still suspicions of British intentions and some were ready to believe that we had instigated or at least encouraged the assassins. Fortunately for us all, the Governor had already achieved a close relationship of mutual trust with U Nu, the most senior of the surviving AFPFL leaders, and a powerful figure on the political scene with a high reputation for strength and integrity. Without hesitation, he threw his support firmly behind the Governor. Both spoke on the radio later in the day and U Nu's unequivocal announcement that he had agreed to form a new AFPFL government did much to restore calm and confidence.

The speedy arrest of the killers also served to increase confidence. They had betrayed themselves when they returned from the Secretariat, shouting in triumph, to report their success personally to U Saw at his home. Unfortunately for them all, his house had been under surveillance since the arms hi-jacking: Saw and the gunmen were immediately detained.

1947 - Departure — Lewis Shaw

The day after we sailed out of Rangoon, 19th July, news was received on board that Aung San, who had hoped to become the future leader of the government and guide Burma to independence, had been assassinated. This was a sad day for Burma, which led to considerable political and civil unrest, from which the country has still not recovered. Many people were arrested in Rangoon, including a REME officer who was suspected of having some association with the supposed killers, and although I had come to love being in Burma, I was glad that I had got away from it at that time.

4th January 1948 - Independence — Nick Larmour

In the last weeks before independence, there were many farewell parties. The Governor allowed his staff to give a Ball at Government House to which we invited our personal friends, and that was a memorable occasion. The date of independence had long been agreed, but after U Nu took over, the exact timing became crucial because he, like most Burmans, believed that important decisions should be taken only at astrologically auspicious times. The astrologists were accordingly consulted, horoscopes were cast, and the creation of the Republic of Burma was fixed for exactly 4.20 am on 4 January.

The Ball at Government House - Nick and Nancy Larmour are left and centre.

So, before daybreak on that date, the Governor and his staff, the President Elect, Ministers, senior officials, newly arrived diplomats and invited guests of the Burma Government, all assembled in what was later to become Independence Square in downtown Rangoon. At 4.20 precisely, in the cool darkness, the Union flag was lowered to the solemn notes of *God Save the King* and the new flag of Burma was raised to the unfamiliar strains of the new Burmese national anthem. Immediately after this dramatic and moving ritual, the cheering and shouting broke out, fireworks soared, bonfires blazed, rifles were fired in the air - a feu de joie, we hoped, but we were not quite sure, for many of us were still apprehensive of the future.

There was a later, more convivial and conventionally British ceremony at Government House in the bright light of day, after which we all drove to the jetty where the cruiser HMS Birmingham was waiting to take the Governor to Colombo. After warm farewells which left many in tears, including most of the Cabinet as they stood in line in their elegant silken national dress, the Governor and Lady Rance embarked, the two national anthems were again played, a 21 gun salute was fired in honour of the new Republic, and, punctual to the last, HMS Birmingham got under way.

1948 - Reflections — Glyn Court

I am bound to regret having known so few Burmese personally. As a sergeant of the British Army, how could I? Every time I walked into Rangoon from our headquarters I paused at the memorial erected to those of my regiment, the Queen's, who had died in Manipur and Burma. But we British in the Fourteenth Army were fewer than the half-million men and women from four continents - Australian fliers, King's African Rifles, Merrill's Marauders from the U.S.A., Punjabis, Sikhs and Dogras from India, Gurkhas from Nepal, and thousands more - who served or fought to free Burma from the curse of Japan, and none of them, certainly, would have consented to have one colonial rule replaced by another, no matter how benevolent.

Least of all would the Burmese people, and the root of the tragedy of Burma since 1947 may be found in 1945, when the British Bourbons who sat out the war in Simla returned believing that nothing had changed, while everything had. And yet, although the Burmese were determined to have freedom, soldiers encountered little overt hostility even in the heart of Rangoon. The death of Aung San was an irreparable loss, but it is untrue to say that it completely perverted the course of Burma's history. The seeds of separation had been sown before, and his death only hastened the severance of Burma from the Commonwealth.

4th January 1948 - Reflections — Nick Larmour

As the cruiser slipped down the Rangoon River to the open sea, we British on the jetty did not have much to say to one another. But we had much to think about. I knew that many of those who had served in pre-war Burma felt a sense of guilt about the British failure to protect Burma from the Japanese. They did however feel an even deeper regret that we should now be pulling out, with the Burmese economy in ruins and its prospects of recovery uncertain. I understood how they felt, but I did not share their feelings. Although I had greatly enjoyed my five adventurous, exciting and challenging years in and out of Burma, and had made good friends, British and Burman, whom I would greatly miss, I was quite content to move on and leave Burma to the Burmans.

1947 - Farewell

Sylvia

And so one morning, with our little family, we embarked on the tender that would take us to our ship, and waved goodbye forever to Mary and Anthony, with baby Philip screaming at the top of his voice for Mary. Soon, from the deck of our tramp steamer as it sailed down the Rangoon River on its way to South Africa, we had our last glimpse of the Shwe Dagon Pagoda, gleaming gold in the bright sunshine. As it disappeared finally from view, with tear-filled eyes we said our last farewells to Burma, land of happy memories!

1948 - Farewell

Nancy Larmour

The last and most enduring memory is of January 1948, as HMS Birmingham drew away from the quayside in Rangoon, bearing the last Governor, Sir Hubert Rance, and Lady Rance, while the entire Burmese Cabinet, resplendent in their gorgeous silken *longyis* and *eingyis* and tasselled *gaungbaungs,* stood in line along the quayside, waving, and - you must believe me! - many of them in tears!

1945 — Glyn Court

I remember a day in the monsoon near Letpanthonbin, a few miles east of Waw, in a hut with three other soldiers, and a man nursing a sick child who was moaning and would not be comforted. The nearest doctor was five miles away, beyond an impassable morass. We had no medical supplies other than mepacrine and water purification tablets, and for a common language, only a few phrases culled from an Army booklet. "*Gowng kaik day?*" (headache) I asked. "*Baik na day?*" (stomach ache). It could not have made any difference, and we were moving on in five minutes' time, but with all his anxiety he responded with a smile, and that, with so much other humanity, has stayed in my mind.

1961 — Sue Fenn

We lived for a couple of months with a weaver's family in the village of Amarapura, by the Irrawaddy river a few miles south west of Mandalay. From them we learnt so much besides the language and how to cook. One important lesson concerned washing. The British had a bad reputation on this subject, going back to the days immediately after the war. Some well-intentioned but ignorant British women had published a leaflet in Burmese on Personal Hygiene. The shocked readers, who bathed at least twice a day, were advised: "You should try to take a bath at least once a week"!

So when we made our twice daily visits to the nearby well we washed very thoroughly and dried ourselves with three towels, one for the head, one for the body and one for the feet. Then we slipped the dry *longyi* over the wet one, aware that there were sighs of disappointment from the giggling children, as we once more achieved this feat with our modesty and dignity intact!

Towards the end of our stay the youngest daughter developed horrible boils and began to vomit up all her food. U Nyunt and his wife, Daw Mya Thaung decided to take Myint Myint Aye to the *Nat Gadaw*. This good lady plastered the boils with a thick black paste, but the condition did not improve. I went to a wonderful doctor in Mandalay, Dr. Guha, and described the symptoms. He gave me a delicious chocolate syrup of penicillin which Myint Myint loved taking. She was soon restored to health and in her usual mischievous spirits.

I asked her parents if they would take her to the doctor in Mandalay next time she was so ill. "No," they replied firmly, "How do you know it wasn't the *Nat* which cured her?"

One of her brothers grew up to become a successful doctor in Rangoon!

1969 Patricia Herbert

I didn't want an *ein-paw* (house companion/maid) - but Burmese friends and husband thought we should have one and in due course Daw Hlaing arrived. She was an older lady, from a village near Kyaukpadaung in the dry zone, and was very poor, barely literate, and the mother of six sons. Her husband was a useless drunkard, and she had come to Rangoon to earn money for her family and to fulfil her greatest ambition which was to enable her youngest son - now thirteen or so - to become a novice monk - a very necessary stage for all Buddhist males. At that time (1969/70) domestic servants were paid very little - about 30 kyats a month - and though they lived-in and had meals provided, they worked all hours and were lucky to get just one day off a month. Working for just two adults and receiving well-above average wages and free time helped compensate for the fact that our household was not a typical Burmese one and was a bit lonely for Daw Hlaing. I learnt to cook very simple village-style Burmese food, but had to rely on Burmese cookery books for more elaborate dishes. A kind of culinary compromise emerged: for instance, Daw Hlaing thought frying an egg an extravagant use of precious cooking oil and I learnt, when cooking a chicken curry, not to throw away the feet but to pop them into the pot with the rest of the chicken. As I peered into the saucepan there, emerging from the simmering curry, would be upturned scaly chicken feet which Daw Hlaing insisted on eating, though in time she was persuaded to eat more meaty parts of the chicken as well.

Then one morning Daw Hlaing did not get up. She lay on her mattress for three days and would take no food and said she was going to die. We called the doctor who, although he could find nothing wrong, gave her an injection since, like many Burmese, Daw Hlaing only had faith in *hsei-hto* (injected medicines). Two days passed with no change and I was getting very anxious about her when at last she sobbed out the following story: that she had been recruited in her village by a broker who had brought her to Rangoon to work in a *shauk-thi hsei-pya* factory (one making sour fruit pastilles), that she had had to work from five in the morning until midnight and that she had run away after her fingernails fell off from being always immersed in salty, lemony liquid. The broker had tracked her down to our place and apparently had come several times to demand money that she claimed Daw Hlaing owed her. On her last visit the broker said that Daw Hlaing must pay a lot more money, claiming her youngest son would go to prison otherwise, and that she had put a spell on Daw Hlaing and she would die. I could not persuade Daw Hlaing that we could sort out this matter and that she would not die until I thought of telling her that I had learnt western *Bo-ma* magic which would counteract the broker's bad magic. I gave Daw Hlaing a special potion (actually, a vitamin tablet dissolved in pineapple juice) and then solemnly recited "Abracadabra" several times. And indeed "hey, presto" Daw Hlaing was cured and rose from her sick bed.

After eighteen months with us Daw Hlaing declared the time had come to go home and hold her son's *shin-pyu* (Buddhist initiation) ceremony. We had great fun together at the market choosing candles and enamelled tin plates, gifts for the monastery and all sorts of things she wanted for the ceremony. As her purchases piled up, I unsuccessfully tried to persuade her not to spend all her savings on the *shin-pyu* but to save something for her own needs. I was slow to grasp that as a devout Buddhist, Daw Hlaing was intent on accumulating much merit, far more precious than worldly possessions.

1971 — Peter Smart

During the early seventies, the Queen's Birthday reception was held on the lawns of the Ambassador's residence at a time of year when torrential rain might well wash things out. I expressed our apprehensions about this when talking to the chief monk of a pagoda in Rangoon's northern suburbs.

He immediately summoned a young acolyte to bring him a candle and a pin with which he forthwith inscribed on the wax an invocation in Pali script. He then advised that, twenty minutes before the reception, I should go with my ambassador to the north-west corner of the residence garden, where we should plant and light the candle.

We shyly, almost furtively, followed the monk's instructions. It was a balmy evening and the reception was a total success.

As the car bearing the very last guests left the residence, there was a deafening clap of thunder, the heavens opened and the lawns were awash within seconds.

I went, a few days later, to thank the monk, who seemed as gratified as we had been at the happy outcome of his intervention.

1983 Daw Kyi Kyi May

The first thing that struck me when I came to England and started reading the daily papers is that most of the tabloids and magazines include horoscopes according to the zodiacal birthsigns. I was very surprised because I never thought the westerners would take these things seriously like us in the east. In the bookshops, too, there are shelves and shelves of books about horoscopes, astrology, birthsigns, numerology, Chinese, Vietnamese and Persian horoscopes, and now, lots of people are into Feng Shui. But I have yet to meet a westerner who admits to reading it or is serious about it. It makes me wonder what sort of people buy and read these books, because none of my acquaintances or friends have done it.

What about me? Do I believe in astrology or do I consult an astrologer, one might want to know? I do read the horoscope of my birth-sign whenever I come across it in the Sunday Times magazine but I do not take it seriously because even if the predictions are unbelievably good they are forgotten in a couple of hours. A typical Burmese to the bone!

Some Westerners think that all Burmese are superstitious and they like to consult a fortune teller. I know many Burmese who have never believed in that sort of thing. My maternal grandmother was one of them. She did not believe in *Nats* either. She considered herself a true Buddhist. She led a very religious life doing good deeds for her family and for others and never felt that she needed to consult and take advice about her own life from someone whom one also had to pay. But, most young people would go to a fortune teller in groups just for fun. I know a couple who decided to get married because the fortune teller's descriptions of the soul mate each of them will meet fitted each other. Most of the time the fortune teller will give you a remedy to get out unscathed from the ill-luck that besets you.

INTRODUCING HELEN WOODRUFF

1936-45 **Helen Woodruff**

My appetite to see Burma was whetted when my brother Eric wrote to me from there in the mid-30s, where he was working for the Indian Civil Service, and said that I must come out when I finished training as a nurse, to see this beautiful country and the lovely people. He found them "very delightful". He thought that when I finished I might like to get a job as a sister in a hospital near Yenan-gyaung - where the oil fields were. Then came the war with Germany - and I had two more years to train.

I joined the Princess Mary's Royal Air Force Nursing Service, and was posted first in the UK and then the Far East - to Bombay, Calcutta and then Chittagong, getting nearer and nearer to Burma. At this time the Japanese were invading Burma and our assistance to the RAF squadrons was needed in small and mobile units as they fought the Japs back. I was sent to 63 Mobile Field Hospital at Chittagong. My brother meantime was walking out with the civil administration, having stayed behind for a while to blow up the oil fields so that the Japanese could not use them.

We did a lot of moving around near the combat zone - much of it by air, and saw a lot of the beautiful country. We were busy, mainly with medical matters - malaria and dysentery, which far outweighed active injuries.

Finally we flew into Burma from Calcutta - down to Rangoon.

I had already met my husband-to-be, in Chittagong actually, then I was posted to '63 MFH' - and he was already on '61'. Later I was on the officers' ward in Chittagong, and he was the medical officer in charge. And that's how we met up again, but only for short spaces of time. He was out there for five years; I was only for two and a half. So we had to get married to stay together! That was the idea. Much to the disappointment of our families in England! But we met whenever we could. The Harvards were the great planes because they could take one or two passengers and they were the links between the various stations. If we had 48 hours leave or I was not too far away from him we managed to see each other. But it was very spasmodic.

Our wedding eventually took place over a year later. I've got a picture, but I haven't got the nice picture, with the Burmese in, I've only got us. We were married in Rangoon. Honeymoon in the YWCA. Three days we were there. At one point Alan was stopped with a gun because he was not allowed in, "Where do you think you're going?" He said "I've got my wife in there!" Oh yes it was great and my brother Eric was back with the Indian Civil Service administration. The wedding was at the Mingaladon garrison church, because I was working in the hospital near there. It was a Burmese military hospital.

My first impressions of Burma are hazy because we were all busy settling into our new RAF Unit living quarters and nearby hospital. The scenery was gentle, pleasant, not dramatic as seen later, and we did not really come into contact with Burmese people. We were only there for a short while, then the military were turned out for the civil administration to take over. Then Alan was posted back to Calcutta and I followed. We had twenty tin trunks, which he coped with. Because the people at home were all on rations, and we were advised to take what we could find on sale - cloth and other provisions

When I flew up to Calcutta we had to go back to Rangoon because the plane couldn't make it all the way. The Dakotas had been worn out. It was Lease-Lend; we bought them from the States. And it was very sad because many prisoners of war had gone through such agonies, through the Jap camps, and were being flown home - and a lot of them lost their lives - those planes crashed because they were not airworthy, often lacking spare parts.

I think it was the *Duchess of Richmond* we came back on and there was smallpox aboard so when we got back to Liverpool the men and women were sent off to different camps. So there were another two days before we got back to our homes.

POLITICS AND RECONSTRUCTION

April 1948 Ken Wootton

At the time of Independence in January 1948, only the most rudimentary repairs had been made to an economy wrecked by war. Ken Wootton was hired to help restore the oil refinery at Syriam, which had been comprehensively destroyed by the retreating British in 1942. Here is a letter he wrote home to England in early 1948:

"Back in 1941 everything was warm and easy in the Burmese oil industry and the guns in Europe were almost out of earshot. Oil was flowing well, money could buy much more than it could at 'home'. The BOC Oil Refinery at Syriam stood capable of producing 6,000,000 gallons of petroleum products per day. The IBP refinery at Seikgyi and the BBP one at Thilawa were intact. Syriam village lights were still on all night, supplied from the BOC power station.

"Then on Sunday 7th March 1942 that security was shattered. As the Japanese penetrated the borders, panic followed. Before the British oil men left they destroyed the whole oil production capacity and the street wires dangle pathetically to this day, lighting not a single lamp. Not a single drop of oil has Syriam processed since.

"Before the smoke of that destruction had cleared Phil Swales and the rest were down the river and out to India. Phil's job had been to destroy the Drawing Office - imagine him strewing the papers from every drawer, dousing them with petrol and striking a match. The denial team worked their way to the jetty, where they boarded the motor launch *Salin* and out to the *Fultala,* bound for Calcutta.

"During the war great plans were evolved in Simla and thanks to Mountbatten and later Sir Hubert Rance the first parts of them were going into action and complete refinery units were being manufactured in the States. This is where I came in, in June 1947. A peaceful withdrawal of the British was made. By the time Independence was celebrated earlier this year (1948), rehabilitation plans were already in motion - oil, electricity supply, railways, hydroelectric power, mines. You could motor from Rangoon to the Fields in a few hours.

"But today (in 1948) I drove up there, and it is as if time has stood still since that demolition in 1942. As I wander over the Refinery's desolation I see the large Refrigeration Plant that stopped on Denial Day. As I pass by the jungle that was a garden blooming with February flowers, or look into the Workshop in which are still lying the chunks of metal that were being crafted by one of the 7,000 pre-war workmen then employed, as I glance at the great electrical generators, silent since Denial, I cannot but feel sad."

24th September 1949 (from W.A.Howe)

By 1949, the Yenan-gyaung oil field was starting to resume limited production. Not much, but this did not stop it being expropriated from the "capitalist" Burma Oil Company by the (Burmese) Oil Workers' League, backed up by troops of the PVO (People's Volunteer Organization). Here is their programme for the "fête and gala" to celebrate this "victory".

Victory Celebrations over Expropriation of the Oil-field

The expropriation of the B.O.C and M.O.C. by the workers will be made ceremoniously according to the following programme on 24.9.49.

PROGRAMME

1. The sweeping and the cleaning of all houses and compounds and weeding in the oil-field shall be finished by the night of 22.9.49.
2. During the forenoon of 23.9.49, offering-to-the-*Nats* ceremony will be held at the two Companies.
3. At 6 o'clock that night there shall be a procession of people bearing torches and shouting slogans. All the workmen should gather at the appointed pandal at 5 p.m. exactly.
4. An orchestra will be in attendance at the pandal.
5. At 5 a.m. on 24.9.49 the workmen shall gather at the pandal wherein the ceremony will be held. (The flags of the companies will be flying near the pandal).
6. At 6 a.m. exactly the authorities of the companies concerned will lower the company flags.
7. Labour leaders will hoist the labour flag. (The Royal Drums should be sounded then).
8. As soon as the flag is at the top of the mast, a salute of guns will be fired and buzzers sounded to mark the expropriation of the oil-field.
9. Saluting the flag (Bugles/Trumpets in attendance).
10. At 6.30 a.m. the authorities of the companies will hand over the oil-field and necessary records/documents to the labour leaders.
11. After the handing over there shall be tremendous shouts.

RECEPTION

12. Music.
13. Tea Party to begin at 7.30 a.m.
14. Speeches.

BOC lived with this situation until fierce battles broke out between PVO and government, when they withdrew to Chauk, dismissing 2,000 workers.

Over the next ten years the economy was not the only problem, as rebel armies swept over the country, and students tried their hand at politics and strikes.

1953 **Anna Allott**

Diary notes and letters on Oct 53 Student Strike

Oct 11th Posters were stuck all over walls of Rangoon University, demanding 1 month's holiday. On Oct 2nd, students had clashed with police at Ava Hall!

Nov 1 Sun Previous Thursday - insurgents blew up Moulmein train, kidnapped (60?) 30 passengers including a student due to sit his exams.

Student politics as explained by girls at Inya Hostel:

Independent Students' Front - upper-class but without financial support from any political party - therefore have no funds. Used to be in a majority in the Students' Union, but were then replaced by Progressives and the government supported Democratic Students Organization (DSO).

My female informants (who are "independent") claimed that the DSO, with money from the government, rigged the Union elections in September 1953, and tried to win by printing 1000 extra ballot papers. Other students found out and burnt the ballot boxes, so the former committee was still in power (or there was no Student Union Committee for 1953-54).

Before the election the DSO had said they would fight for 30 days holiday, but after election they changed to supporting the government who had ordered a 15 day holiday. All other students claimed their full 30 days; it was called a "strike" by the government but the girls thought they were rightfully going home for a month as usual.

Government decided that the communists had instigated the strike; the girls didn't think so - saying that there are not more than a handful of communists among the 7,000 students. But others said the trouble had started because the government had introduced almost free education and so wanted to control the universities in exchange.

Rector Dr. Htin Aung was actually rather "helpless" (my comment).

Nov 21 Maymyo - Lashio train blown up by insurgents. 16 killed, 24 injured. Some students expelled after strike.

Nov 25 Rangoon-Maymyo train again blown up - 6 killed, 25 injured.

Dec 6 Headlines in The Nation about student riots - ! The boys it seems have been pretty violent and destructive - perhaps more should be ruthlessly expelled.

Letter Nov 12 The political situation is not happy, the country is far from being peaceful - the Chinese Nationalist army links up with the Karen rebels and the Communist insurgents, and the Burma army can't cope. People travel all over by plane.

There is a certain amount of unrest in the universities because the authorities are being "strict", and turning off all electric light from 11 p.m. to 6 a.m. - the students are pretty cross. It is claimed it is to save money. The hostel fees have been reduced to 57 Kyats a month.

Letter Dec 6 The student situation has worsened again. After expelling about 40 students 3 weeks ago, the authorities hoped everyone would be suitably intimidated. Far from it. Very soon groups of boys - including the expelled boys and girls - began 12-hour hunger strikes in front of University offices. In the evenings there have evidently been quite serious disturbances in the men's halls - lights have been fused again and again, tutors have been assaulted for carrying out their checking. Quite a lot of wanton destruction, breaking of locks, tearing down wiring over windows etc and finally all the large bulbs in the road lights leading to the convocation hall have been smashed. On several nights, the noise of the boys tramping round the compound and shouting for everyone to put out their lights as a protest against the electricity cuts has been terrific - but not so bad, I am told, as the night of Oct 2nd before I arrived, when the battle of Ava Hall was staged - police, hoses and live ammunition actually being used against the students. This subject of students makes headlines and leaders in many papers, and the general opinion is that the only way to stop it is to expel ruthlessly all offenders and trouble-makers. The girls' halls take no part in this and it doesn't interfere with our work. People say the communist students are at the bottom of it and that they are linked with the insurgents. What is more unpleasant is the fact that since 10 o'clock Thursday morning - it is now Sunday - Inya Hall has had no water!! It seems that our pump which pumps from our artesian well has broken down and so far it hasn't been mended. Goodness knows how long this will last. If it wasn't for the fact that only the matron and I use our lavatory, I should have to leave the hostel. The smell from the washrooms gets pretty bad by the morning - though they use plenty of disinfectant.

1960 — Nick Fenn

In 1960 an Australian agronomist came to the Irrawaddy Delta where the best rice in the world grew by mistake in a kind of wild profusion. He brought to Burma the benefits of the Green Revolution - new strains of rice, new methods of crop rotation, irrigation and fertilisation. He taught them, quite literally, how two blades of rice could grow where one had grown before. The villagers were delighted and eagerly adopted all the new methods.

A year later he went back to see the results of his labours. He found that indeed they had doubled the yield of their paddy fields. But instead of doubling their production they had halved the acreage, securing the same amount of rice for half the work. They value leisure more than wealth. They were grateful to have more time to sit under a palm tree discussing the universe. They were very good at it.

The Director of the Agricultural and Rural Development Corporation was equal to the

Traditional ploughing with bullocks, near Amarapura.

challenge. He introduced western cosmetics into the village store. The younger women quickly developed a taste for make-up. They had ways of their own to make their husbands increase their income to pay for these expensive foreign products. And, little by little, the lost acreage came back into production. The Green Revolution prevailed in the Delta.

1969 **Patricia Herbert**

The Rangoon International Cook Book is not an obvious introductory guide to Burma, but it is the first book on Burma that I owned. Published by the Women's Society of Christian Service of the Methodist English Church in Rangoon, its foreword described Rangoon as "most cosmopolitan of cities", and listed major companies and stores, many founded under British rule - for example, Chas C Cowie, Finlay, Fleming & Co., S. Oppenheimer & Co., Rowe & Co., Dalhousie Stores - and carried advertisements for all sorts of products and services, among them Nescafé, Cow & Gate ('the food of royal babies'), Air-India, the Rangoon Dairy Farm and Golly Milk Bar, Tiger Balm, and the Burma Gem House. The recipes in the book were truly international and had been contributed by ladies of all nationalities from Rangoon's diplomatic, business, missionary, nursing and educational communities, as well as by such eminent Burmese ladies as Daw Khin Kyi, widow of Burma's national hero, General Aung San, and Daw Mya Sein, historian and only woman delegate to the Burma Round Table Conference of 1931-32.

By the time I went to Burma in 1969 the world of the Rangoon International Cook Book had almost disappeared. Under peeling paint on crumbling facades in downtown Rangoon, the names of old trading companies and institutions could sometimes just be discerned. The western recipes in the Rangoon Cook Book required ingredients like fresh butter, milk, cheese, oatmeal and chocolate that were now unobtainable, leaving one free to concentrate on local recipes. But even Burmese ingredients could be a problem since the 'Burmese Way to Socialism' introduced by Burma's ruling Revolutionary Council meant in practise that many items were rationed, families being entitled to fixed quantities of rice, cooking oil, condensed milk, soap etc per month, at the People's Cooperative Stores. Families supplemented their rations by buying in the black market, while the poorest often preferred to sell or barter their inadequate allowance of one tin of condensed milk a month. The Nescafé and Horlicks advertized in the Cook Book's pages were now exotic luxuries, only to be found as solitary jars perched on a blackmarket stall at a price beyond most people's reach. All foreign companies as well as some Burmese enterprises had been nationalized and many Indian traders and immigrants had left, not always voluntarily. The country was effectively closed - a passport for Burmese to travel abroad was only issued under the most stringent and expensive of conditions, while entry visas were initially restricted to a 24 hour transit visa, later extended to a one week tourist visa. The newspapers carried pictures of dutiful citizens joining in street cleaning and other similar cooperative community projects, and of smiling model workers and youth pioneers. At school, children learnt to chant the rhyme:

Tit, hnit - Hsoshelit (One, two - Socialist)
Thon, lei - Lok-a pei (Three, four - Volunteer labour)
Nga, chauk - Ayin-shin pyauk (Five, six - Out with capitalists)
Hkunit, shit - Amyo-tha chit (Seven, eight - Be patriotic)
Ko, Tahse - Aung myin me (Nine, ten - Victory will be ours)

By the 1970s, it was hard to believe the world of the Rangoon International Cook Book had ever existed and indeed a young Burman, born and brought up in the military socialist period, to whom I showed the book thought that it must date from the colonial 1920s, when in fact it was published in 1958. Perhaps only now, some forty years on, is an international presence returning to Yangon.

1969 - Full Moon — Peter Smart

Gentle smiles light up so much of Burmese life, and no more so than at the age-old full moon festivals held at pagodas up and down the country.

In the late sixties, huge crowds converged as they still do on major pagodas in the larger towns. And country people swarmed in their hundreds on foot or by bullock cart to the more modest rural shrines. The festivals, often coming at the end of the busy harvest season, afforded a brief day or two for celebration and relaxation, for dressing up and winding down. Smiles.

For most, the pagoda terrace was the first port of call, to kneel before the small altar representing the week day of their birth, to place a posy of flowers, to light a candle and to breathe a private prayer. Then a quiet perambulation of the pagoda as the sun beat down; men and boys, unusually spruce; women and girls more graceful and pretty than ever in their finest clothes and jewellery and cheeks powdered with *thanakha*; and flashes of saffron from monks mingling with the visitors. Worshippers sharing with all within earshot, the merit they acquired by striking a temple bell. Pi-dogs scavenging, peeing and snapping as they quartered the oven-hot platform. And, wherever one looked, images of the Buddha in stone, wood, plaster, bronze or gilt, serenely contemplating the passing crowds.

Time then, perhaps, to go to the lower grounds of the pagoda to share in the festival's more worldly pleasures: lines of tempting stalls with vendors of wok-fried batter cakes, of sticky sweets, try-your-skill attractions with air guns and coconuts; fortune-tellers revealing your fate whilst telling you how to survive or pre-empt it; tattooists hemmed in by myriad illustrations of their extravagant art. Dust, colour, odours, heat, gentle bustle and the omnipresent smiles.

At sunset and moonrise the entertainments begin. A magician opens his booth and, after some routine trickery, spirits his glamorous assistant into thin air before your very eyes. The *pwes* (sometimes as many as six), which will each entertain until dawn their audiences of some 2,000, get ready for their non-stop programme of traditional dance, comedy and melodrama. And puppet theatres begin their all-night show.

The humbler festival may boast only one of these dusk-to-dawn diversions. Indeed, that at the Kyaikkauk Pagoda, seemingly remote from the capital (but only ten miles distant across the swirling muddy waters of the Rangoon River) had only a single puppet show when we went there. Unaccountably, it was preceded by a jerkily projected, distressingly boring, black-and-

One of the many pagodas near Syriam.

white film of the treatment of cross-eyed children in the England of the 1930s. But the audience was both attentive and happily diverted.

For us the Kyaikkauk experience was a special one, since we viewed the night's proceedings from the top of an ox-cart at the invitation of a landless peasant who had borrowed it for the day and had backed it, alongside many others, into a semi-circle to form a temporary amphitheatre.

At first light, when the crowds began to disperse, we trundled with him, his wife and two children, whom she had been suckling all night, to their one-roomed dwelling, perched on stilts at the edge of a clearing. In a trice she had pursued a scrawny chicken and, within the hour, had converted it into a memorable curry breakfast. Smiles.

In the 1950s and 1960s, the Burmese government strove to get on top of its many problems while rejecting help from abroad. Progress was slow, but it did exist. One outside visitor in the mid-60s was Professor Alan Woodruff - whom we met earlier as husband of Helen Woodruff - a doctor in the London School of Hygiene and Tropical Medicine, and he was very favourably impressed with what was being achieved despite appalling conditions. Here, in abbreviated form, is the article he wrote about it in 1967:

26 August 1967
Article in the BRITISH MEDICAL JOURNAL
by Professor Alan Woodruff

Medicine in Burma Today

Very great developments have taken place in Burma, and particularly in the medical services in Burma, over the past two decades, and a new administrative organization of these services was inaugurated on 1 January 1965. Little has been heard of these developments in Britain or elsewhere, yet they are remarkable and important. Remarkable in that they have been carried out without any considerable amount of external aid and in this way differ fundamentally from those which have taken place in Africa. Important in that very great emphasis has been given to taking medical services to the people in rural areas, an aim which has defeated the health administrators of many tropical countries...

First a word about why comparatively little is known of these developments outside of Burma. The short answer is, of course, that in recent years Burma has been relatively isolated; the passionate and understandable desire which the Burmese have for complete independence led them to leave the Commonwealth and, as a corollary to this, to make themselves ineligible for aid extended to Commonwealth countries. Likewise, in 1953 Burma terminated the arrangements which they then had for aid from the United States Government... No doubt material developments could have taken place more rapidly had large-scale aid been accepted, but this desire for independence, so passionately cherished by the Burmese people, is something which has won widespread respect. They, like everyone else, realize that South-east Asia is now and for some time has been in a highly inflammable state and they have no wish to become another Vietnam. Their country has in the last 20-odd years been torn by war several times. A result is that only recently have they begun to see the end of a phase of national reconstruction.

In reconstructing their country after all this trouble the Burmese people have a great desire to weave all that is best of their ancient culture into national development in its modern sense... Gaiety and a capacity for friendship and hospitality are outstanding characteristics of the Burmese, and colour is one of the most striking characteristics of the country.

This desire for colour is of course very obvious in the dress of the tribespeople from around the periphery of Burma. As we all know, there have been differences of opinion between these groups and the central government, and the present aim is to bring about their integration with the peoples of Burma proper. With this object a school for national groups has been established at Sagaing, and here selected young persons are brought together for periods of a year and trained in local government, so that on returning to their homes they will be able to take a prominent part in running local affairs. I visited the Academy, and certainly they were an exceedingly happy group obviously getting on well together...

Conclusion

Burma is an exciting place to be in; the Burmese are working very hard with comparatively little and they are doing things in a very workmanlike way... The Burmese are keen to have constructive criticism, and throughout my visit it was emphasised that they wanted that, not praise. Behind all this activity is their Prime Minister, General Ne Win, with his solid practical approach. I came away with very great admiration for the approach to medical problems which is being followed in Burma, and I am sure that there are opportunities for cooperation between our two countries in this field. We can probably help with selected personnel, and an epidemiologist for the new school of preventive and tropical medicine has already been seconded from the Department of Clinical Tropical Medicine, London School of Hygiene and Tropical Medicine. The fund of good will towards British people in Burma is immense. If their material resources could match their goodwill, the Burmese would indeed be ideally placed. There is much to be learnt from the way many things are being tackled in Burma, and especially in the medical sphere, where dealing with large problems of disease is being imaginatively undertaken with limited resources. The Burmese have much to be congratulated upon. We for our part can help in various ways in this venture, and it is here, in increasing co-operation between the two countries, that this article may perhaps bear results.

NB - We thank the BMJ Publishing Group for permission to publish this article (see copyright page at the start of this book).

GENERAL NE WIN

General Ne Win, who was Commander-in-Chief at the time of Independence, was the effective ruler of Burma, under various titles, from his military coup in 1962 up to 1988. Yet remarkably few details of his personal life have ever emerged. Helen and Alan Woodruff were some of the handful of people outside his family who knew him well over a long period. This happened because the World Health Organization gave Burma a large sum in medical aid at the end of the 1960s and Professor Woodruff, whose article had helped prompt it, was asked to advise on how the aid could best be used.

1965-85
Helen Woodruff (interviewed by Editor)

Q: When did you first meet General Ne Win?

A: We first met him in the mid 1960s as a result of my husband's job. Alan was Professor of Tropical Medicine, but often asked to travel to overseas medical centres to examine and advise; and so he was invited to go to Burma. He heard that the Burmese Medical Association were doing very noble work as compared with other tropical countries, considering the difficulties, their history and the Japs, they were trying hard and so he wanted to help them. He mentioned that in this paper that he wrote for the British Medical Journal and then he was asked if he could go out with a neurosurgeon from University College Hospital. This was Mr. Bernard Harries' first trip to the tropics and he was quite horrified when he met outsize Burmese insects and frogs and so on - and I couldn't help smiling, and thinking of the difference in atmosphere from his hospital theatre in England, where he was the Big Boss.

We had quite long chats with General Ne Win - my husband particularly - I was there as well sometimes and his wife Katie (Daw Khin May Than) was there too. She was most interested. I think she had a little more time than the general. Alan and Bernard together were suggesting places where the World Health Organization money would be most useful for increasing efficiency. However, the Burmese medical establishment needed help in so many ways, so it was a matter of where they could best give help, and where it was most needed, and whether it was to be money towards a new sick quarters or a small hospital or theatre here or laboratory there. Or staffing of these places - and medical schools started up, or more students able to get help to go there.

Q: You were saying earlier how much General Ne Win relied on the practical talents of his wife Katie. Was she a big help in organising the way the money was employed?

A: Yes, she was wonderful. And General Ne Win was very much backing her up. But I expect she had more time than he did. I know when my husband went back three years later, he was very impressed with what had been done and where it had been done - things that he and Bernard Harries between them had suggested they might do if they could with this money. So that was a big feature in the relationship of the Burma Medical Association and the British Medical Association.

Q: What impression did you form of the General?

A: We stayed at State House several times, with the General and Katie and we used to have quite long talks in the evenings and I was able to ask various things. We were taken to see a place in the Arakan which the General told us about. He was trying to get the various ethnic groups - the Arakanese and the Kachins and the other tribes - I forget which ones now - and was very keen that they should keep their own way of life - but also that they should get on with each other because there have been difficulties - not only in tropical countries - between the different varieties of people that live in these countries. Several institutions had been set up - like a big sort of school. They still had their own way of life, yet lived together amicably, they did a lot of good work on that. And we felt that he was very good.

Q: What did Ne Win think of the British?

A: I had the impression that Ne Win got on well with the British - though of course he was very keen to be independent. Maybe he was too polite to say what he actually thought of us!

Q: Yet he was not keen to ask for aid from Britain?

A: I asked him this once. After being in Burma a while we had noticed the dilapidation of Rangoon, and later this became even more apparent when we were flying back home via Bangkok. And of course Thailand was having a lot of American aid building things up and it looked absolutely terrific after just a year or two. Whereas Rangoon was pathetic. And they were always short of money in Rangoon. The thing I remember asking Ne Win was - whether we could do anything to help - but he said, if we take it from you, we have to take it from China and even from Russia. That's just what he told me. Of course I didn't quite understand it then. And while we were out there the Moscow Ballet came you know - they made a great fuss of that - I thought how extraordinary: out here seeing the Moscow *corps de ballet*! And that was part of it. They did take aid from Australia, which is interesting.

Some people thought the General was something of a communist but I got the impression that he certainly wasn't, I mean he had to fight alongside the Japs at one stage but I think many Burmese thought at the time that when the Japs had got through Burma into India, they would leave it to itself and Burma could maintain its independence. And that's what he was really desperately needing. And he was, I thought, pretty fair. Having met the man I got a feel of camaraderie - well, we were good friends!

General Ne Win accompanying Princess Alexandra around Pagan in 1962.

Q: How did he get on with China?

A: He was not at all for the Chinese. Because they were communists. And the northern part of Burma has got several hundred miles of frontier onto China. We met an awfully nice chap - we called him Mo, I don't know what his real name was, and I suppose he was a sort of bodyguard for the General. My two sons, Arnold and Peter, and my daughter Heather were with us at the time - they were about 13, and he was so kind to them - they adored Mo and he was often sent up near that China border and then we heard very sadly that he was killed up there and we thought that he was just finding out what was happening, because the Chinese used to come over and take some of the villagers from the villages nearby and indoctrinate them and then send them back to their own villages to do a little pro-communist doctrination. So we were led to believe, and because he was such a jolly nice chap we were (*unable to speak*).

Q: You knew the Ne Win family in a social way?

A: Both Ne Win and his wife were very kind and friendly to us. Well, we stayed with them and we used to have meals with them, and there were just the four of us. We were out there for a month or two at a time - and in all I think we must have met five or six times out there, and they came to London, and we had them out to tea and this sort of thing.

Q: Did you have to worry about how you behaved, or what you wore to dinner, or what you said, or anything like that?

A: I don't remember anything like that. Not as if they were royalty inthe UK, nothing like that. One would hope that one would look respectable.

Q: And you all went up to Arakan together?

A: I don't think the general was there, though - the family were. The children did a lot of swimming with our children, a terrific lot of swimming. The children got to know each other very well. The children were normally together, and we were together, but we knew them fairly well. Sanda was a nice child - we knew her best. They all got on well.

Q: How did this work together with the ordinary population?

A: They kept rather... well, there were these - I think they were relations - of Katie and so on. They lived near by and they used to see a lot each other a lot and they took us to see an awful lot of places. Not the General - Katie came with us - and we did go seeing all the sights that there were to see around.

Q: People recognised her?

A: We used to go to pagodas and things. I think sometimes they were greeted by people, at other times not.

Q: Like our own Royal Family, to that extent?

A: Not to that extent, I think, but always friendly. I suppose they were busy with their own work. They had people to look after them. I don't remember a lot of servants around, but I suppose there must have been.

Q: General Ne Win was reputed to have had quite a temper - is that true?

A: I never saw any of that but I wouldn't say... We used to talk with them till 11 at night. But that's different; I can imagine that if he had high ideals about how things were done and people didn't do as he wanted or behaved in a stupid way, I can imagine that he could be like that, but he never was as far as we were concerned. It would come out in his treatment of his family and I don't remember that at all, they seemed to get on well together. They were not all that much together that I can remember. Their children were with our children as I say - but our children only came out twice.

Q: And Katie died quite early, didn't she?

A: Yes, it was very sad. She had kidney trouble and they sent out specialists because at that time it was difficult to deal with kidneys and I know our people in Britain tried to help - and sent one or two very knowledgeable people over, to see if they could do anything, but it was not possible in those days to...

I'm afraid the General took it very badly. He was very fond of Katie - as were we, and we know that she used to read all the British papers before and after breakfast and she had a good idea of what was going on overseas. She was a great help to her husband. And she was a very pleasant person - as were her friends; I don't know if they were friends or relations. I can't remember Burmese names; but they were Margaret and Sue;

and Amy was another. They were always there when we went out - and they came to visit us in Britain - came to tea, etc.

Q Was your husband physician to Gen Ne Win?

A: No. He may have advised him privately, but I wouldn't have known anything about that.

Q: Did you know the General after Katie died?

A: Yes, but I didn't even know he married again after Katie. In 1985 - we were in the Sudan - and we were invited to go back, so we took time off, to see them again. Not Katie of course. General Ne Win came over to Britain at one stage. He did see a doctor, but it wasn't my husband. My son is also a doctor - we went to see him together, purely non-professionally, in his nursing home. We wished him well and so forth but it was quite a short visit and he wasn't feeling too good then.

1982 Patricia Herbert

Rangoon motorists, bus, taxi and sidecar drivers in the 1960s and 70s were accustomed to being signalled to slow down and pull to the side of the road by truckloads of soldiers, who would deploy themselves along the roadsides and occupy front gardens flanking the route taken by a procession of black official cars on the way to the airport or the golf course. The cars swept by so fast that it was impossible to see the shadowy figure of the occupant, "Number One", General Ne Win.

I could not foresee as I waited at the roadside that in the early 1980s I would be invited to meet the general and would hear some of his reminiscences of the 1930s and 40s. One story he told of the early days of the Burma Independence Army during the Japanese occupation was about nine BIA members complaining in a letter about "daily matters" to Bo Mogyo (Colonel Suzuki, the Japanese officer who had recruited and trained the wartime "thirty comrades"). They were summoned immediately to report to Bo Mogyo, but only seven of the nine went and were shown into a room where there were six or seven Japanese standing with half-drawn swords.

Bo Mogyo came clattering down the stairs, like thunder, and entered the room wearing full dress uniform. On a table in the room in a silver bowl on a wooden block was their letter. Bo Mogyo speared the letter with his sword and held it out, saying, "You are like my children. Children do not write such things to their father. Complaints should only be spoken." He was lividly angry and everyone became red-faced as the tension mounted. Aung San was the only armed BIA member present and his hand went to his sword, but was checked by Shu Maung (Ne Win) touching his arm.

Then Aung San replied to Bo Mogyo saying: "We have been complaining verbally for ten days and now you have a letter you can show as evidence of what we say". Only then did Bo Mogyo begin to smile and ordered drinks to be served.

A shorter slightly different version of this incident is given by Dr Maung Maung, a friend and confidant of U Ne Win, in his book *Burma and General Ne Win*.

MORE BURMESE PEOPLE

1983 **Daw Kyi Kyi May**

Burmese elders are very fond of giving nicknames to babies. I'm not sure whether the British are like that or not; but I think a British person will be more restrained to comment openly to the proud parents that their offspring's nose is flat or that he or she has slitty eyes like the Chinese. In Burma, a maiden aunt or an outspoken grand uncle will never hesitate to point out that the baby is very dark by giving him a nickname "*kalar lay*" or "*pho kalar*" right on the spot, superseding the parents while they are racking their brains to come up with the most beautiful name for their child.

As everyone knows we are situated between the two most populous nations of the world, India and China; many Burmese people are either "*kala-sin*" (taking after the Indians) or "*ee-san-kwar*" (of Chinese descent) in the eyes of family and relatives. The funny thing is they never keep their observations to themselves and the parents do not take it as an insult unless it goes too far. Therefore, if one looks around or does a survey, one will find that there are more than a few with nicknames such as "*kalar*" or "*kalarma*", "*tayoke*" or "*tayokema*" (Indian or Indian girl, Chinese or Chinese girl) among the Burmese families with no apparent strain of either blood in their veins. Are we very colour conscious, I wonder?

One of my American friends commented several years ago that the Burmese are very colour conscious. I looked around me and have to agree with her absolutely. Yes, we are very conscious of the colour of our skin as well as of other people! In Rangoon, if you walk through the downtown area you will overhear local girls and boys whispering at each other if there is a tourist with a white skin in their vicinity saying "*hla de naw*" (isn't she pretty or handsome according to the gender). That particular person might not be good-looking at all but in the eyes of the people with brown skin, a white skin is something to be admired and looked at. I felt sorry for the tourist especially if she is a woman because she could not move an inch without being scrutinised by at least twenty pairs of eyes.

It is good to be frank and direct at times but I have often felt that the Burmese elders are quite cruel to the young ones, making jokes of their "not-so-pretty" features. And, names like *kalarma*, *"zee kwet"* (owl due to big eyes), or *"lan bar"* (lanky chap) etc remain with the person throughout their life. He or she may have grown up to become a famous surgeon or a learned professor of mathematics but he would still be addressed as *"lan bar"* by his doting uncle whenever he has to go and pay respects to him.

After getting this far, I suddenly realised that the British are the same, too, after all. Prince Charles, the heir to the throne, has been ridiculed all through these years because of his big ears by the press. I hope his family is more kind towards him than a Burmese family with its extended relatives!

1971 Patricia Herbert

One of my favourite recipes in the *Rangoon International Cook Book* is Daw Khin Kyi's chicken curry. I was not to know when I arrived in Burma that for the next three years and on subsequent return visits I would be invited nearly every week to lunch at Aunty's lakeside home.

I treasure and revere the friendship and true loving kindness that Daw Khin Kyi extended to me. She had enormous presence and dignity, and a most distinctive voice, and lived quietly, seldom going out. After lunch we would walk round her beloved garden and she would point out her favourite plants - arum lilies, and limes on the little lime tree outside a door - and her latest horticultural experiments: growing coffee and pepper. Sometimes we would sip tea in the little pavilion she had built on the lakeside edge.

Not being a brash journalist, I never presumed to ask her about the personal tragedy that was also the nation's great tragedy, the assassination of her husband, General Aung San. She had told me that people often asked her if she was lonely and that she always replied that they shouldn't be so impertinent and that she kept very busy. She said she was conscious that she should set an example and that because of the loss she had suffered and because she had principles she could thereby help others.

When I left Burma Aunty Daw Khin Kyi gave me a beautiful silk *htamein* (*longyi* for woman), in dark green shot with purple, and of a quality no longer obtainable. I treasure it greatly.

1960 **Nick Fenn**

When I was a language student in Mandalay in 1960, I struck up a friendship with Ludu U Hla, the charming and cultivated editor of the local communist newspaper "Ludu - The People". He wrote a marvellous Burmese style, at once elegant and simple, so that even I could understand it. I took to reading the communist newspaper in preference to more pretentious journals which would no doubt have been preferred by my masters in Rangoon.

U Hla did us the honour of dining with us one evening, together with a number of other Burmese language pundits. To my astonishment, he wrote about the evening in his column the following day, amused to find a young Englishman who was trying to learn his language and whose beautiful wife served excellent Burmese food. With much travail, I composed a careful letter of thanks for his kindness - and he published my letter! Thus began a public correspondence which continued throughout our stay in Mandalay and greatly improved my use of Burmese idiom.

My wife and I went to stay with friends in Hong Kong for Christmas. On return to Mandalay, I composed an account of our visit, including the contrast between the wealth of the skyscraper culture and the poverty of the refugees from communism, who lived in shacks clinging to the hillside. I was pleased with myself for getting this implicit reference to the failure of Chinese communism into a Burmese communist newspaper. Unfortunately the Information Officer in the Embassy in Rangoon had this passage translated and included it in the Ambassador's weekly summary of the Burmese language press. This drew a formal rebuke: British officials should not attack colonialism in communist newspapers.

My correspondence with U Hla was more circumspect thereafter.

1985 **Daw Kyi Kyi May**

I have many English friends with whom I would go out for picnics during the summer months in London. After laying down our food and drink etc under a shady tree my friends will choose to sit right out in the blazing sunshine while I and other friends from the East will try and find excuses to stay in the shade. My French and German friends want to get their skin tanned as much as possible while we, who already have a year-round tan, do not want to give ourselves a headache by sitting in the sun. They tease us with not wanting to get our skins more tanned while we jokingly retort with Noel Coward's "mad dogs and Englishmen go out in the midday sun." Oh, that reminds me of something else. When we are asked what sort of drink would we want to have when being invited to British homes I have found the Burmese to be reluctant to say outright what they want. A westerner might think we could not make up our minds even on a simple matter like choosing beverages. We would just say "*ya-bar-de*" which means "Anything you have will do", so that the host need not lose face if what we demand might not be available. As a Burmese guest, the rule is not to embarrass the host by asking for this or that, but take what the host has to offer. There has been many an occasion when people who do not eat beef at home will close their eyes and swallow down pieces of meat because they do not want to offend or embarrass their host by not eating their specially cooked meal. Mind you, that is just between Burmese themselves. I think most of the British who have friends in Burma have sometimes been unable to refuse Burmese hospitality and have to eat plate after plate of admittedly delicious cooking.

1936 **Maureen**

As for my mother, I try to see her as others did, but I was so attached to her that I would fail. She was very pretty, pale and had a gentle, serene appeal, even when her face was in repose. Clothes, jewellery and pretty flowers were her delight and long was the time spent dressing her ankle-length hair. It was such a treat to be allowed to watch her getting ready to go out. She seemed to have three separate styles for doing her hair. For every day it was coiled into a gentle knot on the nape of her neck, held in position with an ivory comb with a circlet of jasmine. For festive but informal occasions it would be wound into a topknot, but a loop of it was allowed to trail over one ear. For very formal affairs a great deal more attention had to be paid and some help from her mother or a friend enlisted as her hair would have to be coiled most carefully and smoothly on the top of her head in a sort of cylinder shape and kept in place with hairpins and ornaments.

A Burmese maiden.

1983 **Daw Kyi Kyi May**

Burmese people are very polite by nature but we do not use the expression "thank you" as often as westerners do. Especially when someone comments on my scarf or my jacket or the flower I am wearing on my hair, in Burma, I would not need to say anything except a shy smile as acknowledgement. Sometimes just out of shyness a woman would softly say "*ma hla bar bu*" (I'm not pretty) after someone praises her good looks. But here in Britain people say "thank you" if someone comments on something about you. In the beginning it was a bit awkward for us to accept the praise by saying thank you because it means that we are pompous enough to accept that we are pretty or what we are wearing is good.

AND FINALLY...

1965 - Cheroots — Helen Woodruff

Q: You once said "Burmese cheroots were nearly the ruin of me!"

A: They were the first things we were taken to buy, on our first visit to Burma. I'd heard about these cheroots before we went out - so we got some. I must say I was a heavyish smoker of cigarettes, and wanted to give them up very badly but couldn't - and then I got myself onto cheroots. And people were most generous - and thanks to the General, we always came back to England with boxes of cheroots, and I found they kept longer if you took them out of the boxes and put them in these big tin plaster containers that we had in hospital and we used to keep them for quite a while. They were the last things I gave up when I was giving up smoking and they were supposed to be less poisonous than cigarettes - the nicotine in cigarettes was stronger than the cheroots, which were larger and more loosely packed.

I used to smoke more when I was doing things that I didn't like than when I was relaxing, and I hated washing up, so I always used to smoke a cheroot over the washing-up bowl. It's very difficult to wash up with a cheroot in your mouth but I got quite skilled. They were about seven inches long - quite big and thick.

Q: Did you smoke cheroots in the Ritz?

A: No, we were not regulars at the Ritz, but I used to smoke them at home, and one or two of my friends smoked with me and Alan. I sometimes offered them around. Mind you, people were rather scared of them, but once they'd smoked them, yes, well, I wouldn't let them get in the habit of it!

1971 - A Rare Climb — Peter Smart

In the early seventies, Rangoon was rattled by minor tremors and the umbrella (*hti*) at the top of the Shwedagon Pagoda was knocked slightly askew. The authorities decided it should be examined and resecured. Bamboo scaffolding soon enveloped the pagoda and work began.

Through the good offices of a monk living at the Shwedagon I was permitted to scramble to the top in stockinged feet to see, at eye level, the incredible profusion of inlaid precious stones on the umbrella and on the bud and vane above it.

My new ambassador had just arrived in post and I contrived to arrange an ascent with him. As we looked down dizzyingly at the pagoda's subsidiary buildings and its surroundings and as we marvelled at the rich encrustations of diamonds, rubies and emeralds, the repair work was declared complete and three workmen began dismantling the scaffolding, beginning with the topmost bamboo poles on which we had just been steadying ourselves.

We were, I believe, the last of very few Westerners to enjoy the immense privilege of such a climb - and one which His Excellency Edward Willan later confessed he had completed only by struggling against a life-long terror of heights.

1979 - Water Festival — Kenneth Watts

Each year, the Burmese Foreign Office invited the Diplomatic Corps to take part in the Water Festival in Rangoon, and, as UNDP Resident Representative in the late 1970s, my wife and I were included in this invitation. The following is my diary entry for Sunday, the 15th April 1979, which gives an account of this occasion.

"We are up early and off to the Foreign Office grounds, where we indulge, and are indulged, in water festivities. U Kauk, our driver, takes us and as usual drops us on the welcoming line, where immediately buckets of water are tipped over us. This dowsing - the first among many - really does make me shiver as the water goes down my spine. About ten people on the line leave us all thoroughly wet to the skin. There is a dance troupe entertaining us with drums, a very happy atmosphere prevailing. A long boat is set up full of water, and people are encouraged to splash the other guests. I find myself opposite Daw Than Han (a senior diplomat in the FO), who, equipped with a small bowl, contrives to drench me very efficiently. The boat is surrounded by the crowd (of ambassadors and foreign office staff), and becomes a flurry of flung water. The dance goes on, now performed by a transvestite dancer, squatting down with that strange bent-arm, puppet-like style that the Burmese have. The beat pervades the gathering, heightening the excitement. We are invited to take tea and some fried confections. We laugh and joke, the girls come round with bowls of water and pour it down our backs...

"Eventually, we embark on buses, and drive up Prome Road, where pandals (decorated stage-like constructions) are set up along the side of the road. In the most primitive form, these are no more than bamboo shelters with palm fronds draped around them. But the most elaborate have stages with bands, and in front are lines of young people equipped with hoses.

"The town is full of open jeeps and trucks, densely packed with other youngsters who caper and shout and blow whistles. They line up at the pandals to have water squirted at them - in fact the scene with its concentrations of hoses, its devotion to the making of an object wet, and its single-minded, whole-hearted attainment of this objective, reminds me of a fire brigade dealing with a particularly difficult fire. Except that no fire ever receives the concentration of effort that these vehicles do in sheer volume of water, and no fire is the object of such jubilation. Water pours down on the dancing, shouting, whistling throng. Each wagon gets its share and it then moves on; and as they pass, they gesticulate and cheer. There is no malice here - or at least, I could see none - just a controlled release of high spirits, a splendid display of exuberance, which leaves them exhausted.

"Our buses arrive at the Lanzin Youth pandal, and we run the gauntlet of those merciless hoses and sit in our soggy seats, and a young girl - miraculously dry - announces in English that the Lanzin Youth are the future leaders of Burma, that they welcome us and will display some dances. The band strikes up and the dancers come on, capering gaily, and cups of coffee are handed round. We watch for 20 minutes, and then go through the hose cannonade once again. But the tales of water cannons that we heard from last year were much exaggerated. These hoses transmit the maximum amount of water to the victim, but as gently as possible.

"We drive down Prome Road to City Hall. Our buses are always parked in such a way that we have to walk past the hose barrage... An elaborate pandal has been erected in front of the Hall, and there are dances going on. We are given seats in the sun across the road in front, and the drenched procession of possessed youths in their jeeps passes between us and the stage.

"Afterwards, we go on the Customs House, where the dance performance is better. As we arrive, a young girl is giving a solo, singing to herself but her words are drowned out by the band. In her elaborate gown, she shuffles and elbows her way through the dance, totally absorbed. A troupe comes on, and then the puppet dance, very well done. We are set up on a covered-in stage to one side, off Strand Road, where the dripping trucks pass by, pausing in front of the stage with their passengers executing in unison the grotesque movements of the dance amid shrieks of applause from the onlookers. We are given soup here, cooked in enormous metal quallies over open fires inside the building...

"Off we go again, this time to the Construction Corporation, where U Soe Aung receives us. We are given soup and watch the performance. They perform the Karen dance, not with the same verve as the Karens themselves, but the catchy music is infectious. So that when people come round and ask us to go on the stage, I agree to go with Vlado Sestan (the Yugoslav Ambassador) and break the ice. We caper around for about 5 minutes or so, and then come down again. The dance goes on and on, and Joan (my wife) joins in as many others go up. And there's an end to it.

"We drive back to the Foreign Office, to a renewed barrage of water on arrival, more splashings at the boat, a good meal and at 1 p.m. it is all over.

"I am left with a very pleasant feeling about the whole thing. I was somewhat dreading it -

a duty to be undertaken, something to be endured. But the light-heartedness of it, the utter but controlled abandonment, the lack of ugliness in any form - all this I found quite unusual. Only in Burma, perhaps, could such an event take place peacefully and with such joy. Coming back, we pass vehicles with their delighted passengers, trailing water from every part. We return home and subside."

Dancing in the street - a Buddhist festival.

1971 **Peter Smart**

The leading dancer at the *pwe* had lived briefly in England some years before and spoke a precise English. I had met him in Rangoon. When he learnt that I was shortly to visit Mandalay, he invited me to go back-stage during the week that his *pwe* would be a central attraction of the town's major pagoda festival.

At two in the morning, it was his turn to perform a traditional dance before the all-night audience of some 3,000, squatting on mats in the company's cavernous temporary theatre of bamboo. As the curtain fell there was prolonged and tumultuous applause.

I remarked that it must be extremely satisfying for him, in the setting of Burma's ancient capital, to evoke such an enthusiastic response for the performance of a dance of such venerable tradition.

"Yes", he replied, "it is rather rewarding. But you know, Peter, my heart - my heart - is in Ipswich."

I was too taken aback to probe further.

1987 - Mandalay **Gerry Abbott**

When lectures were over or there wasn't any work to do, one of my greatest pleasures was to drive over and join the Burmese at their devotions in the nearby Hpaya-gyi. This was the name that my Mandalay University colleagues generally used when referring to what the guide-books called the Arakan (or Mahamuni) Pagoda. The original building had been erected on the orders of King Bodaw-hpaya to house the coveted Mahamuni Buddha-image, the greatest of the spoils brought back from Arakan in 1785 by the king's victorious army.

Having kicked off my Mandalay slippers and put them in my Shan shoulder-bag, I would stroll up one of the pagoda's four cool, shadowy arcades. To the sides were flower-sellers and vendors of artifacts, and astrologers and soothsayers, and dim alcoves with frescoes of various ages in all stages of dilapidation; nearer the shrine there would be a warm golden glow ahead, the smell of incense and flowers, murmurings of devotion and sometimes the sonorous tones of monks chanting. In the central hall, dimness gave way to colour and light. Coming into view like some massive sunken treasure lying on a sunlit sandy sea-bed was the Mahamuni image, bathed in light, encrusted with the gold deposited by wave on wave of humanity, and continuing to beam upon an ever-changing and never-dwindling congregation.

Here in front were the gold leaf sellers, always doing a roaring trade. I would stand to one side and watch the devout, mostly women it seemed, sitting quietly with their feet tucked respectfully away from the Enlightened One's sight. They would then kneel forward in an attitude of prayer, holding flowers or fresh *thabyé* leaves between their palms, the fingers splayed and held before the brow which they bent down to touch the ground. Then they would rise from their meditations, go to a little counter to buy a packet of gold leaf that they could ill afford and take it to the attendants, who would apply the gold according to the wishes of those making the offering. A rough measure of the Burmese people's veneration of this Buddha was the fact that in places the brass figure was coated with several inches of gold.

No-one ever found it odd that I should bend my awkward European frame so as to join the congregation, but unfortunately my joints were soon aching. I would rise stiffly from the marble floor, walk down a colonnade of massive square pillars with vermilion bases that supported a row of lofty gilded arches and wander outside in the blazing sun. Often I would hop across the scorching paving stones to strike my favourite bell three times with the butt of a stave so as to share *kutho* with all humankind, then retreat into the shade to observe the faithful as each washed one of the eight small marble Buddha images - the one that represented the sign under which he or she was born. Finally I would scamper across to the Cambodian bronze statues that had accompanied the Mahamuni image on its journey from Arakan to Bodaw-hpaya's court. If you had a bodily ailment you could cure it by stroking the corresponding part of one of the bronzes. I would always stroke the trunks of the three-headed elephant. My nose still gives me trouble, though.

1946 Glyn Court

Even as I write this, new memories appear out of the shadows, but they must wait. Old men forget, said the king, but some cannot forget Burma. Like Falstaff and Shallow and other greybeards now at rest, I too have heard the chimes at midnight - but more than that, I have feasted on *khow swe* - cooked over charcoal and eaten off banana leaves - at midnight in the Sule Pagoda Road;. and such memories, like the songs of the 'pleasant-voiced' nightingales for the Greek long ago, the years can never, never take.

1998 Pat Herbert

When I lived in Burma, puzzled Burmese friends occasionally asked me why I chose to be there - especially as some of them thought they would prefer life abroad - and tended to assume that I must have had colonial ancestors. I did not know myself why Burma so tugged at my heartstrings and will always be so dear to me, just as it is for many other *kala hpyu* (white foreigners) whom fate has brought into contact with that distant land and its people. But a very venerable aged Buddhist patriarch, U Wiseitathara, once told me that in the cycle of existence I was a daughter of Burma - words which touched me deeply and make me content to feel that in another life I must have truly belonged there and will one day return.

Appendix I: Britain-Burma Society - Notes on the Contributors

1. **Gerry Abbott**
He was nominated by the British Council for the job of senior lecturer in English at the University of Mandalay in 1986, and taught there for almost two years. Since 1965 he has been lecturing in The Teaching of English Overseas at the University of Manchester, but is now semi-retired as honorary fellow. He is married to Daw Khin Thant Han - formerly a lecturer in English in Burma. Books: *Back to Mandalay* (Impact Books, 1990); *Inroads into Burma*:(OUP; 1998); *'There Before You': The Traveller's History of Burma* (Orchid Press, 1998).
Pages 194-195.

2. **Mrs Anna Allott, OBE**

Her mother's country is Czechoslovakia. She started studying Burmese in 1952, at the age of 22. Her first visit to Burma (described here) was for nine months from Oct 53, to learn the language, and she has visited again in 1976, 1981, 1983, 1985, 1986, 1988, 1993, 1995 and 1998. She was Lecturer in Burmese at the London School of Oriental and African Studies till the end of 1990, and was Hon Secretary of the Britain-Burma Society for 16 years - from 1980 to the end of 1996. She was awarded an OBE in the 1998 New Year Honours "for her services to British-Burmese relations".
Pages 51, 71-72, 169-170.

3. **Mrs Elizabeth Bagshawe**
Née Melville, she married Clement Bagshawe in 1865 at the age of 26, and they set off straight away for the tea estate which he was to manage in Cachar, a remote corner of Assam just across the border from Burma. Our text starts with a quote from her diaries, which were considerable. After the period she describes, she and her husband managed the estate in Kuttlee Cherra for a number of years and their children were born there. This extract was contributed by her grandson, Leonard E Bagshawe, who lives in North Carolina, and is the translator of several important Burmese historical sources.
Page 1.

4. **Mrs Maureen Baird-Murray (née Rossiter): "MAUREEN"**

Born in the Shan States in 1933 of an Irish Assistant Superintendent and the beautiful Burmese village girl who was his wife. She went to school in Burma and stayed on through the Japanese occupation. Her story is told in *A World Overturned*, published in 1997 by Constable at £15.95 - from which all her accounts in these pages are taken.
Pages 11, 15, 24, 25-6, 45, 56, 66, 75, 129, 131, 132, 141, 142, 143, 187.

5. **Mrs Jessie Beale**

Née Bruce. Much of her story has already been told in these pages. Born into a poor family in Lambeth in 1906, she grew up in the grim years that surrounded the First World War; then spent several years in Burma married to a Forestry Officer; returning to the UK before World War Two. She died in 1985. Her autobiographical account is contributed by her son, Bruce Beale.
Pages 5-10.

6. **Evelyn Broughton-Smart (née Gaudoin) - "EVELYN"**

The daughter of a Shan princess and a Deputy Commissioner, she was brought up in 1930s Burma and was studying at Rangoon University when the war started. She spent the war in her uncle's palace in the Shan States; then won a scholarship to Michigan State University in the USA. She next married a superintendent in the Indian Police Service from Burma whom she had already met, and went with him to South Africa for two years. Since then Evelyn has lived in London, where she has been a teacher and brought up a family.
Pages 18, 27, 34, 49, 68, 103, 104, 130, 132, 133.

7. **Derek Brooke-Wavell (editor and contributor)**
Spent ten years managing the BBC's Burmese-language section. In this capacity he visited Burma in 1985, 1987, 1993 and 1994. Hon Secretary of the Britain-Burma Society since January 1997. Takes photography very seriously - with his own dark room since 1981, and has exhibited photos of Burma and China.
Pages i, 42.

8. **Dr Glyn Court**
After serving in the British Army in Burma from 1945-47, he took up modern language teaching, and took a Ph.D. in *The Literary Inspiration of Hector Berlioz*. From 1973 to 1989 he chaired a number of committees in Somerset County Council. Publications include: *Exmoor* (for the Countryside Commission); *West Somerset in Times Past*; *Carols of the West Country* (with music), plus more than 500 articles on the West of England, environment, rural problems, Anglo-Saxon England, music, history and languages.

Pages 41, 135, 139, 141, 155, 159, 161, 195.

9. **Mrs Mavis Edwards**
She arrived in Burma at the age of one - her father shuttled between there and India for the Post and Telegraph organization. From 1919 she went to a series of schools in Burma - and then attended the Teacher Training College in Maymyo. After the war, her husband Robert was Civil Surgeon in Myitkyina, where they settled. She returned to England in 1965, has eight grandchildren, and is on the Council of the Britain-Burma Society.
Pages 30-31.

10. **Sir Nicholas Fenn, GCMG and Susan Fenn JP**

Now retired after 37 years in the diplomatic service. Burma was his first post: vice-consul in Mandalay, then Third Secretary in Rangoon; then on to a series of extremely prestigious posts for such a young man, serving as Assistant Private Secretary to four British Foreign Secretaries in succession. He was Britain's Foreign Office Spokesman from 1979-82; then Ambassador in Burma from 1982-86. From 1991-96 he was British High Commissioner in India. In addition to his Presidency of the Britain-Burma Society he is now chief executive in Marie Curie Cancer Care, and chairs Encounter - a high-level forum on Ireland.

Lady Fenn, who gave her husband strong support in all his postings, is an accomplished photographer, and is now a Justice of the Peace. They live in Kent.
Pages 17, 21, 22, 60, 61, 73, 171, 186 (Sir Nicholas).
Pages 31, 44, 62, 73, 161 (Susan Fenn).

11. **Mrs Amy Fitzgerald (née Forbes-Mitchell)**

She left Rangoon in 1942 at the age of 11 - and has never been back, thus severing a long family connection with Burma. She was evacuated on an army plane from Shwebo, with thirteen other children and four mothers, on the return run to Calcutta of a Dakota that was bringing in relief supplies. Her family stayed in India till 1947; then came to the UK, where she went to school, and has devoted her life to nursing and bringing up a family. She lives in Hampshire.
Pages 56, 102.

12. **Tony Foucar**

Born in Burma, where his family had founded Foucar & Co, the teak firm. All this was lost when the Japanese invaded. Both he and his father served in Burma during the war. Since then he has had a successful career as a barrister, working in the insurance industry. He has a keen interest in modern military history.
Page 57.

13. **Patricia Herbert**

Patricia Herbert has lived several years in Burma - her last visit was in 1983 - and examined many an old Burmese manuscript. After returning from Burma she became Curator of the Burmese Collections at the British Library. She has published works on the Hsaya San rebellion of 1930-32, on the life of the Buddha illustrated from Burmese manuscript sources, and an annotated bibliography of Burma. Her own book collection on Burma, which began with the *Rangoon International Cook Book,* now numbers some 900 volumes. She is a Britain-Burma Society Council member.
Pages 162, 172, 182, 185, 195.

14. **Noel Holmes**

Born in 1931 in Maymyo. Now retired and living in the Midlands, after forty years working in market research for British Gas. He is a qualified umpire at cricket. He recently returned to his birthplace for a visit after fifty years.
Page 38.

15. **Bill Howe**

Who contributed the "programme of celebrations" to mark the takeover by the Burmese workers of the oil field at Yenan-gyaung in 1949. He first went out to Burma in 1931 to join the Anglo-Burma Rice Co. He had an "interesting" war, much of which was spent moving behind Japanese lines in the Kachin Hills, and for which he was awarded an MC. He then married in Rangoon, and returned to England to work in his family's market-garden business for 25 years, after which he sold up and worked for a housing association. He is now an insurance broker.
Page 168.

16. **Pat Kelly (now Maeve Reid) and Desmond Kelly MD, FRCP, FRCPsych**

Born in Loilem, Burma, in 1933 and 1934. Children of Norman Kelly, OBE, who stayed on in Burma behind Japanese lines to organize the Chin Levies, which with the 17th Indian Division held the Chin Hills from May 1942 until the spring of 1943. Maeve has worked all her life as a journalist, and now lives in Pembrokeshire. Desmond is Visiting Professor of Psychiatry at University College, London, and Medical Director of the The Priory Hospital, London. He lives in East Sheen, London.

Pages 106, 109, 114, 117.

17. **U Khin**

He graduated from Rangoon University in 1938, and later picked up MAs (in journalism and SE Asian history) at the universities of Minnesota and London. During the war he was in the civil service in what is now Karen State. He then worked for three years in Voice of America. Under U Nu he was Burma's Information Officer, then Deputy Director of Press and Public Relations. He was seconded to the BBC in 1966, but returned to be Director of Information. He retired from that in 1977 - and spent another 11 years with the BBC Burmese section. Former Deputy Chairman of the Britain-Burma Society and still on the Council, he is patron of three Buddhist viharas in the UK.

Pages 137-138.

18. **Sir Nick Larmour, KCMG and his wife Nancy**

Sir Nick was in Burma from 1945-48 - during the last part of which he was Deputy Secretary to the Governor. After Burma he worked in the diplomatic service for nearly 30 years; peaceful times barring some excitements over Suez and Nigeria. In his last three years in Whitehall, he was Assistant, then Deputy Undersecretary of State in the FCO. His greatest and longest contribution has been to Britain's process of decolonisation.

"Diplomatic wife" is a full time job, but Lady Larmour also found time for fund-raising, and teaching Braille in Singapore and Shakespeare in Jamaica.

Pages 148-149, 151-152, 156, 157-158, 159 (Sir Nick).

Pages 70, 160 (Nancy Larmour).

19. **Daw Kyi Kyi May**

Born in Burma and lived there until 1983. She read for B.Sc. and M.Sc. degrees in Zoology at Rangoon University; she was an information assistant in USIS Rangoon from 1977 to 1983 - and editor of *Lin Yaung Kyi*. Then in 1983 she joined the BBC Burmese Section in London, rising to Head of Section in 1997. She is well known in Burma for her "Paddy-Bird Club" children's programmes, which she created for many years. A Council member of the Britain-Burma Society.

Pages 164, 184, 187, 189.

20. **Stella McGregor - "STELLA"**

Born 1913 in Rangoon, where she lived (when not at school) till 1935 - when, at the age of 22, she suddenly had to leave Burma after the death of her father. She went on to marry and raise children in the UK - but when her husband died, she started to tell the story of her early life in Burma to her daughter Pauline, in a series of letters. These letters make the basis of Stella's contributions in the present anthology, and the complete collection will later be published under the title *Radiant Star*. Stella died in 1995.

Pages 2, 13, 27, 33, 34-38, 48, 49, 51, 52-54, 65, 66, 68-70, 79, 83-85, 96-100, 119-128.

21. **Mrs Sylvia Molloy - "SYLVIA"**

In Burma only from 1940 to 1942, though she came back briefly after the war. Her full story of those years can be read in *Burma Bride* (1996), obtainable from Molloy Publications (44) 1462 627986. Her husband was an Assistant Superintendent in the Shan States. After leaving Burma they went to India, the UK and South Africa, returning to England in 1963. Sylvia is an artist with scores of canvases to her credit - many of the subjects taken from visits to Egypt, Italy, Tunisia and other foreign destinations, as well as from her time in Burma.

Pages 2, 12, 19, 24, 28-29, 41, 43, 54, 60, 62, 74, 75, 78, 82, 87-95, 101, 104, 105, 107, 110, 160.

22. **John Okell**

Lecturer in Burmese at London School of Oriental and African Studies since 1959 - where he has passed on his enthusiasm to many groups of students. Latterly he has taught summer schools in the USA too. went to Burma in 1960-61, travelling on the same boat as Nick and Sue Fenn. He returned to Burma in 1969 (for 1 year), 1980 (3 months), 1991 and 1997. He is known among Burma computer users as the designer of the Avalaser Burmese font. Winner of the 1996 Tuttle Language Grant for East Asia Publication, for the quality of an all-audio Burmese language course. He is the Chairman of the Britain-Burma Society.
Pages 3, 46, 74.

23. **Philip Plumb**

He came into Burma with the British armed forces in 1945 and left in 1947. After that he worked in Hertfordshire County Library; he married and had five children. After a varied career as a librarian, he became Librarian of the University of East London, and in 1992 was President of the Libraries Association, in which capacity he paid an official visit to Burma. He was a Justice of the Peace for twenty-four years. He co-founded the WS Gilbert Society. He is now retired and lives in Hertfordshire.
Pages 20, 47, 145-146, 150, 153, 154.

24. **Edward Rossiter - father of "MAUREEN" (Baird-Murray)**
An Assistant Superintendent whose job took him over a wide tract of the Shan States. He took the northern - and quite untried - route into India at the time of the Japanese invasion. He survived the horrifying trek into Assam, and managed to shake off the effects of beri-beri, but died in Calcutta in 1942.
Pages 112-113, 115-117.

25. **Lewis Shaw**

In Burma 1945-47 as a member of the British forces. After leaving the Army he put his professional skills as a mechanical engineer to use in the plastics division of ICI, where he worked for 30 years. He had also acquired an interest in Burmese coinage, on which he has talked to the Britain-Burma Society. He revisited Burma briefly recently. He has three children and two grandchildren. Since retirement, he has been active in local organizations in the area of Poole, Dorset, where he lives. Book: *The Coins and Banknotes of Burma* (1981).
Pages 30, 81, 86, 134, 136, 140, 142, 144, 147, 154, 157.

26. **Elizabeth Shepherd**

A Britain-Burma Society member who now lives in Toronto. Born in Burma, she has had a successful career in acting - first in the UK, then the United States and now Canada. In the early days she had roles in a number of popular TV series like *Emergency Ward Ten*, as well as West End stage roles in *Inherit the Wind* and *War & Peace.* Then she emigrated to the United States in 1965, again combining television acting with Broadway. She has been working in Canada since 1991, where she is an active member of the Canadian Friends of Burma.
Page 63.

27. **Peter Smart**

He was Head of Chancery in the British Embassy in Rangoon, from 1968-71. From there he went to be assistant head of the SE Asia Dept. in the Foreign and Commonwealth Office, then to a series of diplomatic postings ending with British Ambassador to Fiji. He retired in 1992.
Pages 163, 173-175, 190, 193.

28. **Kenneth Watts**

A town planner by training and profession, Kenneth Watts joined the UN in 1962 and became UNDP Resident Representative in Rangoon in the late 1970s, which is when his diary entry on the Water Festival dates from. He retired in 1982 but went on a number of further missions for the UN throughout the 1980s, and was Resident Representative *ad interim* in Pakistan and Thailand. Book: *Outwards from Home - a Planner's Odyssey* (The Book Guild, 1997). He lives in Hertfordshire.
Page 191-193.

29. **His Excellency U Win Aung**
Ambassador of the Union of Myanmar to London since 1996, he is *ex officio* (and energetic) Patron of the Britain-Burma Society. He studied Chemistry at Rangoon University; graduated at the age of 19 and went into the Army - but switched to the diplomatic service in 1985. Postings in Laos and Singapore; then Ambassador in Germany. He is a proficient pianist, and specially interested in Burmese history and traditions.
Pages 20-21.

30. **Professor Alan Woodruff CMG, OBE and Helen Woodruff**
Professor Woodruff unfortunately passed away in 1992; for thirty years he was Professor of Clinical Tropical Medicine at the London School of Hygiene and Tropical Medicine, and, with his wife Helen, had a special role in developing relations between the British and Burmese Medical Associations in the 1960s and 1970s. He was also President of the Britain-Burma Society.
Pages 175-177 (Alan Woodruff).
Pages 165-166, 178-182, 190 (Helen).

31. **Ken Wootton**
A mechanical engineer, he worked for the Burma Oil Company for several years, and took part in efforts to restore Burma's oil refining capacity after the war. After that he returned to the UK and took up a new career with the large contractors George Wimpey. He has three children and three grandchildren, and lives in Surrey.
Page 167.

ABOUT THE BRITAIN-BURMA SOCIETY

- The Britain-Burma Society is non-political by constitution, and welcomes all who come in a spirit of goodwill and interest in Myanmar/Burma whether they think of themselves as Burmese, Myanmar or western.
- It was founded in 1957 under the distinguished patronage of Lord Louis Mountbatten of Burma.
- Our President is Sir Nicholas Fenn; our Patron is HE the Myanmar Ambassador, U Win Aung.
- We hold seven meetings a year in the Medical Society in London - additional get-togethers often include *Thingyan Pwes* and summer river trips.
- Meetings at the Medical Society are usually slide shows - or sometimes a video - by an expert with recent knowledge of some aspect of Burma.
- Typed summaries of talks are very often available to members who are unable to attend a particular meeting.
- The annual subscription is £5.00; and an additional £4.00 at the door for meetings. *(NB - true as of May 1998).*
- Members receive seven meeting notices a year - which also include items of relevant news.
- The Society also has a web site, which offers a primary reference point to all people with an interest in Burma. Some material - such as colour pictures and book reviews - it provides for itself; in other cases, it refers the visitor to more specialist web sites. It also includes a reference source for all Society activities.
- The address of the web site is: <http://www.britainburma.demon.co.uk>.

- If you are interested in joining, contact the hon secretary, Derek Brooke-Wavell, at:

  40, Kidmore Road,
  Caversham Heights,
  Reading
  RG4 7LU
  UK.

- Application for membership should be made in the awareness that the Society is non-political and inspired by (a) interest in Burma/Myanmar, (b) a desire for friendship and understanding with its people, and (c) devotion to their interests.

SUGGESTIONS FOR FURTHER READING ABOUT THIS PERIOD

Books published before 1992 (and therefore, unfortunately, likely to be out of print).

- There are vast numbers of really good books on this and other periods in Burma. Rather than list them here, we would refer you to Patricia Herbert's wonderful annotated bibliography, *Burma* (volume 132 in the World Bibliographical Series; Oxford: Clio Press, 1991.) It lists some 1,700 works on Burma (books and articles) - each described, commented on, cross-referenced and indexed. It is available through Plymbridge Distributors Ltd, Plymbridge House, Estover Road, Plymouth PL6 7PZ, or good university libraries.

Recent books still likely to be in print.

1. Gerry Abbott, *Inroads into Burma: a travellers' anthology.* (Kuala Lumpur; Oxford: Oxford University Press, 1997). A delightful and informative selection of extracts from 16th-20th Century travel accounts of Burma.
2. Gerry Abbott, *There before you: the travellers' history of Burma.* (Bangkok, Orchid Press, 1998). A history of Burma based on both published and manuscript accounts by previous visitors to Burma, with the emphasis on places of interest to travellers.
3. Louis Allen, *Burma, the longest war 1941-45* (London; Melbourne, Australia: J.M. Dent, 1984; London: J.M. Dent, 1986. 686p, 36 maps.) Well, this one is pre-1992 but is impossible not to mention, as a superb book about the war in Burma.
4. Maureen Baird-Murray, *A world overturned - a Burmese childhood* (London, Constable Publishers, 1997). Irish father, Burmese mother - a sensitive story of the pre-war and war years in Burma, seen through the eyes of a young girl.
5. Alastair Dingwall, ed., *Travellers' literary companion to South-East Asia* (Brighton: In Print Publishing, 1994.) The Burma section to this guide (pp. 1-54) is by Anna Allott and introduces readers to Burmese literature as well as Western writing on Burma.
6. Sylvia Fraser-Lu, *Burmese crafts: past and present* (Kuala Lumpur: Oxford: Oxford University Press, 1994). A huge, profusely-illustrated guide to the subject.
7. Ian Lyall Grant, *Burma the turning point;* the seven battles on the Tiddim road which turned the tide of the Burma war. (Chichester: Zampi Press, 1993)
8. Nicholas Greenwood, *Shades of gold and green: anecdotes of colonial Burmah 1886-1948* (New Delhi: Asian Educational Services, 1998). An unusual selection of extracts from little-known writers and sources on Burma in colonial times.

9. John Hill, *China Dragons: a rifle company at war, Burma, 1944-45* (London: Blandford, 1991)
10. Sylvia Molloy, *Burma Bride* (Letchworth: Molloy Publications, 1996). The day-to-day life of a young English wife in remote areas of the Shan States just before the war.
11. David Rooney, *Burma victory: Imphal, Kohima and the Chindit issue, March 1944 to May 1945* (London: Arms and Armour, 1992).
12. Noel F. Singer, *Burmah, a photographic journey 1855-1925.* (Gartmore: Kiscadale Publications, 1993). A wonderful illustrated study of early photographs (and postcards) of Burma.
13. Noel F. Singer, *Old Rangoon, City of the Shwedagon.* (Gartmore: Kiscadale Publications, 1995). A beautifully illustrated (from old and contemporary photographs, prints and postcards) history of Rangoon from earliest times to the onset of the war (1941-42).
14. Martin Smith, *Burma: Insurgency and the politics of ethnicity* (London: Zed Books, 1998; 2nd rev edn.). An outstanding major study of the complexities of modern Burma and the unresolved problems of national unity, military rule and opposition movements.
15. Paul Strachan, *Mandalay: Travels from the golden city.* (Gartmore: Kiscadale Publications, 1994). An entertaining account of more than a year's residence in Burma, covering not just life in Mandalay but travels to many out-of-the-way places.